EMOTIONS

TRANSFORMING
ANGER, FEAR AND PAIN

EMOTIONS

TRANSFORMING
ANGER, FEAR AND PAIN

*Creating Heart-Centeredness
in a Turbulent World*

Marilyn C. Barrick, Ph.D.

SUMMIT UNIVERSITY PRESS®

We gratefully acknowledge the following for permission to reprint excerpts from their copyrighted material: "The Criteria of Emotional Maturity," by Dr. William C. Menninger, reprinted with permission of the Menninger Foundation. From *Going to Pieces without Falling Apart,* by Mark Epstein, copyright © 1998 by Mark Epstein; reprinted with permission of Broadway Books, a division of Random House, Inc. From *A Return to Love,* by Marianne Williamson, copyright © 1992 by Marianne Williamson (portions reprinted from *A Course in Miracles,* copyright © 1975 by Foundation for Inner Peace, Inc.; all chapter openings are from *A Course in Miracles*); reprinted with permission of HarperCollins Publishers, Inc.

EMOTIONS: *Transforming Anger, Fear and Pain*
by Marilyn C. Barrick, Ph.D.

Visit Dr. Barrick's web site at www.spiritualpsychology.com

Kuan Yin Riding the Dragon, facing p. 188: by Roxanne Duke

Library of Congress Control Number: 2002102790
ISBN: 0-922729-77-8

SUMMIT UNIVERSITY 🕉 PRESS®

The Summit Lighthouse and *Pearls of Wisdom* are trademarks registered in the U.S. Patent and Trademark Office and in other countries. All rights reserved
Printed in the United States of America

08   07   06   05   04   6   5   4   3   2

I dedicate this book to the spirit of freedom
alive and well in good people everywhere. May we
mobilize the courage to overcome the tyranny of evil—
within and without.

As we plumb the depths of our heart and soul,
may we free ourselves from emotional bondage.
As we face and strive to overcome the denizens of the
deep, may we be victorious. And as we seek to heal
the pain of our soul, may we be made whole.

May we face fearsome circumstances with valor
and endurance. And may we shine the light of the
heart as a beacon of hope to a world and a people
weary of suffering and discontent.

This is my prayer for all who would serve life
with gladness and keep on moving toward
the victory of the Good.

Contents

Acknowledgments

It is with eternal gratitude and devotion that I offer this book to Kuthumi, Jesus, Maitreya, Gautama and all the masters of the wisdom flame. I am deeply grateful to El Morya, Lanello and Mother, faithful mentors of my soul; Kuan Yin, mother of mercy; and Saint Germain, sponsor of the Aquarian age. And I acknowledge with gratitude every adept who has ever walked with God and left footprints to guide us Home.

I wish to thank the following special people whose dedication, expertise and professional assistance have brought this book to the finish line: Karen Gordon for her skillful edits and compassionate assistance; Carla McAuley for her valuable concepts and input; Lynn Wilbert for her expertise in designing and formatting; Roxanne Duke for the beautiful painting of Kuan Yin Riding the Dragon; *and Annice Booth, Nigel Yorwerth and Patricia Spadaro for their helpful input.*

I also wish to thank my clients, whose courageous work in therapy is the inspiration behind all of my books. Truly, they are examples of victors walking the path home to God. And I especially thank my friends and family, whose love and support has helped to make it all happen!

Preface

The quality of mercy is not strained;
It droppeth as the gentle rain from heaven
Upon the place beneath. It is twice blessed—
It blesseth him that gives, and him that takes.

—WILLIAM SHAKESPEARE
The Merchant of Venice

When I began writing this book in the spring of 2001, I had no idea we would soon be facing a worldwide crisis. I had planned to awaken the reader to the power of emotions and to offer a process for healing deep emotional pain. I would include spiritual teachings, techniques of psychological transformation and case histories to illustrate my points. And then came September 11.

The tragic events and aftermath of that heart-stopping day impacted all of us emotionally, and we are still dealing with anger, fear and pain. As I worked as a therapist with people suffering from that trauma and all that occurred in the months that followed, I came to a crystal-clear realization: In perilous times what we all need most is strength, wisdom and a merciful heart.

We have seen a great outpouring of compassion in the way people rallied to help the victims of tragedy in New York City, Washington, D.C., and Pennsylvania. They did whatever they could—from driving all night to deliver supplies to the burn unit in Washington, D.C., to giving

blood, to children making peanut butter and jelly sand-
wiches for the rescue workers.

Many touching stories have been told, but one particular story is a living example of the largesse of heart that
ennobles the human spirit.

On the morning of September 11, Howard Lutnick
arrived at his job late, having taken his son to kinder-
garten that day. Lutnick is CEO of Cantor Fitzgerald, a
bond-trading company that occupied several floors near
the top of the World Trade Center, Tower 1. To his shock
and horror, he saw fire, smoke and the towering icon
crumbling in ruins. Some seven hundred of Cantor Fitzgerald's employees were in the office, including Lutnick's
brother, Gary. All were killed.

As was true of many others, Lutnick felt grief and guilt
when family, friends and employees died and he was still
alive. But he turned it around. Instead of burying himself
in guilt, he set up a relief fund for the families of his employees and personally donated $1 million. This honor-
able man spent many hours comforting the grieving
families and promised 25 percent of profit from the next
several years for their support.[1]

We saw a tide of selfless giving and people's willingness to put their emotions aside to help with the rescue.
And miracles that comforted the soul and uplifted the
spirit happened right in the middle of the devastation.

Only a block away from the collapsed towers,
St. Paul's Chapel, where George Washington visited in
1789 after his inauguration at nearby Federal Hall, still
stands. It doesn't even have a broken window. The dedi-

cated minister who serves there called it a miracle—
"a metaphor of good standing in the face of evil." [2]

Rudy Giuliani, mayor of New York at that time, also
spoke of the preservation of this historic building during
New York City's memorial service: "It's a small miracle in
some ways," he said. "That chapel, standing defiant and
serene amid the ruins, sends an eloquent message about
the strength and resilience of the people of New York
City and the people of America." [3]

We saw that emotional resilience in people all over the
nation who came together in the face of adversity. And we
have seen a growing unity of nations all over the world
striving for an end to hatred and violence.

Each of us can do our part by healing our wounds,
offering compassion to others and moving forward. This
is emotional transformation at its best. I believe that one
day we will look back and see the year 2001 as a never-to-
be-forgotten turning point. And we will realize we have
seen the mirror of the divine in people's noble response to
disaster.

Introduction

*Intellect is to emotion as our clothes are
to our bodies; we could not very well have civilized life
without clothes, but we would be in a poor way
if we had only clothes without bodies.*

—ALFRED NORTH WHITEHEAD
Dialogues

When we look at the varying emotions we experience
in the course of a day, we realize they often come up suddenly, as a rush, a wave of energy. We flush with anger,
tremble with fear or cry out in grief or pain. We melt with
love and tenderness. At times we dissolve into our emotions. At other times, we succeed in staying in the pilot's
seat of our emotional being.

Emotion itself is an inner energy triggered by some
phenomenon inside or outside the body.* Along with it
comes the arousal of the brain and nervous system; they in
turn stimulate thoughts, feelings and propensities to act.

Our emotions can either move us into purposeful
activity or emerge as a chaotic outburst. Yet chaos itself
moves toward order. The big bang theory tells us the
entire physical universe emerged out of chaos.

The infinite mind of the Creator patterned the energy
of chaos into orderly galaxies, planets and the stars, sun

*The word *emotion* is derived from the Latin *movere*, meaning "to
move," plus the prefix *e*, denoting "to move away."

and moon in our sky. Out of chaos came spring, summer, autumn and winter—life cycles of birth, growth, maturation, decline and preparation for rebirth.

The question before us is, Will we use our higher mind to guide our emotional energy into creative cycles of inner rebirth and renewal? or will we allow those seemingly chaotic emotions to toss our lives into frantic disarray?

The Inner World of Emotion and Feeling

To begin to answer this question, we explore the relationship between "emotion" and "feeling." They are often interchanged, but we intuitively understand some subtle differences.

When we talk about feelings, we are referring to subjective reactions to a particular event. Often these reactions suggest an absence of reasoning, a rambunctious primal response. So we might find ourselves saying, "I can't trust my feelings" or "My feelings got away from me."

Emotions, on the other hand, involve not only intense feelings but also accompanying physical and mental activity. As author Daniel Goleman says, "Emotions are, in essence, impulses to act, the instant plans for handling life that evolution has instilled in us." [1]

Each emotion prepares us for a different kind of response. When we are frightened, we experience a momentary state of "freeze" ("frozen with fear," we say), a built-in quick-stop reflex that gives us a second to decide the action to take. At the same time blood is rushing to our arms and legs, preparing us to fight or flee the danger and propelling us into movement. Our whole body is on instant alert.

When we get angry, our heart rate accelerates and a thrust of adrenaline gives us the necessary energy for strong action. In the same instant, blood rushes to our hands, making it easier to strike out or fend off an assault. We are ready to fight, to defend our turf.

In contrast, love, with its gentle and tender feelings, creates what has been called the relaxation response—a set of reactions that bring about feelings of calmness and contentment.

When we feel happy, our brain is actively releasing endorphins, tiny peptides that relieve pain and stir good feelings. We experience an increase of positive energy. We feel it as a sense of uplift, enthusiasm and an inner readiness to get on with the goal or task of the moment.

Sadness, on the other hand, is accompanied by a slowing down of body metabolism—a drop in energy. This physiological response creates an opportunity for us to slow down, to feel the full impact of a disappointment or loss and to grieve. As the grief cycle moves on, our energy picks up and we feel a lifting of the weight of sadness. Gradually we move on to new beginnings.*

Who's in the Driver's Seat?

All of us have emotions; all of us have feelings. But the real issue is whether or not we are aware of them and in the driver's seat. Most of us are in that driver's seat part of the time and tossed and turned like a passenger without a seat belt at other times. Yet each of us can learn to guide

---

*For a spiritual understanding of the transformational stages of grief and renewal, see pp. 291–94.

our emotions creatively once we set our minds and hearts to the task.

When strong emotions stir us, we can choose to take a time-out, to calm our tumultuous feelings, to think through a potential approach and to use the power of our uplifting emotions to make it happen.

By doing this, we put ourselves in the driver's seat of our emotions. Now we can move forward without risking the potential disaster of being driven by anger, fear, grief or any other runaway emotion. The vehicle of our consciousness is no longer out of control.

When we learn to handle our emotions, we can be true to the self we really want to be. We can make wise choices. We can move on with our lives instead of being tumbled or immobilized by our emotional ups and downs.

Throughout this book we'll be investigating the nuances of our "inner dragons" and the methods of our Real Self we can use for taming them. We'll explore ways to exchange the different faces of our defensive self for the miraculous essence and integrity of who we really are.

Who Is Your Real Self?

Many people speak of their Real Self as the Higher Self, or Christ Self or Buddha Self—the source of higher values that prompts them to benevolent motives, thoughts, words and deeds. And it is that level of selfhood that gives us the impetus to be strong, wise and loving in the face of adversity.

At an energetic level, your Real Self* is brilliant white light, the divine light of Spirit. That light moves through

*See illustration of "The Chart of Your Divine Self," p. 335.

your chakras and meridians—spiritual energy centers and pathways that govern the flow of electromagnetic energy in all levels of your being. As the light flows through the chakras, it is refracted in a similar way to sunlight passing through a prism, forming the colors of the rainbow. (Perhaps this is why we enjoy a shimmering waterfall with rainbow colors dancing in the mist—it reminds us of our inner essence.)

In the very center of this wellspring of light is a fiery spark that burns as a threefold flame (pink, blue and gold) hidden away in the secret chamber of the heart. This chamber is beyond the physical dimensions of time and space. Thus the threefold flame is typically unseen by human eyes. However, we can envision it, and people blessed with inner sight have seen it.

How does the threefold flame connect with our memories, thoughts, emotions and physical reactions? This spark of divinity carries the divine thrust that energizes our four lower bodies: the etheric (or memory) body, the mental body, the emotional (or desire) body, and the physical body. These bodies are vehicles that the soul uses during her* journey in time and space.

The etheric body is like a temple for the soul. This energy body houses the blueprint of the soul's identity and the memory of all we experience during our earthly embodiments.

The mental body is the repository of the cognitive

---

*The soul, whether housed in a male or female body, is the feminine counterpart of Spirit. Our spirit (lowercased *s*) is our masculine essence; thus we say the spirit of a person is joyful, lethargic, melancholy, and so forth.

faculties—our thoughts, ideas, plans and reveries. When purified, it can become the vessel of the mind of God. The emotional body houses our emotional reactions and reflects our higher and lower desires. And the physical body is the miracle of flesh and blood that enables our soul to progress in the material universe.

Understanding all of this, we can think of the Real Self as the quickening essence of the Creator within us—nudging us to become the creative, compassionate person we can be when we are heart-centered. When we are true to our Higher Self, we not only feel good about ourselves but also become more genuine in our relationships with others.

As Shakespeare aptly phrased it, "To thine own self be true, and it must follow, as the night the day, thou canst not then be false to any man." [2]

PART ONE

Heart-Centeredness:
Courage in the Face of Adversity

Emotional Balance in a Turbulent World

We never know how high we are
Till we are called to rise
And then, if we are true to plan
Our statures touch the skies.

—EMILY DICKINSON
Complete Poems, No. 1176

Keeping one's emotional balance is a major key to being true to one's self. Such stability is relatively easy when life is on an upswing but more difficult in troubling circumstances. Anger, fear and pain can emerge unexpectedly when we are confronted with emotionally charged situations.

Often this occurs when we have a major change in the status quo of our family, job or relationships. And through the worldwide media, we are quickly impacted by happenings thousands of miles away. All of this came to an instant crescendo in the world-shaking events of September 11, 2001.

Many people became sharply aware of fear, even a sense of panic and terror, during the terrorist attacks on the World Trade Center and the Pentagon. As we watched our TVs that day and in the weeks that followed, our fear often gave way to a tremendous anger at the senseless destruction going on before our eyes and toward those responsible for it. Publicly and privately we wept tears of pain and grief for lost loved ones and for the heroic people who perished trying to save them.

For many, an underlying sense of fear, apprehension, anger and grief has become an unpleasant daily companion. Things we take for granted—going to work, taking a vacation, opening the mail—have become problematical.

Yet we do not need to stay submerged in the darkness of fear or anger or other reactive emotions. We can learn to mobilize ourselves to face turbulent times with an ongoing posture of strength, courage and resourcefulness. This is a large part of what I hope you will learn from this book.

As you read and reflect on the heroic actions of others, and the psychological underpinnings of such actions, ponder what taking that kind of action would mean in your own life.

Being in the Now

Think about the men and women through history whom you consider to be heroes or heroines. In reality, they were ordinary people, like you and me, who mobilized themselves for courageous action in the face of extraordinary circumstances. They didn't just think about it. They acted.

Author Eckhart Tolle talks about such courageous deeds as normal behavior if you are totally present (with all your faculties) in the moment, in "the Now." Athletes call this state "being in the zone" and writers talk about "the flow of inspiration." What this means is total focus in the moment, in the Now.

In relation to fear, Tolle says, "If you have ever been in a life-or-death emergency situation, you will know that it wasn't a problem. The mind didn't have *time* to fool around and make it into a problem. In a true emergency, the mind stops; you become totally present in the Now, and something infinitely more powerful takes over. This is why there are many reports of ordinary people suddenly becoming capable of incredibly courageous deeds....

"A great deal of what people say, think, or do is actually motivated by fear, which of course is always linked with having your focus on the future and being out of touch with the Now. As there are no problems in the Now, there is no fear either." [1]

Of course, this doesn't mean we may not shrink back momentarily in situations of real danger. But that is different from the psychological condition of fear that comes upon us in the absence of immediate, concrete danger. In this case, we are not continually faced with danger yet we tend to walk around in a state of fear because our mind ruminates upon fearful possibilities. And that is an inner drama we can do something about.

We have all been heartened by the courage and selflessness of firefighters, rescue workers and ordinary people in the very face of the September 11 horrors. There were many heroes and heroines during and after the terrorist strikes, people from all walks of life who acted instantly in the face of deadly circumstances.

Would we have done the same? Very possibly, because we are all endowed with that same courageous potential. What it takes is practicing the consciousness of being in the Now. And this is a stance that we can begin to practice on a daily basis.

A Beloved Chaplain's Courage and Dedication

Father Mychal Judge, a monk and Fire Department chaplain, immediately rushed out of his room at St. Francis of Assisi Friary to offer comfort and assistance to those injured at the towers. He didn't think twice about going. He just moved, quickly and courageously, because that's the kind of man he was.

In 1993 Father Judge had helped Chinese immigrants stranded at Rockaway Beach when their ship had washed ashore. In 1996 he had been at the crash scene of TWA Flight 800, comforting victims' families. And on that fateful day in 2001, as he was giving last rites to a fireman at the World Trade Center, falling debris struck and killed him.

More than three hundred firefighters died in that disaster. Commenting on Father Judge, one firefighter said, "I just think God wanted somebody to lead the guys to heaven."[2]

Father Judge was so cherished by the firemen of

Ladder 24-Eng ... that they carried his body to a nearby church and later to their firehouse. "We brought him home," said one firefighter.[3]

This beloved priest was a living example of courage and comfort, a servant of Christ in all, who gave of his heart and soul and physical strength up to the end. In the midst of turmoil, he brought God's love home to those beleaguered, weary firemen. All who knew him loved him because he practiced what he preached. He walked his talk. And he set a heroic example for all of us.

Courage in the Face of Certain Death

Another inspiring story of courage under unthinkable circumstances came to light in phone calls from those aboard United Airlines Flight 93, the hijacked plane that crashed in a Pennsylvania field.

Approximately an hour into the flight from Newark to San Francisco, Flight 93 made a sharp turn south that put it on course for Washington, D.C. The plane was now on a trajectory toward the White House and the Capitol.

Terrorists had seized control of the cockpit and moved the passengers to the back of the plane. A group of men apparently banded together to divert that plane from its terrorist target. They included Mark Bingham, a public relations executive, Tom Burnett, an executive with a medical research company, Jeremy Glick, a salesman for an Internet company, Todd Beamer, a sales account manager, and Lou Nacke, a manager of a toy-store distribution center.

Before the crash Bingman phoned his mother in

Sacramento to say he loved her. Glick called his wife to say goodbye to her and their infant daughter, Emmy.

In phone calls Burnett made to his wife and in a brief conversation Beamer had with the GTE AirFone supervisor, it was clear the passengers knew about the attacks on the World Trade Center and realized Flight 93 was headed on a mission of death.

Burnett told his wife, Deena, "I know we're going to die. Some of us are going to do something about it." Glick told his wife, Lyzbeth, they were going to "jump the hijackers." And Beamer's final words heard by the Airfone supervisor were, "Are you guys ready? Let's roll."[4]

We have to piece together what happened next, but from the screams, yells and commotion heard over the phones, the five men likely charged the cockpit. Flight 93 never made it to Washington. When it crashed into a field eighty miles southeast of Pittsburgh, all aboard were killed. But the heroic intervention foiled the terrorists' plans. That plane did not strike its intended target.

As Glick's wife, Lyzbeth, said, "As long as I've known him, he was the kind of man who never tried to be the hero but always was. . . . I think God had this larger purpose for him."[5]

Others on Flight 93 undoubtedly played their own heroic role. Relatives of the captain, Jason Dahl, say he would never have allowed hijackers to take control of his plane without a fight.

We ask ourselves, "How did they mobilize the courage and strength of heart to do what they did in the face of certain death?"

I believe that whether or not they realized it, they drew upon the light of the heart, their inner connection with God and the angels. As they focused one-pointedly on what they had to do, they tapped into their inner power and allowed God to work through them. They were in the power of the Now, as Eckhart Tolle calls it.

A Brave Woman's Journey

One little baby, born the day after the terrorist strike, was "a miracle arrival." Her mother, Jun Lee, a United Nations lawyer, faced circumstances that called for quick-thinking as well as courage. When the planes crashed into the buildings, she was shopping in a World Trade Center bookstore. She acted immediately.

She hurried out of the World Trade Center and cautiously moved through the fallen rubble and terrified crowds. She found shelter some ten blocks away in a hotel and phoned her husband, lawyer Thomas Letsou. He joined her at the hotel late in the afternoon.

By early evening there was no electricity or phone service in the hotel. Around midnight, Jun Lee felt birth contractions. The only way to get to the hospital was to walk. As she labored, she and her husband walked two miles through the darkened, smoke-filled streets. It took an hour and a half to make their way from lower Manhattan to Beth Israel Hospital, but they arrived safely. Eight hours later, Jun Lee gave birth to Elizabeth Letsou, their first child.

I'm sure Jun Lee's harrowing experience faded quickly when she looked into the eyes of little Elizabeth. To me this child symbolizes what America is fighting for in the war against terrorism. This little one has a God-given right to grow up and to fulfill her mission in life. She represents children the world over who have the same right to seek their destiny in a world free of terrorism.

Psychological Tools to Help Children Outwit Fear

How do those of us who are parents, teachers or simply friends help children grow up courageous instead of fearful?

By being courageous in our own actions, by helping our children face smaller fearsome situations and by being loving and kind in the process, we become role models for them.

Parents have said to me, "I worry about my kids watching all of this stuff about terrorism and anthrax on TV. But they need to know what's happening because their friends talk about it, and they hear about it at school. How can I make sure they are not psychologically damaged by it?"

We help our children feel secure when we answer their questions honestly with simple explanations. We comfort and reassure them when we give smiles and hugs and follow normal routines at home. And we give them an opportunity to experience and appreciate civility when we model integrity, courtesy and kindness in our words and actions.

Some parents wonder, "How do I figure out when I am or am not being kind? For example, if I march my kid to the front door and say, 'Get on that school bus!' am I being kind?"

I say yes but with some qualification. This kind of firm action does teach the child to fulfill his or her responsibilities, and that will be kindness in the long run. By insisting that a child fulfill his learning responsibility, you are preparing him to be successful. And by facing a relatively simple situation early in life, the child learns the kind of firm stance that he will need in difficult situations later on.

However, this type of action needs to be preceded by talking with the child about his uneasiness in riding the bus. Is it the bus ride itself? Is it something else? Find out. Maybe he's connecting the bus ride with something scary he saw on TV. Or maybe there's something wrong at school or with his friends that you can help him straighten out. Once he feels your support, he may very well decide on his own to hop on the bus.

If it isn't that easy, try brainstorming together about how he might handle it. Maybe he will decide to whistle to himself or give himself a pep talk or buddy up with a neighbor on the bus ride. If you have a really good talk, you likely will not have to march him to the bus. He'll accomplish it by himself, and be proud of himself for doing it. In this way he builds the courage to face difficult moments.

Courage Is a Quality of Heart

The English word *courage* derives from *coeur,* French for heart. Thus courage can be understood as "heart-age," or the "coming of age of the heart."

Spiritually, courage is a spark of fire from the Creator's heart—our divine passport to heroism, if we so choose.

Psychologically, courage is a balance of inner fortitude, wisdom and compassionate action in the face of threat or peril.

Courage is the quality of heroes and heroines, who greet danger or crisis with valor. And courage is a quality of ordinary people who strive to meet the challenges of their daily lives with fortitude.

Most of us would agree that courage is a necessity in our turbulent times. Yet we may unwittingly carry a subtle sense of apprehension that can interfere with living life to the fullest. For example, a couple who had been planning to vacation in Europe in the fall of 2001 became apprehensive after the terrorist attacks and didn't go. Another couple, however, had a choir commitment in England and chose to make the trip.

Now whether either of these couples made a right or wrong decision is not the point—it's how such a decision is made. You might ask yourself: "Am I making decisions today from a baseline of fear or a baseline of courage? Am I allowing fear to control my life? Or am I taking positive action in fearsome circumstances?"

A baseline of courage is what empowered Mychal Judge, Jun Lee, the men on Flight 93 and the firemen and rescue workers. It emboldens our military men and women and all who are fighting the battle against terrorism. And it strengthens all of us when we have health problems, financial difficulties or face setbacks at home or on the job. We, too, can claim courage as our heart's coming of age.

Aspects of Courage

How do we claim courage? We train ourselves to respond courageously when danger calls. And we do that by developing the basic elements of courage—inner strength, wisdom and love.

Inner Strength. What is inner strength? How does it relate to courage? And how do we access it?

Inner strength is spiritual strength—a moral fiber that we garner and reinforce by prayer, meditation and other spiritual practices. Think of this as opening wide a highway to God. As we move along on that upward trek, we are nourished and empowered from on high. And we find it easier to walk our talk, to stand for what we believe in.

Here is an exercise to help you mobilize inner strength:

1. Take a moment to envision an inspiring experience where your soul feels uplifted and invigorated (e.g., a snow-covered mountain illumined by the sun, a strengthening moment of prayer, a glorious rainbow arcing across the sky, the awesome grandeur of a redwood forest). Attune your heart to the majestic power of the Creator.

2. Now imagine yourself in some kind of daunting circumstance and ask your Higher Self, "What would be a powerful, centered way to approach this situation?" Make a note of whatever intuitive image arises.

3. Access your strength of mind by developing a well-shaped idea and focusing on a steady mind-set to follow through on your imagery. Write it down.

4. Mobilize your emotional strength by attuning yourself to that inner calmness, centeredness and self-assurance that accompanies control of your emotions. Write a note to yourself about it.

5. Focus your attention on your physical heartbeat and take several slow, deep breaths, releasing any tension while exhaling. And quietly take positive action.

6. Enhance your inner strength by staying physically fit and taking regular exercise. If you don't already have a favorite practice, consider walking, biking, hatha yoga, T'ai Chi or aikido, the martial art of harmlessness.[6]

Put all of this together and you will be well on your way to claiming your inner strength.

Wisdom. A second component of courage is wisdom. What does wisdom mean? It's more than "smarts." It's good judgment, which leads to a balanced course of action.

How do we tap into it? Think of some situation you are apprehensive about or an activity you want to do but are avoiding. Then try this exercise:

1. Center yourself in the heart and ask your Higher Self, "Is this a wise or foolish thing to do?" Notice your intuitive response.

2. Think about what additional information you might need in order to make an educated decision, and determine to get those facts.

3. Forestall any unruly emotions by including reasonable precautions in your plan.

4. Stay centered in your heart while you take balanced action. If worry and doubt arise, try reciting positive affirmations or mantras until you feel centered again.

Put all of this together and you will have mobilized wisdom, the second component of courage.

Love. The third aspect of courage is love—love as compassion and caring. Let's look at how we might ready ourselves to express love more fully.

1. Think back to a special moment when you were loving and compassionate (or someone was loving and caring toward you).

2. Contemplate what love and compassion mean to you. Spell it out for yourself mentally or on paper.

3. Center in your heart, put your arms around yourself (or someone you love) and give yourself (or your loved one) a big hug—and revel in the good feelings.

4. Practice loving behavior toward another person. And remember, this means behavior the other person considers loving—which may or may not match your own definition. (You might think it's loving to take your daughter to Tahiti for a week, but she might think it's more loving if you go with her to a soccer game.)

Put this all together and you will have mobilized love.

When we focus on inner strength, wisdom and love, we prime ourselves to handle courageously whatever situation we encounter. On the other hand, when we allow ourselves to give in to fear, we tend to immobilize ourselves.

As we practice these steps we build a momentum. Ultimately, we do not even have to think about mobilizing courage; we have become courageous people.

Understanding the Physiology of Fear

Sometimes fear is a good thing. In the face of danger it quickens us so we take the necessary measures to survive. When we look at fear in this way, it can be useful— if we know what to do with it.

What happens in the physical body when we are fearful? Our heart rate accelerates, our muscles tense, our digestive functions slow down and epinephrine (adrenaline) pours into the bloodstream. These physiological changes enable us to act quickly and decisively.

When we were children, we didn't necessarily call these sensations fear. We just felt excited. But if we got hurt in the middle of that excitement, we may very well have decided that it was pretty scary.

Let's say a small child builds up a rickety pile of boxes, and he's teetering on top playing king of the mountain. He's feeling great. And his king-of-the-mountain game is just fine until something startles him and he falls off and bumps his head.

Now he has all that adrenaline surging and his head hurts. The next time that adrenaline starts surging, he remembers playing king of the mountain and hurting his head when he fell. Now he's likely to feel frightened when he has that adrenaline pumping and to say, "I'm scared." His response is both physiological and emotional.

A race car driver feeling the surge of adrenaline might say, "I'm up for the race." And performers on stage say, "I don't do a good show unless I have a little stage fright."

Most people new to public speaking have "butter-flies" in the stomach. People learning to sky dive, to compete in athletics or to handle conflict on the job have similar physical sensations. Whether or not they call the sensations "fear," and get panicked, hinges on the way they interpret them.

If we remember that this is the body revving up for action, we can turn it to our benefit. We can transform those butterflies into a signal that says, "I'm ready for the challenge. My body is set for action!"

Sometimes, however, our fears and physiological reactions do not have an objective reason—they are the product of our own imagination. The only way we can outwit these phantoms of the mind is by realizing them as such.

In a sutra, the Buddha says,

> He who has awakened is freed from fear; he has become Buddha. He knows the vanity of all his cares, his ambitions, and also his pains.
>
> It easily happens that a man, when taking a bath, steps upon a wet rope and imagines that it is a snake. Horror will overcome him, and he will shake from fear, anticipating in his mind all the agonies caused by the serpent's venomous bite.
>
> What a relief does this man experience when he

sees that the rope is no snake. The cause of his fright lies in his error, his ignorance, his illusion.

If the true nature of the rope is recognized, his tranquility of mind will come back to him. He will feel relieved; he will be joyful and happy.

So many times we frighten ourselves by conjuring up a fearful image or remembering a past trauma and projecting it into today. Once we realize what we are doing, we can let it go and be at ease.

Freeing Ourselves from Emotional Burdens

To a greater or lesser extent, we all carry some degree of fear and anxiety. We may remember traumatic happenings that account for such feelings, or these traumas may lie hidden in the subconscious and unconscious levels of being.

Frequently, when my clients pursue their uneasy feelings and probe their emotional depths, they recall repressed experiences from earlier in life. Often these go back to infancy or early childhood—or even to experiences in the womb or in a past life.

Once we have a glimpse of such a traumatic memory, we can begin the work of healing that younger part of our being. In the process, we come to understand ourselves at deeper levels. We can touch with kindness the wounded aspects of our soul and spirit crying out to be healed.

As we seek to free ourselves from the emotional pain and bondage of past trauma, we embark on a transformational journey. Through the ups and downs of the journey, we develop new insights and creative ideas that lead to our emotional healing. We begin to shed outmoded habits and physical tensions. And we experience a renewal and expansion of our inner love nature.

If instead of freeing ourselves from emotional pain of the past we allow emotional baggage to accumulate, it can adversely impact our life. We all know how worry and overconcern can ruin our day and put a damper on relationships with family and friends. Fear and superstition can paralyze us at the very moment we need to take action.

When we dwell in negative emotional states, we don't notice the laughter of children at play, the beauty of flowering trees, the grandeur of the mountains, the warmth of the sun or the twinkling of the stars. In short, fear and its wayward emotional companions hold us captive and bar us from enjoying the good things in life.

What are your specific personal fears? Do certain situations trigger anxiety? Do you fear someone in your life? Are you afraid of something in yourself? Are you fearful about trying new activities? What do you worry about? Make some notes to yourself about what comes to mind.

Now ask yourself, "What fear do I most need to conquer in order to be happy and productive?" Perhaps it's a part of yourself that you're afraid will get out of hand and wreak havoc. You might be afraid of your temper—or someone else's. Or you might be fearful of interacting with bossy, critical people. That can be a big problem if your boss or a co-worker on a project is that type of person.

One Woman's Victory over Fear

Jessica, a client of mine, faced exactly this kind of situation at her job as secretary for a high-powered executive.* She would get up in the morning with a sense of dread about going in to work. And frequently her worst fears came true as her boss critically nitpicked her work to the point that she lost confidence in her ability to do the job. Of course, that didn't help a bit. When she came in to see me she was on notice that she could lose the job if she didn't shape up.

Jessica burst into tears as she tried to explain her feelings. "I can't live this way," she cried. "I'm almost hoping Austin fires me because then I'd be out of this office. But I can't afford to lose my job. My husband is doing the best he can, but with three kids to support we need the double income to make it."

"Jessica," I responded, "I understand how you feel. It must seem like your world is coming down around you. Let's see what we can do to turn this situation around."

"I don't think that can happen," she said despondently. "I've been making too many mistakes, and Austin is past the point of even being civil to me. The minute I see him I get the shakes."

"I realize it's tough, but you wouldn't be here if you didn't want to at least give it a try, right?" I replied.

"Well, that's true," she sighed. "What do you suggest?"

"We're going to have to partner on this," I said. "What is it about Austin and the job that scares you the most?"

---

*I have changed names, places and certain details to protect the anonymity of the individuals whose stories I have included in this book.

Jessica was silent for a moment, but I could see she was beginning to ponder the situation.

"I think it's that I can't take criticism, even constructive criticism. As soon as Austin gets after me for something, I go blank instead of retaining what he's telling me." She sighed again, "It's just like I used to do when my dad would try to teach me something. I was never quick enough to understand what he wanted, and he would get totally exasperated with me. One time he told me, 'You're never going to amount to anything if you don't try.' I tried to explain that I was trying, but he didn't believe me."

"How did you do in school?" I asked. "Was it the same situation there?"

"It kind of depended on the teacher," she responded. "If the teacher picked on me, I'd go blank and that made it worse. But if the teacher had more patience, I did just fine."

"So it's not that you couldn't do it," I said. "It's more like you're scared you can't if someone gets picky or demanding. Is that right?"

Jessica was looking slightly relieved. "I guess so," she answered. "I hadn't really thought of it that way."

"I wonder what would happen if you conquered your fear of a picky, demanding kind of person?" I asked.

She thought for a few minutes, "I think I'd do okay. It really is the fear that immobilizes me."

"Jessica," I responded, "many of us carry over fears from our childhood or youth that hamper us in our work or family life. This is something we can do something about."

"Well, I have my doubts, but I'm all for trying," she said.

"Good!" I answered. "Let's see how you do with the emotional freedom technique."

"What's that?" she asked.

"It's a method of psychological reversal in which you acknowledge your fears but affirm your desires. As you do that, you tap certain meridian points to release the energy that is blocking you[7]—in your case, the fear that's making you blank out in the face of criticism."

"Would that really work?" Jessica sounded interested but skeptical.

"Let's go for it," I responded. "You don't have anything to lose, do you?"

"No, I'm already in the duck soup," Jessica said with a tiny smile. "Things can't get much worse than they are now, and I do want to get over being such a scaredy-cat. I'm actually pretty smart when I'm not scared."

"So it's not all of you that's scared," I commented.

I could tell that Jessica was beginning to make her turnaround. We did some inner child work first so that she could get in touch with this younger part of herself that was still reacting to her critical father. She practiced being her loving adult self while she dialogued with her fearful inner child.[8]

What she discovered was that her inner child had decided she simply couldn't stand up to authority figures —they were just too scary. And her adult self had been going along with that decision. As Jessica gave voice to her childhood fears while centering herself in her loving adult, she began to understand more clearly the origin of her fears.

I asked her, "Do you feel ready now to begin letting go of this fear?"

"Yes," she said. "I can see that it isn't really me as an adult that's scared of Austin; it's this carryover from my childhood. I'm ready to work on letting it go."

"Okay," I replied. "Let's decide on your psychological reversal affirmation." The affirmation she began with was, "Even if my inner child is scared of Austin's criticism, I deeply and completely accept myself."

We went through the meridian-point tapping as Jessica voiced her affirmation. When she began this session, her fear of Austin's criticism was a nine on a scale of zero to ten. As we went through the energy release, it dropped to six.

So I asked her, "What's keeping it from going to zero?"

She responded, "Well, it feels a little more manageable, but I'm still scared he'll fire me."

So then we shifted to another affirmation: "Even if my inner child is afraid that Austin will fire me, I as the adult choose to stay calm."

This time as we went through the process, I watched Jessica begin to smile. When we concluded it, she said spontaneously, "Well, that's really something. I realized I am *not* that child; I'm an adult. It's like I'm separating out from that child part."

"Good," I said. "Where is the fear of Austin now on the scale of zero to ten?"

"It's a three," she replied, "because I have some trepidation about whether Austin will keep me on even if I lick this. I'd like to keep the job, even if it's just to prove to myself that I can do it."

"That sounds like a move in the right direction," I said. "Let's keep going."

Her next affirmation was, "Even if I have some trepidation about Austin keeping me on, I deeply and completely believe in myself."

As we went through that set of affirmations and the meridian tapping, I observed Jessica firming up. Her voice became stronger and her tapping firmer.

"So how bothersome is the fear now," I asked, "on the scale?"

"I can't quite believe this," she said, "but it feels like a one. I just don't feel all riled up about it anymore. I do feel peaceful. If this job works out, fine. If it doesn't, I'll find another one."

"Okay," I replied, "that's a real shift, isn't it?"

"Yes," she laughed. "I can feel the difference between staying centered in my adult self versus falling into my child self."

Jessica came in for several more sessions to do additional inner child work and some more emotional release work as needed. But she had indeed made a major turnaround. It wasn't that she didn't make any mistakes, but she was doing so much better and had such composure that even Austin commented on it.

As he told her, "I guess I've been pretty tough on you, but it seems to have paid off. I'm impressed with your work these days as well as your shift to a positive approach. I believe we're beginning to be a good team. And, frankly, that's a relief to me because I don't want to have to break in a new secretary."

Jessica smiled when she told me, "I'm perfectly willing to let Austin take the credit. I did tell him that I'd discovered I was twice as efficient when he didn't yell at me, and he took that.

"We're getting along pretty well now. And I'm impressed with the fact that he hasn't been as critical— only when he gets stressed out. That's been a lesson for me. It isn't all about me. A big part of it is Austin getting uptight when we're under the gun with a client. He just reacts a different way than I do. I've been doing the fear thing; he does his critical, demanding thing."

She added, "I ought to send him in here because I can see that he criticizes me or anyone in sight when he's worried that something isn't turning out right. Anyway, now that I've calmed myself down, I am doing a good job. And that feels great!"

A Man Wins His Private Battle in the Workplace

Lest you think that fear in the workplace is restricted to women, I'll give you a quick look at Connor, who had a problem similar to Jessica's.

Connor was an enterprising fellow who worked in the advertising business. He was good at what he did, but underneath his surface composure, he was uneasy about interactions with his boss and co-workers. He knew it was a fear of being put down that he had carried since childhood.

As he told me, "My dad and brothers were real buddies, but I didn't seem to fit in. They were macho types and

I wasn't. They liked to roughhouse; I didn't. They'd be out throwing the football, and I usually had my nose in a book.

"That part of it wouldn't have bothered me so much, but my brother Bill got it into his head that I was a sissy. He'd say, 'So you're scared to do the man stuff, are you?' And then he'd punch me. When I didn't punch him back, he'd either punch me again or pronounce with the greatest scorn, 'You're nothing but a wimp!' Sometimes I wondered if I was. And over the years I got sensitive to criticism from him or my dad.

"One of the worst memories I have was overhearing my dad talking to my mom one time. What he told her really got to me. He was saying, 'Connor doesn't know how to hold his own, even with his brother. He's going to have trouble in a man's world.' I remember feeling shocked and hurt and wondering if he was right."

He went on, "My mom defended me, but that almost made it worse. She shouldn't have had to. Anyway, I'm on my own now, but I've got a boss and co-worker who are so much like my dad and brother that it's not even funny. It's a real macho atmosphere at work. Whenever we're taking a break, it's all about contact sports and who's topping who in the advertising game. I catch myself feeling 'one down' again, and it's beginning to affect my creativity."

I knew Connor had an inquisitive bent, so I responded, "It seems like a replay of your childhood misery, doesn't it? What can you learn from it this time around?"

Connor reflected. "I suppose the lesson is to believe in myself. They're not really directing their banter at me like

Bill and Dad used to. I guess I'm worried there really might be something wrong with me. And that kind of takes the wind out of my sails."

"Is there something wrong with being different?" I asked.

"Well, no, but there's something wrong with me not being a man," he responded quietly.

"Let's look at that," I suggested. "What is being a man from your point of view?"

He thought for a bit. "I always thought being a man was standing up for what I believed in. It didn't have so much to do with physical prowess or being on top.

"Of course, now that I think about it, in a situation that required me to be physical, I'd do that. I remember rescuing this little kid who'd broken through the ice when he was skating. I didn't even think about it. I just did it."

"That was a manly action," I commented.

"Yes, I guess so," he responded. "What shakes me is realizing I'm still scared of potential put-downs. That's what's bothering me—not so much the physical stuff. I don't like thinking of myself as a wimp just because I'm not combative."

"Now you're putting your finger on it," I replied. "It sounds like a leftover reaction to your dad and brother, and it's surfacing with the boss and co-worker because they're similar in their approach to life. Tell me this, would you want to be like them?"

"Absolutely not," he grinned. "Maybe I've been scaring myself for nothing. I actually like who I am, and I am good at what I do."

"So what is it going to take to chase those fears from your childhood and teen years out the door?" I asked.

Connor was looking more relaxed. "Just doing it!" he laughed. "Somehow seeing so clearly that I've been caught in my old childhood movie helps. I have noticed that my boss values my ideas; he's actually more critical of Ken, my co-worker. Maybe that's why Ken joins in with the boss's macho stuff, trying to get a footing with the boss that way."

He was quiet and thoughtful for a moment. Then with a visible sense of determination he said, "I'm going to focus on my own ideas and forget about the office horseplay. I was hired for my creativity, and that's what I'm going to go for."

Connor did exactly that. And it worked. These days he's highly valued for his creative ad copy, and he's got a sense of humor about the macho atmosphere. He's even been able to capture the humor of that macho attitude in some of his ads. That's when he found out his boss has a sense of humor about himself as a boss.

It really lightened Connor up when his boss kidded him, "Hey, you trying to make me famous through your ad copy?"

What about the childhood fears? Connor says, "I can tell that my inner teenager feels a lot more secure now. I can hold my own, and he knows it."

A Process for Taking Command of Your Fears

Maybe, like Connor or Jessica, whatever fear or uneasiness you experience relates to painful circumstances earlier in life. Perhaps a loved one went through a tragedy and you identified with his or her pain and fear. Or maybe you read about a disaster in the newspaper (or watched it on the news or even saw it in a movie) and thought to yourself, "I don't think I could handle that. It's too unnerving." Here is a self-help process for taking command of that fear:

1. Take a moment to get in touch with your fear or sense of anxiety—that inner shakiness or sinking feeling in the pit of your stomach.

2. Once you get in touch with that feeling, take a few slow deep breaths, relaxing with each out-breath, and allow your intuition to guide you as you explore the feeling and allow it to intensify.

3. Ask yourself, "When have I felt this way before?" Make a few notes to yourself about the memories, thoughts and physical sensations that come to mind.

4. Give this mantra out loud: "I AM loving, I AM wise, I AM strong." Feel the words as you say them until you feel centered, focused and invigorated.

5. Set up an action plan for handling yourself in a scary situation. For example, you might take a quick time-out, focus on your heart and take a few slow, deep breaths, formulate a constructive response and initiate firm, positive action.

Keep in mind that when you are having a good time or thinking about pleasurable experiences in your life, you feel happy and contented. That is a baseline to remember.

How quickly we can exchange scared or anxious feelings for uplifting ones when we are immersed in the beauty of nature or a peak experience—or when we simply remember a happy time or focus on positive imagery.

Imagery is a great way to shift your consciousness from negative to positive, and it doesn't require being able to visualize per se. As Dr. Martin Rossman, author of *Guided Imagery for Self-Healing,* says,

> While imagery certainly includes what you see mentally, it also consists of what you hear in your inner ear, sensations and emotions that you feel inside, and even what you smell and taste in your imagination. Some people imagine in vivid visual images with color, sound, smell, and sensation, while others may experience sounds, songs, or thoughts in their heads without any pictures. Some will be more aware of senses or feelings that guide them and let them know when they are close to something meaningful.
>
> It doesn't really matter how you imagine, just that you learn to recognize and work with your own imagery. Your purpose is not to get pretty pictures, but to pay attention to what your body/ mind is trying to tell you. Imagery is a vehicle to this understanding, which may come through inner pictures, words, thoughts, sensations, or feelings.[9]

A Moment of Renewal

Here are some examples of uplifting imagery. Imagine each one happening (with your eyes open or closed) and discover which ones appeal to you. Or create your own.

- Think of a little baby, cooing and smiling as mom and dad look on in adoring appreciation. Feel their love and affection.

- Bring to mind the bubbling joy of children tumbling happily down a grassy hill or laughing with delight as they squirt each other with water from the garden hose. Let the corners of your mouth turn up!

- Envision a graceful figure skater, gliding, leaping into the air and whirling over the ice in perfect rhythm to a rising crescendo of orchestral music. Feel the flow of the music within yourself.

- Think about how you feel in inspirational moments. Perhaps it's a moment in nature or in your place of worship. Maybe it's a moment of bonding with a loved one that is so beautiful it touches the sacred.

- Call to mind one of those moments of truth in a heartwarming movie or a humorous TV show. Remember how you feel when you watch something that comforts, inspires and cheers your soul.

- Reflect on the inner essence of divine love, that perfect love that pours like a waterfall into your heart from your Higher Self. Feel the invigoration and the awakening of your spiritual senses. Listen for the gentle whisper of the angels saying over and over again, "God loves you." And allow yourself to feel their gentle nurturing of your soul.

- Sit back, relax and remember the feeling you have when the sun is shining, the birds are singing and all seems right with your world. Allow yourself to feel it all over again—the warmth of the sun, the chirping of the birds, that comfortable sense of inner peace.

- Imagine any comforting situation that gives you a sense of uplift and joy. Stay with it for a few minutes. Bask in the reassurance and solace of this moment of imagery. And enjoy the positive shift in your feeling world.

Celebrate the good feelings. Stand up and stretch, smile at yourself in the mirror, sing to yourself, play a tune on your guitar or piano. Make up a poem or a song that celebrates your happy feelings. Draw some happy faces or fun-loving cartoon figures. Enjoy the moment of renewal.

2

Mastering the Shadows of Fear

Fair seedtime had my soul, and I grew up
Fostered alike by beauty and by fear.

—WILLIAM WORDSWORTH,
The Prelude

*L*et's take another look at the dragon of fear. As we do so, keep in mind your true identity as a child of the universe, a son or daughter of God. As the apostle John put it, "Beloved, now are we the sons of God, and it doth not yet appear what we shall be: but we know that, when he shall appear, we shall be like him; for we shall see him as he is."[1]

Think of yourself as a bearer of spiritual light, which emanates from your threefold flame and invigorates every dimension of your being. Only when fear distracts you from that inner pulsation of light do you identify with that fear and lose track of the loving, courageous person you really are.

Fear is like a shadow that slips in between you and the sun—the sun in the heavens and the sun of light and happiness within you. It clouds your true identity.

Yet it isn't real, in the true sense of the word. It's a lot like Peter Pan's shadow, which he keeps trying to see and getting exasperated with when he can't. We ourselves get pretty exasperated with our "shadow" when we can't seem to hold on to it and see it for what it really is.

When we identify with fear, we deny our selfhood. If in fear we think or say, "Maybe I won't make it, maybe I'm a lost cause, maybe God doesn't exist," we identify with the "not-self," the antithesis of our real being. That creates even more fear.

Our fears relate not only to current situations in our lives but also to whatever karma and soul pain we may be carrying from past events or past lives. Each of us has records of fear hiding in the folds of our garments of consciousness.

Fear Is a Pollutant

Fear is at the core of ignorance and superstition. We tend to fear whatever we don't understand, so we create superstitious myths and beliefs to explain it to ourselves. We even create an inner myth that we are unlovable—and turn it into a self-fulfilling prophecy by behaving in unloving ways.

On an energetic level, fear is one of the most active pollutants on the planet. When a horse smells it on his rider, he gets jumpy. A frightened animal will charge. Dictators and terrorists take control by instilling fear. And when we're afraid, we induce fear in others—scaring ourselves even more.

Thus, fear begets more fear. Ultimately, we create an inner chain reaction that builds a momentum of fear that can culminate in panic and hysteria. Our fears harbored over this life and long-forgotten past lives become a tremendous force of disintegration within us. That force of disintegration also impacts people with whom we interact. And it adds to the planetary momentum of fear.

Personal and planetary fears act as negative nutrients to the different levels of our consciousness. Over lifetimes of experiencing fear—sending out fear, taking in fear—we have been saturated with this toxin. Even our physical cells are accustomed to being fueled with fear.

Reconnect with Your Original Nature

In my clinical practice, I have noticed that after years of being fueled with fear, many people have a fearfulness that penetrates the depths of their spiritual, mental, emotional and physical being. A pervasive sense of terror lives in their heart and soul.

When we so identify with fear, we tend to forget our spiritual origin. And when we are out of sync with our spiritual nature, we feel a deep sense of soul pain and disconnection.

How do we reconnect? How do we turn our consciousness around? Many people on the spiritual path fast* and pray in order to overcome fear. Through physical

---

*I advise limiting a fast to one to three days. If you are under a doctor's care or have health problems, consult your doctor before fasting.

and spiritual purification, they gradually clarify their consciousness.

In their purified state, every atom, cell and element of their being begins to vibrate in attunement with the presence of God within them. They are able to fully realize their oneness with the Creator. And in that state of oneness, fear has no power.

We can think of every cell in our body as a star, a consciousness that has a focal point of the mind of God. The streams of light emanating from those cells reach all the way to the stars in the heavens, and the stars return the current.

I believe this is the reason we enjoy an energizing uplift when we look up at a brilliant starry sky on a clear night. As we gaze upon the stars in the heavens, we connect with the infinite flow of cosmic energy and affirm our heritage as sons and daughters of God.

Now we can seek to understand and resolve the source of our fears. As we do so, we can take to heart these enduring words: "There is no fear in love; but perfect love casteth out fear: because fear hath torment. He that feareth is not made perfect in love."[2]

We take courage to be true to our original nature of divine love. We reawaken our love for God, for ourselves and for those we meet along the highway of life. We remind ourselves that divine love and peaceful contemplation are antidotes to fears and doubts that have been our inner tormentors.

When you are feeling fearful, try this exercise to help connect with these antidotes:

1. Offer a prayer to the angels and your Higher Self to help you reconnect with divine love and peaceful contemplation.

2. Focus your attention on your heartbeat and on your breathing. Remember (or imagine) a beautiful nature scene or an uplifting moment in your life as you continue to stay in touch with your heartbeat and breath.

3. Softly murmur words of love and comfort to your soul, your inner child.

4. Envision the sunlight of your Divine Source flowing through you, enlightening you, invigorating you.

5. Now ask yourself, "What is the best way for me to maintain this experience of divine love and tranquility?"

6. Write down whatever intuitive answer comes to you. And follow through with it on a daily basis.[3]

Generating a Whirling Sun of Inner Peace

We all realize that instantaneous fear can be injected into a crowd of people. For example, when someone yells, "Fire!" in a crowded place (or we get news of an earthquake or terrorist attack), we feel the grip of that emotion.

Why does this occur? That message of fear polarizes with fear we already harbor within ourselves. If we didn't have our own fear to ground it, that fear-laden yell would rouse us to appropriate action, not panic.

We usually feel that fear in the pit of our stomach,

which connects directly to our solar-plexus chakra.*
Sometimes the fear can get so strong we are quaking all
over. What is the opposite of such inner fear and trembling? It is an ongoing sense of the inner peace and qui-
etude we just practiced.

Our solar-plexus chakra is meant to be a place of peace
—a whirling sun of peace, spinning so fast that it appears
to be utterly still. That whirling action transforms our
inner trembling. And it deflects all that is unlike itself—
just as a fan might blow away the dust. Try this mantra
when you feel that shivering in your solar plexus (visualize a band of white fire around the chakra):

COUNT TO NINE

Come now by love divine,
Guard thou this soul of mine,
Make now my world all thine,
God's light around me shine.

I count one,
It is done.
O feeling world, Be still!
Two and three, I AM free,
Peace, it is God's will.

I count four,
I do adore
My Presence all divine.
Five and six, O God, affix
My gaze on Thee sublime!

---

*The solar-plexus chakra, or spiritual center (located at the navel), is
directly connected with our emotions.

I count seven,
Come, O heaven,
My energies take hold!
Eight and nine,
Completely thine,
My mental world enfold!

The white-fire light now encircles me,
All riptides are rejected!
With God's own might around me bright
I AM by love protected![4]

When we have a powerful energy of peace whirling in our solar plexus, we do not tie into the fear when fear-inducing energies come at us. Those energies are deflected and transformed by our tremendous momentum of inner peace.

How do we keep the chakra whirling? By moving with the flow. What does that mean? Socrates knows.

The Way of the Peaceful Warrior

Socrates is Dan Millman's teacher in the book *Way of the Peaceful Warrior*. He instructs Dan not only about the illusion of death but also about the power of peace and moving with the flow in the middle of mayhem. He teaches Dan in unique ways—playing tricks on him, challenging him, scaring him, laughing at him—all the time impressing him with a true warrior's compassion, wisdom and humor.

At one point, having enraged Dan by confronting his "poor me" act, Socrates teaches him to use anger in a positive way. He tells him, "Anger can burn away old habits. Fear and sorrow inhibit action, you see; anger generates it. When you learn to make proper use of your anger, you can transmute fear and sorrow to anger, and anger, to action. That's your body's secret of internal alchemy."[5]

This is a thought-provoking teaching. Anger is a form of power energy; it can be used for good or ill. And for most of us, fear or pain underlies our anger. Anger is typically our attempt to gain power in a frightening or overwhelming situation. Socrates was showing Dan that converting anger into positive power is more fruitful than shivering with fear or playing "poor me."

He goes on to instruct, "When your mind creates a problem, when it resists life as it unfolds in the moment, your body tenses and feels this tension as an 'emotion,' variously interpreted by words like 'fear,' 'sorrow,' or 'anger.' True emotion, Dan, is pure energy, flowing freely in the body."[6]

Socrates likens this process of flow to the way a baby responds. As he puts it, "When a baby is upset, it expresses itself in banshee wails—pure crying. It doesn't wonder about whether it *should* be crying. Hold or feed it and within seconds, no more tears. . . . Babies let it flow, then let it go."[7]

We can learn a lot about energy flow from babies. They don't get all tied up in ponderous tangles of thought. Nor do they hold grudges. In their innocence and basic goodness, they simply express their immediate feelings and flow from one state of emotion into another. They are fully present in the moment.

As Ramakrishna says, "The anger of the good is like a line drawn upon water. It does not last long." Most of us relate to babies as "the good," but in essence all of us are. We simply see that basic goodness more readily in babies.

Energy flow, smooth or rough, is what our emotions are all about. In other words, we have universal energy flowing through every compartment of our being. On a feeling level we experience that energy flow as emotion—energy in motion—and we direct it in accordance with our state of consciousness. How we express that energy and what action we take is our choice—consciously or subconsciously.

Taking Balanced Action

Eastern teachers tell us that every action we take is karma-making, for good or for ill. When we take positive action, we make good karma. When we take destructive action, we make bad karma. And destructive action is often the result of trigger-happy emotions.

Good or bad karma is the result of our consciousness and the way we spend our energy. It is the consequence of our motives, thoughts, emotional reactions, words and deeds of this and previous lives.

We've all heard the phrase "What goes around comes around." This is the way karma works. Whatever we send out returns full circle to our own doorstep. As Paul taught the Galatians, "Whatsoever a man soweth, that shall he also reap."[8]

So how do we take action that is balanced? It has a lot to do with our intention. If our intention is for good, then we intuitively want our action to be balanced and constructive. The fire of God will propel us in the direction of our intent. And the sacred threefold flame burning in the secret chamber of our heart offers the balance.

When we exercise wisdom in the face of crisis, we draw upon the wisdom (golden) plume of our threefold flame. When we stand strong in the face of serious challenges, we are inwardly bolstered from the power (blue) plume. And when we are compassionate as well as heroic, we have accessed the love (pink) plume.*

Let's look at what happens when we do not exercise a balance of these three qualities. If we overemphasize wisdom, we can end up with a great idea that lacks compassion or appropriate action. In an extreme case, we might withdraw into an ivory tower of intellectual pursuits and ignore our responsibilities to our family, city or nation.

In today's world this might result, karmically, in our being ignored in time of need. We might ask ourselves when we feel abandoned, "Have I neglected others? Perhaps even those who are now neglecting me?"

If our love nature is overdone, we may end up being a sweet namby-pamby who doesn't take responsibility and makes a lot of dumb decisions. Now we risk the karma of irresponsibility and ignorance. No matter how great our loving intentions, if we do not fulfill them wisely and responsibly, we do not move forward.

When our power thrust is out of balance, we run the risk of becoming unreasonable, overbearing tyrants. That doesn't go over well with family, friends, business associates—or with God. And we can accrue much negative

*For more on the threefold flame, see p. xviii.

karma through a misuse of power.

Until we learn to balance power with wisdom and love, we remain tyrants—and we continue to make a lot of karma. One day that karma will return full circle, and we may find ourselves under the bondage of tyranny.

How do we keep that from happening? We cook out our karma. And how do we do that? We stoke our three-fold flame so we can take balanced action.

Stoking Our Threefold Flame

I teach my clients to use visualization, meditation and affirmation to activate the fire of God within them. They visualize their threefold flame in a sphere of white light and meditate upon that imagery. And then they make an affirmative statement, "I AM a threefold flame. I AM the balance of love, wisdom and power in action here." They repeat the affirmation until they begin to experience the truth of it.

Another effective way is by giving prayers or decrees. We all have our favorite prayers. One that many people find comforting is Psalm 23:

> The LORD is my shepherd; I shall not want.
>
> He maketh me to lie down in green pastures: he leadeth me beside the still waters.
>
> He restoreth my soul: he leadeth me in the paths of righteousness for his name's sake.
>
> Yea, though I walk through the valley of the shadow of death, I will fear no evil: for thou art with me; thy rod and thy staff they comfort me.
>
> Thou preparest a table before me in the presence of mine enemies: thou anointest my head with oil;

my cup runneth over.

Surely goodness and mercy shall follow me all the days of my life: and I will dwell in the house of the LORD forever.

When I offer this psalm as a prayer, I feel protected, comforted and empowered.

What is a decree? It is a dynamic form of spoken prayer used to direct God's light into individual and world conditions. Here is an example:

> I AM the light of the heart
> Shining in the darkness of being
> And changing all into the golden treasury
> Of the mind of Christ.
>
> I AM projecting my love
> Out into the world
> To erase all errors
> And to break down all barriers.
>
> I AM the power of infinite love,
> Amplifying itself
> Until it is victorious,
> World without end![9]

As we center in our heart and give this decree a number of times, the sacred fire increases in intensity and begins to transmute (or transform) the energy of our wrong motives, thoughts, feelings and actions. We may even feel a sense of physical heat around the heart area when this transmutation is going on.

Elizabeth Clare Prophet, teacher and author of profound books on New Age spirituality, says every cell in our body receives the fervent heat of our devotion—in proportion to how purified the cell is. The heat from the sacred fire in the heart actually causes a change in the chemistry of the physical cells.

Here's how it works. The sacred love fire in the heart is magnetized to the "sun" of the cell through the flow of our devotion. This love fire begins to build and eventually reaches a "boiling point"—much as fire under a teakettle boils water. When the kettle whistles, the water is boiling and turning into steam, which eventually evaporates. In the same way, the sacred fire of love in each cell dissolves the fear through an action much like evaporation.

This process occurs cell by cell. It is the way fear can be transmuted and released—by being "cooked out" by the fires of love. When we open our hearts to love, fear is dissolved and our soul and body are left intact. This is one way every form of darkness on earth, and the negative karma each of us carries, can be transformed—by God's perfect love, by transmutation.

No matter what we may have done in the past, we can turn around our consciousness. We can balance the karma of overdriven power moves, wrong decisions and unloving behavior. We can determine to stand tall for what is right, to make wise, balanced decisions and to practice the art of loving-kindness.

The Practice of Loving-Kindness

Buddhists teach the practice of *metta,* which means loving-kindness. Sharon Salzberg, an American Buddhist teacher, explains:

The Pali word *metta* has two root meanings. One is the word for "gentle." Metta is likened to a gentle rain that falls upon the earth. This rain does not select and choose—"I'll rain here, and I'll avoid that place over there." Rather, it simply falls without discrimination.

The other root meaning for *metta* is "friend." To understand the power or the force of metta is to understand true friendship. The Buddha actually described at some length what he meant by being a good friend in the world. He talked about a good friend as someone who is constant in our times of happiness and also in our times of adversity or unhappiness. . . .

Once, when someone described to the Dalai Lama how much fear they were experiencing in their meditation practice, he said, "When you're afraid, just put your head in the lap of the Buddha." The lap of the Buddha epitomizes the safety of a true friendship. The culmination of metta is to become such a friend to oneself and all of life.[10]

The meditative practice of metta allows us to embrace all parts of ourselves, as well as other people. In this practice, we first send thoughts and energy of loving-kindness to ourselves. Second, we send metta to a person who has been good to us, our benefactor. Third, we send metta to a friend of our choice. Fourth, we send metta to a neutral person. And fifth, we send metta to a person we find to be difficult (Buddhists speak of this fifth type of person as the enemy).

Here are the classical phrases that are used in the formal practice of metta, but you may also develop your own.

May I be free from danger.
May I have mental happiness.
May I have physical happiness.
May I have ease of well-being.

Repeat this four-line mantra with total focus until it rings true within you. Then begin sending loving-kindness to your benefactor: "May my benefactor be free from danger," and so forth. Continue with the friend, the neutral person and finally the "enemy."

Loving-Kindness Is Not Human Sympathy

Sometimes people confuse loving-kindness and compassion with human sympathy. Sympathy is not divine love; it is commiseration with the human condition. The world is full of human sympathy, that "poor you" kind of love, which fails to uplift or elevate the other person's consciousness. Instead, it deepens the victim's self-pity and takes the rescuer into the same morass.

Perhaps you have heard the story about the fellow who is sinking in the quicksand. A sympathetic passerby runs to his assistance. He jumps in to pull him out, and they both get caught in the quicksand. As they are both about to go under, a compassionate passerby grabs a branch from a tree, hangs on to the tree and pulls the unfortunate men to safety without endangering himself.

This is the way the inner drama of victim and rescuer works. When we try to rescue our victim self* by

---

*This is an aspect of inner child work, a type of therapy where we center ourselves in the loving adult and work with vulnerable parts of ourselves that need healing. The victim self is the part of us that feels helpless and overcome by difficult circumstances or the hurtful actions of other people.

sympathizing with its "woe is me" attitude, we get drawn deeper into a helpless, bogged-down frame of mind.

If we are compassionate instead of sympathetic, we help our victim self without getting caught in its plight. How? By taking a step back and seeking to understand the predicament. The light of understanding helps us see the way out, and compassion gives us comfort. Now we can climb out of that unhappy bog of consciousness.

Sometimes all we need is loving attention. If we suspect this is the source of our quagmire, we ask ourselves, "What is staying in this muddle doing for me?" Our victim self may very well reply, "Well, at least I'm getting your attention!"

Now what would happen if we simply hugged and reassured that woebegone victim self, as one would do with a child who is hurt or discouraged? We'd put our arms around ourselves and say, "It's okay. I love you and I understand how you feel." Pretty soon our victim self would be feeling loved and cared for. Then we can brainstorm to see what kind of action to take. All of these ways of offering compassion to ourselves can free us to move on to whatever is the task at hand.

Compassion as Tough Love

Sometimes compassion means to "deliver a good swift kick" to get our victim self moving forward. That's when the quagmire of self-pity has us so bogged down we essentially refuse to do anything about it—but we complain to whoever will listen.

At that point, the most compassionate action we can

take is to propel ourselves forward. We can do that by focusing specifically on a constructive plan of action. If we're too stuck to get ourselves moving, that kind of mandate may very well come from a friend, colleague or family member. Instead of getting angry with that person, we can breathe a sigh of relief that someone noticed. And we can take it for what it is—tough love.

How do we recognize that we have fallen into the sympathy and self-pity trap? We won't literally find ourselves going down in the quicksand. But there are signals. When life isn't going our way and we sulk, weep, wail or throw a tantrum, the signal light is flashing.

Sometimes a volatile reaction goes off with a bang and we ourselves can't imagine what set it off. All that happened was we were misunderstood, or we didn't get something we wanted or thought we deserved. And all of a sudden we became unglued.

Of course, such a disappointment can be frustrating, but it hardly merits our overreaction. Yet that is what can happen when our attitude toward ourselves or others is sympathetic rather than compassionate.

The way out of the dilemma is to express compassion. This is the way of love that lifts us up and sets us down on our own two feet. It is relating to the higher potential in ourselves and other people, no matter what may be going on with the "shadow" self. It is showing our love for people by telling them the truth, lovingly, and by helping them.

A verse from scripture says it well: "Let us not love in word, neither in tongue; but in deed and in truth."[11]

God's Gentle Love Touch

An article from *Guideposts* tells how a couple, Patti and Jack, experienced the compassion of the Creator alive and well in animal life.[12] It all came about from their move to northern Minnesota, black bear country.

One day a black bear cub appeared in their yard. Jack was concerned; Patti thought she was cute. As she said, "As I watched the little animal, my heart just melted." Little Bit, as they named her, would come right up onto their porch. Patti fed her nuts and seeds, and she seemed to feel right at home. She even brought eight other yearlings to visit. They made Jack and Patti's place their home away from home.

As time went by, Little Bit brought a large male bear to visit and the following spring appeared with a cub. One day when Patti's hand shook as she offered nuts to Little Bit (a side effect from blood pressure medication), the bear gently cupped her big paw beneath Patti's hand to steady it.

A year later when her father died, Patti wrapped her arms around Little Bit, letting tears of grief flow. The mother bear sighed and gently rested her head against Patti's. God's gentle love touch.

In the same way, we can recognize and accept that grace of divine love we carry within us. We can think loving thoughts and extend loving-kindness to ourselves and to others. We can gentle the fear-dragons by being compassionate to ourselves, our family and friends, neighbors, team leaders and co-workers—even our adversaries.

Love softens us, comforts us and helps us feel safe. In stormy weather, love is like an inner fire that warms the soul. As we exchange fearful avoidance for loving-kindness, we create an inner support that allows us to move on.

Master the Turbulence of Your Inner World

Some days are sunny; some are cloudy or stormy. Sometimes it is an outer storm of conflict or physical danger. At other times we scare ourselves with fearful thoughts, painful memories or uneasy forebodings about the future.

How do we cope with life's storms? How do we deal with the turbulence without and the surging waves within?

Our challenge is to ride the waves with love and grace, to so master the turbulence of our inner world that we remain courageous, balanced and serene in the midst of the storm. And sooner or later, the sun will come out.

Is courage the absence of fear? No, it is not. Courage is a mobilizing of the "can do" spirit. It needs to be accompanied by a compassionate heart and a willingness to take action in the very presence of fear.

Here is a five-step strategy that my clients have found helpful to outwit the culprit of fear in a challenging situation:

1. Find a private space and allow yourself to become fully aware of your feelings of fear, anxiety and vulnerability.

2. Be kind to yourself; take care of yourself. If you aren't sure what that means, ask yourself, "What

would I like someone else to do for me right now?"
Do that for yourself.

3. Ask for divine guidance and claim an inner stance
   of strength, courage and calm resolve.

4. Keep yourself informed about the situation that
   concerns you, and take constructive action in your
   own sphere of influence.

5. Be honest, forthright, kind and helpful to everyone
   involved.

When we handle challenging situations with courage
and compassion, our heart begins to come of age. And
when we strive to become the fullness of who we are
meant to be, we begin to fulfill our *raison d'être,* our
reason for being. Hand in hand with our Higher Self, we
become the captain of our ship.

3

Mustering the Courage to Face Our Dark Side

In a dark time, the eye begins to see,
I meet my shadow in the deepening shade.

—THEODORE ROETHKE
"In a Dark Time"

Carl Jung, the famous Swiss psychiatrist, named our dark side the shadow.[1] He taught that when we do not recognize our shadow side, or are unwilling to look at it, it tends to become demonic.

We need to realize that our fears are part of that shadow side. And when we do not bring those fears to light, they do tend to take us over in ways that seem crazy or demonic.

Fear is expressed in a thousand ways. Fear is closely related to apprehension, uneasiness, anxiety and out-and-out panic. Fear is behind rigidity, intolerance and fanaticism.

Fear is at the root of indecisiveness and hesitancy to take action. Fear is behind much of our disorganization, disorderliness or sloppiness—or their opposites, nit-picky organization, compulsive cleanliness or an obsessive need for order.

When we bring our fears up for air and look at them in the light of day, they often are not as fearsome as we thought they were. Unconscious forces gain power when we hide from them, when we say, "I don't want to look at that. It's too frightening." As we shrink from them, they increase their negative hold over us.

When we face and name those dark motives, thoughts or feelings, they become less daunting. As we mobilize our heart's higher power, wisdom and love, we turn the light on in that dark space of consciousness.

Shedding Light on Your Scary Dark Side

Take a moment now to tune in to your scary dark side. It's probably been coming up anyway since you have been reading about it. Name it. And write a page to yourself about it. Then choose a spiritual antidote to that point of darkness. (We've talked about some antidotes in chapters 1 and 2.)

As an example, perhaps you have a tendency to shade the truth, to lie. Hiding under that tendency is your fear of what might happen if you tell the truth. Your spiritual antidote could be to take the following steps.

1. Pray for the courage to speak the truth.[2]

2. Muster up courage a second before the lie sneaks out.

3. Take a deep breath and speak the truth.

4. No matter what happens, congratulate yourself for winning a victory over your dark side.

Take courage to look into your subconscious, to look into the unconscious, to bring your shadow parts to your outer awareness, to give them a name.

Remember how Jesus named the devils before he cast them out? He would say, "What is your name?" For instance, before he cast out the devils from the Gadarene man, he asked the unclean spirit its name. And the unclean spirit answered through the man, saying, "My name is Legion: for we are many." And the devils then entered a herd of swine.[3]

This naming of the inner devils becomes a teaching for us today. Once you name a point of fear, it is no longer an unknown controlling force. You have defined it, circumscribed it and started to detach from it.

The fear loses some of its negative power in the very process of being recognized and named. It becomes a manageable energy that you can cast out and replace. And in that process of replacement you have a turnaround in consciousness.

You can replace fear with enlightenment. You can replace it with faith in yourself and your inner walk with God. You can replace it with equanimity in the face of misfortune. You can replace it with loving care for yourself and others. And you begin to realize it's a great life if you don't weaken!

Mastering Fear of the Unknown

Many people have an underlying anxiety, or apprehension, about the unknown. Some years ago I began to explore fear of the unknown as it revealed itself in people's negative attitudes toward the mentally ill.

Through research and clinical work, I have learned that people are frequently apprehensive about what they don't understand. The unfamiliar itself can trigger uncertainty and fear. And out of fear we tend to become negative toward whatever is unknown. It becomes a vicious circle.

Thus, a hostile reaction to people we don't understand is often our porcupine way of handling fear. We, as it were, shoot quills of negativity to protect ourselves from a fearful unknown. I believe this is one of the dominant fears on the planet today.

Yet the unknown presents us with an opportunity—to discover, to grow in confidence, to increase in self-mastery. When we explore unknown territory, we take a giant step toward mastering our fear.

How can you begin to master fear of the unknown?

1. Ask your Higher Self or guardian angel to help you master that fear in a specific situation, for example, a change of job or location, a reversal of health or finances, a loss of an important relationship, and so on.

2. Name and define whatever it is that you fear. Write it down.

3. Come up with a tentative plan for handling the situation. Write it down.

Now the situation is no longer completely unknown because you have defined it. The next step is to quiet any emotional or physical agitation before taking action:

1. Take several slow deep breaths, focusing on the breath as you exhale.

2. Put your attention on your physical heartbeat. Place your hand over your heart if it helps you locate it. Notice the breath and the heartbeat together for a moment or two.

3. Remember an uplifting experience or inspiring scene. It might be a personal victory you have achieved or a beautiful moment in nature. Relax into the good feelings as you envision moving forward with your plan.

4. Take action accordingly.[4]

Roar at Your Dark Side

Remember the cowardly lion in the all-time favorite movie *The Wizard of Oz*? That cowardly lion knew what he most needed was courage. And when the wizard gave him a medal of valor, then and there the lion's mind-set shifted. He decided, "Now I am courageous. I have a medal to prove it." And he went out and roared at what he previously ran away from.

Even though the wizard was actually a fake, the lion's belief that the wizard could do magic brought about his shift from fear to courage. It reminds us how influential our mental attitudes are. A negative outlook gives rise to negative emotions and physical reactions. And the converse is also true—a positive frame of mind brings about positive emotions and reactions.

We can learn to roar at our dark side. Mark Prophet* used to do that. He would tell his students to beat on their chests and roar like lions. *Roarrrr.* Try it. It's both fun and effective.

Now what puny dragon of fear can stand up against that? Keep your sense of humor. The shadow forces can't stand to be laughed at. That's another thing Mark used to say. He'd quote Sir Thomas More: "The devill..., that prowd spirite, he can not endure to be mokqued [mocked]."[5]

One time Mark informed his staff that inner forces of darkness were about to invade their spiritual retreat, La Tourelle, in Colorado Springs. So he took them all up to the tower room, the highest point on the property. And then he said, "Now, everybody, laugh!" They laughed and laughed. They laughed until tears of laughter were rolling down their cheeks. And the laughter dispelled the darkness.

You can follow their example. You can laugh away your fear of the unknown. You can claim the coming of age of your heart and soul. With courage, with calls to the

*Mark L. Prophet was a visionary and a pioneer in modern religious thought. Mark, along with his twin flame, Elizabeth, served as messenger of the ascended masters for this age. He founded The Summit Lighthouse, a worldwide organization that embraces the great truths of all the world's religions.

angels of fearlessness, with laughter, with joy, you can free yourself from fear. You, too, can claim the light to confront your dark side—and win.

Opportunities for Self-Mastery

People fear not only the unknown but also sudden change in personal circumstances. We get attached to our way of life. Yet change in lifestyle is inevitable in changing times, and it is an initiation* we can pass.

We can either allow ourselves to be submerged in the darkness of fear or we can choose to pursue the light of opportunity. Of course, we want to take the opportunity. But it's not always as easy to do as to say.

Most of us fear letting go of what we are used to, and we fear what may be coming in the future. We fear to make major life changes in the face of international unrest, possible terrorist attacks and the ups and downs of the economy.

We fear all kinds of possible disasters: financial reverses, sudden job changes, having to relocate, ill health, loss of friends or family, the onset of middle age or old age. You could add to the list, I'm sure.

Yet every one of these situations is also an opportunity for self-mastery. The adversary is not change in itself but our fear of its impact on our life.

Let's say we finish our schooling—high school,

---

*Initiation refers to the spiritual testing of soul and spirit that we encounter on the initiatic path, that strait gate and narrow way that leadeth unto life (Matt: 7:14). As we pass our spiritual tests, we overcome, step-by-step, the limitations of selfhood in time and space and ultimately attain reunion with the Infinite One.

college, perhaps some advanced training. And then we start looking for a job. Let's see what fears we are likely to conjure up. How about the fear of being on our own? Or the fear of having to go through job interviews? Or perhaps the fear of not having enough experience or not being able to do the job once we get it?

Once we get a job, we fear not learning fast enough, not being productive enough and not pleasing the boss. We hear about someone getting laid off, and we fear the ax will fall on our own head. If we succeed in the job, we fear having to surpass our successes. We fear going up that corporate ladder because it brings more responsibilities.

Then we have relationships. I'm sure you'll recognize these fears and maybe have your own to add to the line-up. We fear the beginnings and endings of relationships—not to mention all that comes in between. We enter a relationship, and now we encounter the fear of revealing ourselves: What if my partner really gets to know me? Then maybe he or she won't like the real me. We fear losing ourselves. We fear commitment. We fear rejection and loss.

Perhaps we lose the relationship or get divorced. Fear is waiting just around the corner. Now we fear our change of circumstances. And we also fear there is something basically wrong with us. We fear meeting new people, and we fear getting into another relationship that might fail. We fear the rejection, we fear the loneliness; we fear for our children.

We fear the midlife crisis. Here we are with our life half over. We fear the future; we fear losing our vitality.

We fear not fulfilling our dreams, not fulfilling our goals. We fear getting old.

We enter our senior years. We fear the loss of friends and family, loss of our faculties, the unknown realms of death and the afterlife.

Yet when we take courage to banish our fears, we realize that each phase of life, even in retrospect, offers a gift. When we shine the light of understanding upon our life events, we see opportunities for self-mastery, for victory, for spiritual growth.

And now we know directly from people with near-death experiences that we needn't fear that initiation either. Dannion Brinkley tells us we have nothing to fear when we cross over. And he should know. He's been there —several times!

Dannion Brinkley, D.O.A.

Dannion Brinkley offers a great gift to all of us, born of his near-death experiences and the mission of healing given to him by beings of light. Dannion, who works with the terminally ill and has his own healing center in South Carolina, knows what it is to be frightened of death.

He also knows how to help people move through fear of death and dying into spiritual understanding and self-acceptance. He has been there himself. And he has accompanied many people who are crossing over into the realm of Spirit.

Dannion's first near-death experience occurred on September 17, 1975, when he was struck by lightning while talking on the phone. He went through a tunnel of light, met loving beings of light and experienced a life review where he was on the receiving end of what he had given out to life. Some had been good experiences; many were not so good. And he learned the wisdom of the Golden Rule: "Do unto others as you would have them do unto you."

As Dannion relates in *Saved by the Light,* he came back to life in a whirl of pain, confusion and opportunity. He was so sensitive from the lightning burns that it felt like torture to live in his body. He remembered the communications from the beings of light and experienced a constant stream of visions while sleeping. But he was unable to explain all of this coherently to anyone else.

At times he was confused and sometimes overwhelmed by his ability to read other people's thoughts, especially when he touched them. He experienced premonitions that turned out to be accurate predictions. As he states in his second book, *At Peace in the Light,* "I soon realized that I was in three worlds: the spirit world, my own world, and the world of whoever was around me."[6]

By Dannion's own admission, he didn't know what to do with his gifts for a while, but he learned. He even played around with gambling for a while because he was good at it, but he came to realize a gambler's paradise is an empty world. On the positive side, he realized that if he could get people as excited about spiritual matters as they were about slot machines or the dog races, he could make a positive change in the world.

He got back on track with his mission of the centers he was to build. The beings of light had told him these centers were destined to show people they could be in control of their lives through God. He was relieved and excited to realize that his near-death experience was a gift he could offer to others who were approaching death.

In Dannion's hospice work with the sick and dying, he tells people about the tunnel of light, the beings of light and the afterlife review. More than that, he helps them do their own life review ahead of time by talking over the happenings in their lives and putting them in perspective. He sits at the bedside of people who are dying—comforting, listening, sharing with them, learning—as he tells his story and they tell theirs.

In 1989, Dannion had a second near-death experience. This time he was undergoing a heart valve replacement to correct damage the lightning strike had caused in 1975.

He remembers going out of his body, watching the doctors working on his heart and once again going up the tunnel and into a place of brilliant light. He had another life review, one in which he could contrast the first twenty-five years of his life (before his first near-death experience) with the years that followed. He realized that in the years after the lightning strike he had made a positive difference in people's lives. He saw the good he had done and felt joy, happiness and love.

And in September 1997 he was back in the hospital and very near death—again.

In talking about life and death, Dannion has kept a sense of humor. In response to a rather pompous M.D./Ph.D. who challenged his "credentials" to comment on near-death experiences, he replied, "I am Dannion Brinkley, D.O.A."[7]

As Dannion humorously comments, "D.O.A. stands for 'Dead on Arrival,' which is what I have been. Although you won't find a D.O.A. on any university degree, having one does mean that I have a rare form of expertise."[8]

He also discovered that in Peruvian culture he is considered to be a "lightning shaman," meaning a person chosen by God. As a Peruvian shaman told him, "My people believe that God chooses people by striking them with lightning."

The shaman explained, "He does it just like a shepherd chooses a sheep. He reaches out with his rod and touches it. To be touched by God's love, power, and wisdom is the most extraordinary experience that man can ever have. . . . What has happened to you is special. . . . But you also receive a tremendous responsibility that needs to be accomplished. Otherwise, that wonderful beam of light that God has put into you fades away and disappears."[9]

Dannion took this counsel seriously. He continues to work on the centers, to do hospice work with the dying and to encourage others to do the same. He fully understands that his first near-death experience was a wake-up call and the others, extended opportunities. And, most important of all, he knows that "the goal of a life review at the end of a person's life is to evolve as a spiritual being."[10]

Dannion anticipates that future healing practices will be much more about manipulating the subtle energy fields of the body, as has been done in ancient Chinese practices, such as Qi Gong and acupuncture. Adjusting personal energy fields also has its place in energy psychotherapy, meditation, imagery, biofeedback, music therapy, therapeutic touch, prayer and spiritual healing. We are seeing much of this happening today.

He has also learned the usefulness of color, breath and fragrance. He understands that colors are waves of light, individualized in the aura of each person. He has discovered that breathing is a key to spiritual unfolding and understanding. And he has learned that certain fragrances bring peace and calm. He continues to work on the centers, trying to improve them, complete them.

As Dannion says, "We as a people are finally becoming aware of our subtle spiritual bodies. No longer do we view our physical bodies as being separate from our spiritual selves. We now know that the health of our bodies and minds relies heavily upon the health of our spirits too. It is through the subtle energies of the spirit that we can affect the greatest healing."[11]

Let's take Dannion's example and turn every one of our fearful dilemmas into an opportunity for self-mastery. This is what he has done, it's what the adepts have done and it's what ordinary people can do.

What does it require? A shift in mind-set and choosing to greet major and minor change as an opportunity to learn, to grow, to become more of who we are as spiritual beings. The challenges inherent in today's changing circumstances propel our inner growth—when embraced with faith in the Almighty and in ourselves.

An Adept on the Path of Fearlessness

An inspiring story of overcoming fear comes from an ancient adept on the spiritual path.[12] He spent an entire night on a mountaintop imploring God to show him the divine antidote to fear. This adept sought enlightenment not just for himself but for everyone who would ever suffer from fear.

Here is the remarkable tale of how a man became an adept of fearlessness and received the divine dispensation of that quality:

> Would you like to know how I inherited fearless-ness flame? . . . I was also embodied [on earth]. I also walked the path of initiation, and when I came to the place where all of the demons of the night and the fallen ones assailed me to take from me my own blessed Christ-awareness, I knelt in prayer.
>
> I called out to God, as God gave . . . me the aware-ness of these hordes of darkness in their array . . . come to attack the soul—the soul that is about to be set free in the ritual of overcoming.
>
> God showed me the horror of the night and of the fallen ones. And I cried out to him in my prayer and I said, "O God, you are greater than all of this. Your flame and your light [are] able to consume the darkness!"
>
> And I called to God for the specific action of the Christ consciousness that I knew must exist; for no thing, no shadowed one could occupy time and space without God providing the counterpoint of light, of freedom!

And I called forth the dissolving action of the light of the Christ. I called forth the ray that I knew would dissolve all that would assail me in the hour of my victory.

And I would point out to you that in that moment I faced, as you will face in the moment of your over-coming, the entire momentum of fear on [the planet]. ...All of that fear [was] upon me as the clouds of the night. Yet I concentrated on [having] faith in the element of grace that was able to counteract that dark-ness....

I received, after many, many hours of prayer, the vision of fearlessness flame...as a pencil-light across the sky, descending.

And I gazed and I saw, and, lo, the descending of that fire came unto me—to the very place where I knelt in prayer. And as that ray descended, I saw the com-ponents of the inner light. I saw something of the chemistry of God....I saw the piercing white light and the action of the emerald ray, piercing all of that darkness!

And...as the ray descended, I saw the dissolution of worlds of fear and doubt and all separation from God. And in the place where darkness was, I saw, lo, angels, hosts of light; and I heard the music of the spheres carried in fearlessness flame....

As the ray descended, it burst as a fire around me and I was enveloped in that fire, that fearlessness flame! And it burned through me and through my soul and through my chakras and through my four lower bodies. And it burned until I became that flame.

And I surrendered all vestiges of lesser awareness

outside of the great God flame, and I saw that God called me to be the fullness of that flame to many life-waves. I saw that God placed upon me the greatest initiation of fear, that I might receive the greatest blessing of its antidote.

This master of fearlessness knows how we feel when we are frightened. And he understands how difficult we believe it is to overcome that fear. He voices our fears:

You say, "I am caught. There is no escape! I must do this and this and this and this, and how will I do it all? It is too vast for me, for I do not have the understanding of the illumined ones."

Fear not, I say, for God in you is the overcomer. Let God be the fearlessness flame and you will discover. . . who is desiring to be the overcomer within you.

And he takes us on a journey of vivid imagery:

You stand in time and space. Before you is the great highway of life. And there will be times when you feel yourself as in a snowstorm, with your staff that is the teaching to guide you on your way. And in the robes of the pilgrim, you will move against the wind and the storm, scarcely able to see a foot before you. And you will press on, making, as it were, scarcely little progress on that path.

And there will be days when the storm will cease and there will be a calm and you will see the rays of the sun. [Then] once again the rain will come, the lightning and the thunder will be heard and the crackling of the storm.

Each step you advance, you advance by the action of fearlessness. That fear which you must conquer is the conglomerate of your own human consciousness amplified by the fallen ones [people who embrace evil] who live by fear not love....

This is the path which Christ walked. He cast out fear as the demons, as the palsied one. He cast out fear of death and want. He cast it out in every form and lived to prove the law of excellence and of love.

You must fulfill the life of the Piscean conqueror ere you can fulfill your divine plan in Aquarius.[13]

How do we fulfill our mission as Aquarian love-conquerors? We cast out the inner dragons of fear or refuse to give them the time of day. We take another major step forward by following the teachings of Master Jesus to embrace perfect love, which heals and displaces fear. Perfect love not only casts out fear but also positions us for our victory in Aquarius.

As Franklin Delano Roosevelt once said, "The only thing we have to fear is fear itself."[14] And fear can be quite subtle and pervasive. Some people spend hours in front of their television sets every day, partially because they're afraid to face real life. They fear life with all of its challenges, love with the risk of disappointment, relationships that might fail, the responsibilities of family. Instead of embracing life, they immerse themselves in a succession of TV dramas, in which they can participate vicariously— with no risks.

Living life does mean taking risks. Some people think it's a risk to get out of bed every day. But we do it. It's *how* we do it that's important. When we get up with a good attitude, accept the day's challenges, make constructive decisions and face our karma, we take a step forward in fulfilling our destiny.

In order to do this, we must outwit the fear of taking risks. How do we do that? We determine to love ourselves and our mission so much that fear fades into the background. We replace it with a stance of fearlessness. This does not mean an absence of fear—but being courageous in the face of fear. So we get out of bed and pray for love, courage and fearlessness. And we get on with our day.

On an energetic level, fearlessness is a spiritual fire, a brilliant white light tinged with emerald green, as the master of fearlessness described it. We can pray for that light of fearlessness to fill our soul and our etheric, mental, emotional and physical bodies.

Blessing Is Preceded by Initiation

When we make a call for a great blessing, as this adept of fearlessness did, we can expect to face whatever is its counterpoint of darkness. The patterns of light and darkness are always juxtaposed.

Before this adept could receive the dispensation of fearlessness he had to pass his initiation of encountering the conglomerate of fear of everyone on the planet. Only then did he receive the great blessing of the divine antidote, fearlessness. As he describes it:

> In order that I might carry that fire [of fearlessness] and be worthy to carry it, I must . . . first perceive

all that would oppose that fire. I [must] give answer unto the LORD whether I would stand fast to focus that flame in the face of all that would oppose it until the ultimate consummation of the planes of [matter].

You see, . . . whatever virtue you invoke from the heart of God, you must first slay the darkness that will assail that virtue. And God will not lower into the chalice of your heart the elements of that flame until you have stood by your own light, your own determination, your own momentum—until you have stood to conquer those who would challenge you the moment you would receive that energy. . . .

When you enter the [spiritual] path and you begin to call forth the light of God, that light will come forth as a strong energy. It will penetrate your being and the vast canyons of your subconscious. It will penetrate. It will cause to be ejected from your subconscious those very elements that are incompatible with the light.

And you will find yourself as the disciple moving in the storm, [in] the hail and the snow, unable to see before you. Then you will realize: This is not from without; it is from within!

That's quite a realization. All of a sudden in the middle of this tremendous storm he is describing, he has a profound insight: "This storm is not from out there. It's coming from within me."

We all need to come to that realization. Each of us is an individualization of the God flame, a unique spark of the divine. Yet in our exercise of free will, we have made mistakes, and we carry within us whatever darkness we have created through those mistakes.

God possesses the antidote to all of our darkness. So the adept of fearlessness flame summons his courage and says to himself, "I will conquer, for I know God possesses the antidote to all darkness in my world. I will have the courage to conquer."

Remember, courage in itself doesn't mean we have no fear. It means the fear does not immobilize us; we take action in the very face of fear. So we turn on the light of fearlessness flame. We beam up the light of our heart. And we take courageous action.

Where does the fear go? It is displaced! Just like turning on a light in a dark room. Courage and fearlessness take the place of the fear.

Keep On Moving!

This adept of fearlessness willed himself to be courageous:

I will have the courage to conquer! I will not shrink as the coward. I will not be the will-o'-the-wisp and allow myself to be blown hither and yon. I will take my stand. I will be firm and resolute! And I will pray and I will fast and I will commune with my God until he provides the fullness of that response which will be the healing, the regeneration and the liberation of my soul!

This is what it takes to be a Piscean conqueror. It takes sticking to that work, that work of the ages. And just at the moment when all other mortals would give up, that is the moment to press on. And you will find, when you press on, that suddenly, when the

LORD comes into the habitation of your being, the storm will cease and you will say, "Was it only sound effects? Did I imagine myself in a movie set? Was it all unreal?"—so quickly does the darkness vanish....

Here is the key, then, to overcoming that fear... that stiffens the flow of life, the fear that ultimately is the death of self-awareness. The key is to keep on moving!

When you find yourself in a snowstorm or a blizzard, you will not curl up on the side of the road, for you know instinctively you will freeze to death. You keep moving. This is the key to the conquering of all fear. Keep moving! Keep active! Move through the elements, move through the mirage of fear! Pierce it! ...and discover the island in the sun, the place of light, the Garden of Eden.

From his personal experience, this master of fearlessness has given us the spiritual formula for victory over fear: We choose to become fully aware of the challenges of inner or outer darkness. By faith, we trust that there is a divine antidote. We go to God. We kneel in prayer. We ask God to help us. He answers us. He sends forth the light. We see the light. We become one with that light. And we keep on moving!

The darkness this fearless adept encountered was like a mirage. Have you ever driven down a hot desert road where heat waves appear in front of you? This is the way light refracts from the heat, especially around sand dunes. It forms patterns that look like real images. But it's all a mirage, an illusion.

Fear is like that. Inside of us, we have a mirage of fear. But instead of so scaring ourselves with our human creation that we come to a screeching halt, we can put our trust in God and move forward. We can act as if we aren't scared—until we come to believe it ourselves. And when we keep on moving, we move through the mirage into reality.

It takes the same kind of determination that the master of fearlessness is describing. At that moment when we most want to quit, we don't. We press on. When we most want to stop and curl up in the snow, we stand up and keep our feet moving.

So when we feel immobilized with fear, with un-easiness, with panic, we gather up our courage and invoke the divine antidote—fearlessness flame. And we keep on going, one step at a time.

Scattering Dad

Recently I saw an amusing TV movie called *Scattering Dad*.[15] After dad's death, he appears to his wife to tell her she must scatter his ashes. His body, however, is already buried in the garden. She has to get it exhumed, cremated and then scatter the ashes. Dad tells her he can't get in the pearly gates until the ashes are scattered from a high mountain peak. The problem is that she is terrified even to leave the house and has been immobilized by her fears.

The entire drama is particularly problematical because the wife has inner sight, which no one else understands except the Native American shaman who helps her. Although she can see dad and the special guides who show her the way to fulfill his request, no one else has a clue. They think she's just plain crazy.

One of the most humorous and touching incidents is the way she gets herself to leave the house and begin her trek up the mountain. She tremulously puts one foot in front of the other and counts, "One!" Then she puts the other foot forward and counts, "Two!" Step-by-step, counting each step to herself, she inches her way out of the yard carrying dad's ashes in a coffee can.

It's a movie worth seeing, so I won't tell you the whole plot, but this woman gains her victory over fear by simply moving forward, one step at a time. Ultimately, dad's ashes get scattered, her fear is resolved and she even uses her own technique of counting each step to talk one of her daughters, frozen with fear, off a high ledge on the mountain.

We can see that the process of conquering fear is really the mastering of our self-limitations, our human consciousness. The enemy is within. And that is actually very good news. Why? If it's inside us, we can mobilize ourselves to overcome it.

When we draw upon the strength, wisdom and compassion of our Higher Self, we can stand, face and conquer our scary thoughts and feelings. We can shine the light of understanding upon those shadowy fears that enter our consciousness from the dark side. And that light banishes the shadows.

Riding the Tibetan Wind Horse

Another way of moving beyond fear is described in the enlightening book *When Love Meets Fear,* in which David

Richo tells the story of the "wind horse."[16] As Richo explains it, the wind horse is a Tibetan image for the marriage of effort and grace. In other words, when we make the effort to ask God for help and then swing into the saddle and take action, the grace of the Holy Spirit descends to speed us along.

Despite the power of the wind, we remain steady in the saddle when we ride the wind horse. Both the wind and the horse help us move through time and space. The wind pushes us; the horse carries us.

The horse symbolizes the visible choices we make by our actions, our efforts to handle fear with courage. And the power of the horse is amplified by the invisible winds of the Holy Spirit—winds of grace that move us beyond what we have the power to do through human effort alone.

With our own mighty effort and the powerful winds of the Holy Spirit propelling us, we can claim an attitude of fearlessness, we can exercise courage and balance, and we can stay in the saddle in the face of every challenge.

We see the phenomenon of "riding the wind horse" in every situation where people have called upon the Spirit of the living God to help them and have acted courageously and victoriously.

We have seen it in the actions of soldiers, sailors and marines who fought for freedom in two world wars and in Korea, Vietnam and Desert Storm. We see it today in the men and women fighting the war against terrorism, in journalists risking their lives to bring the news to the world and in Red Cross workers bringing aid to suffering people.

We see it in people who face and overcome physical disabilities, mental handicaps or emotional anguish to live productive lives. We see it in hospitals and hospices where people dying of cancer are praising God and comforting loved ones up to the end.

When we call upon the LORD and mobilize the strength and courage to do our part, the grace of the Holy Spirit lifts us up and beyond our human frailties.

Exercise: Facing Fear

Let's try an exercise in facing fear. We are going to ride the wind horse. And we set the tone for it with a favorite meditation, affirmation or prayer. That's the foundation for this kind of spiritual-psychological work.

1. Ask your Higher Self and the angels to help you face a specific fear you want to overcome. Take a look at that fear; name it. Then ask yourself, "What is its purpose? What is its lesson?" In every point of inner darkness there is a lesson the soul needs to learn. Take a moment to contemplate what you might learn from that particular fear.

2. Ask yourself, "What quality do I need to summon to replace that fear? What is the higher quality of my soul and spirit that is its divine antidote?" The antidote may be the quality of faith, courage, fearlessness, fortitude, nonattachment, resourcefulness, and so on.

3. Now write a letter to your fear: to the fear of pain or fear of poverty, fear of embarrassment, fear of

relationships, fear of failure, fear of being controlled, fear of being a terrible person, fear of sick-
ness—whatever you fear. Explain that you appreciate its purpose, its intention. You understand that
it is coming to warn you of some danger, to help
protect you (or so it thinks).

4. In your letter, tell that fear that you are claiming
your courage to handle any seeming danger, so
you don't need fear anymore. You might write
something like, "You can retire from duty because
I have hired courage and fearlessness, and I am
partners with the love, wisdom and power of my
Higher Self and my angels." You are politely
informing that fear-dragon that you no longer need
it, that you are ready to handle the fearsome situation.

5. Conclude your letter by telling that retiring fear
that you will be riding the wind horse through that
fearful scenario with masterful aplomb.

6. Do it! And remember, "Practice makes perfect."

If there are a few quakes in the tummy, you say, "Fine,
quake away. But I'm revved up and choose to move on."
You have told that fear-dragon that its job is done. You
have kindly but firmly fired that dragon. You have decided
to replace it with boldness, faith and focused action. With
effort and grace, you can ride the wind horse through
situation after situation—to victory.

4

Banishing Fear-Dragons from the Psyche

No coward soul is mine,
No trembler in the world's storm-troubled sphere:
I see Heaven's glories shine,
And faith shines equal, arming me from fear.

—EMILY BRONTË
"Last Lines"

*A*ll of us are aware that we live in a time of continuous change and turmoil. As we pick up the newspaper or turn on the TV news, it is often with a sense of apprehension. Will there be a report of violence or terrorism? Will there be a new threat to America's economic stability and our own?

Overcoming fear has been a major initiation for the past two thousand years and more—an initiation that adepts, saints, sages and ordinary men and women have

passed. The master of fearlessness, whose story we re-
viewed in chapter 3, was one of them. In following the
footprints of these indomitable ones, we discover that
fear is rooted deep in the human psyche.

Let's consider four archetypal fear-dragons buried in
the psyche of humanity and how they impact our lives.
Their mischief can keep us from fulfilling our higher calling, looking to the future with hope, greeting change as
opportunity and outwitting the dark side—in ourselves
and wherever we encounter it.

We can chart these four archetypal fears on what Elizabeth Clare Prophet has taught as the cosmic clock.[1] To
illustrate the concept, draw a large circle representing the
face of a clock. Then divide it into four quadrants. Each
quadrant represents a specific dimension of consciousness
and an underlying core fear that plagues humanity.

On this clock, the first quadrant (12:00–3:00) represents our etheric, or spiritual, being. The second quadrant

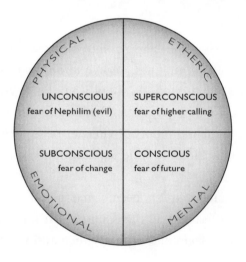

(3:00–6:00) charts our mental functioning. The third (6:00–9:00) corresponds to our desires and emotional reactions. And the fourth (9:00–12:00) stands for our physical body.* You can picture these dimensions of consciousness as interpenetrating, vibrating cylinders of energy—as four energy bodies.

We are most aware of our physical body, which vibrates at a slow enough rate that we can see and touch it. But we also have an emotional body, which makes itself known through our feelings and desires. It vibrates faster than we can see or touch.

Our mental body vibrates still faster. It is in a dimension we cannot see or feel but are quite aware of as concepts, thoughts and ideas. Our etheric body, the highest in vibration, is the arena of soul and spirit, which is ethereal. It expresses itself through intuition, insight, imagination, meditative reverie and spiritual experiences.

These "bodies" also relate to different aspects of our consciousness. The physical body correlates with the unconscious mind, the level of our psyche that contains repressed experiences and residue of long-forgotten memories.

The emotional body correlates with the subconscious mind, where we find those experiences that are emotionally charged. They are just below the threshold of awareness (what we mean when we say, "It's just on the tip of my tongue").

The mental body correlates with the conscious mind. This level contains our conscious thoughts and impressions

---

*These quadrants also relate to the elements: the first quadrant represents fire; the second, air; the third, water; the fourth, earth. The elements correlate with the etheric, mental, emotional and physical bodies.

as well as the ability to label and consciously direct our actions.

The etheric body correlates with the superconscious mind, the realm of intuition, inspiration and artistic, spiritual and ethical inclinations toward humanitarian and heroic action.

All of these levels of consciousness are bathed in an energetic sea of what psychiatrist Carl Jung described as the collective unconscious. We share this arena of experiences in time and space with all evolutions of humanity from all ages—past, present and future.

Fear of Our Higher Calling

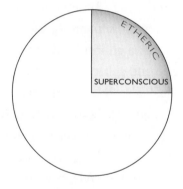

Our first core fear resides in the etheric quadrant, our spiritual body. This dragon is the fear of meeting our soul's higher calling.[2]

Through the flow of divine light, we are awakened to a higher calling, the calling to fulfill a special mission. It may be in any arena—in science, religion, education, healing, politics, communication, the arts, the trades, family life, and so forth.

To fulfill that higher calling, we need to continually move toward our goal and not look back, except to learn from our victories and our defeats. Yet a whole range of fears can spring up, such as: What will happen to me if I go for it, if I pursue that new direction? Will I be able to do it? Will I have to give up my old lifestyle? Will I miss it? Will I want it back? Am I going to make a fool of myself? What if I try and fail? What if everyone rejects me?

Psychologists call this type of fear, fear of success. It's the fear of pursuing our inner dreams, of reaching for the stars. We may fear that high reach because we might not be able to hang on to it, or we might be expected to top it. We may be concerned that friends or loved ones will scoff at our new endeavor. Perhaps we will have to leave behind someone or something we have relied on for security. We may be uneasy about letting go of an old dream or our familiar way of life.

Most of us realize that if we are going to make our dreams come true, we need to reach high with all the zest, enthusiasm and faith we can muster. Yet when we begin to do so, we often encounter an inner inertia—a reluctance to extend ourselves beyond our comfort zone, to go beyond what we are used to doing.

Isn't this especially true when we suspect that a new venture will rock our comfortable boat—or cause waves for other people's boats and the backwash of reaction will flood us?

We can resolve our hesitation once we determine, hand in hand with our Higher Self, what our higher calling is. Often it has to do with a talent, skill or interest we already have or with some new aspect of life that attracts and intrigues us. People discover their mission through education, meditation, contemplation and by cultivating a variety of interests.

Once we figure out our higher calling, we can go for it. We say to ourselves, "I'll take the plunge and do it—no matter what!"

Julie Takes the Plunge

When Julie, one of my clients, was moving on in her life, she said, "Okay, I know my higher calling is to share my spiritual journey with others, but how do I translate that into my daily life?"

I suggested, "Why don't you tell me what you already do on a daily basis that is specific to your spiritual journey and what you would want to convey about that to others? Then step-by-step we can brainstorm what it might take to make it happen."

Julie pondered aloud, "Well, I always talk to God first thing in the morning. That sets my day. I also like to write poems and letters to God. It might be kind of neat to put my poems and spiritual practices into some kind of artistic form. If I design it beautifully, I could give copies to anyone who is interested. But I'm not really good at art and design. That's kind of a block for me."

"Okay," I responded, "how about when you hit that block, figuring a way around or through it? If you need more skills in artistic design, you could either get some training or find someone who already has those skills to help you. Actually, that would be a way to start sharing your spiritual journey with another person."

Julie was a bit hesitant. "I'm not sure I can take time to do all of that. I have to earn a living, you know."

I smiled at Julie's typical excuse. We both knew it was her favorite way of avoiding a challenge—even if it was her own idea.

"Okay, okay," Julie laughed. "You never take my dodge seriously, do you? How about giving me an assist here?"

I offered some input. "All right, let's think this through. If your higher calling takes more time than you think you have, you need to cut something out—and I'm not talking about your job. How many hours a day are already filled, including work?"

Julie thought for a moment. "Well, I know I need about eight hours sleep, and it takes me a half hour both to and from work. When I add in basics like personal care, meals and telephone calls, I probably need another five hours. Counting my eight hours at work, twenty-two hours are already spoken for. That leaves me two hours a day, plus weekends. And on Sunday I like to go to church and visit friends."

I added, "Could you see yourself spending those extra two hours a day during the week plus Saturdays doing what it would take to create materials and begin to share your spiritual journey?"

Julie was looking relieved. "Yes, I think that's actually doable. And Sunday after church would be a great time for me to do my sharing. I could start with friends and move on from there. It's amazing how when we spell it out, it looks possible."

I agreed. "Sounds good, Julie. One more idea comes to mind. If you run into money problems, you could either cut your spending or take an extra half-day job on Saturday to bring in additional funds. In fact, you are doing so well you might just cut your sessions with me to once a month. That would save some money."

Julie laughed. "Okay, I get it. I'm up for it. I really do think I can make it happen. But my family will think I'm crazy to put myself on that tight a schedule—especially for spiritual stuff."

That was her last ditch defensive maneuver, so I replied, "If your family think you're crazy, love them anyway and keep on going for it. It's *your* higher calling, not theirs."

Julie agreed to try. She went on to make it happen. She now delights in sharing her spiritual journey with others and has created several lovely pamphlets and a book of poems that she gives to people who are interested.

As she told me later, "I learned that whatever happened, I had to keep my eye set on my goal. Once I did what I didn't think I could do, at least once, I realized I could do it again. And so I just kept on doing it, one step at a time. I'm still doing that."

As Julie learned, the fear that you can't do something or take the next step or do it again is usually a veil of illusion. When you march right through that veil, it disappears.

Our Higher Calling Is a Moment of Destiny

What Julie has done, you can do. Put your hand in God's hand. Ask the angels to help you. Do your best. And celebrate your victories, big and small, every day.

When you pray for guidance, you can affirm: "Through the inspiration and guidance of my Higher Self and the angels, I will envision my higher calling. I will determine to move onward and upward. I will trust in the great God flame within my heart. And I *will* realize my higher calling!"

As you move toward your new calling, pray to be imbued with fearlessness. Surrender all that you fear and hand it over to God and your Higher Self. Then visualize a bonfire of violet flame—that high-frequency spiritual energy that transforms negativity into light. Toss that bundle of worries into it and watch the violet fire consume them.

Here is a simple violet-flame mantra you can give:

> Radiant spiral violet flame
>   Descend, now blaze through me!
> Radiant spiral violet flame,
>   Set free, set free, set free!
>
> Radiant violet flame, O come,
>   Expand and blaze thy light through me!
> Radiant violet flame, O come,
>   Reveal God's power for all to see!
> Radiant violet flame, O come,
>   Awake the earth and set it free!
>
> Radiance of the violet flame,
>   Expand and blaze through me!
> Radiance of the violet flame,
>   Expand for all to see!
>
> Radiance of the violet flame,
>   Establish mercy's outpost here!
> Radiance of the violet flame,
>   Come, transmute now all fear![3]

All of us can benefit from setting and achieving positive goals, especially about our higher calling. As Elizabeth Clare Prophet says:

> There is a moment that will come, and it comes to all of us, when the calling we have been pursuing will not be enough.
>
> We get content with our best. We get content that we are on top of things—everything is in control, everything is going right, we're in command of our job, we're in command of our soul. And all of a sudden, God comes along, pulls the rug out from under us and says, "It's not enough. You have a higher calling."
>
> At that moment in our lives, the best up to that moment is no longer good enough. And we say, "What have I done wrong? I tried my hardest; I did my best. What happened?"
>
> It's never easy to take the next step. We must let go of many things, shed them, turn our backs on them. We must understand that the higher calling is there, that it is the moment of our destiny.[4]

We can't define our new calling if our mind is clouded by fear. So we make up our mind that we want to fulfill our higher calling, and we aren't going to let an old fear-dragon stand in our way. Like Thomas Edison, we determine to keep on creating our light bulb until on the umpteenth try, it lights up!

Think back in time for a minute. Ask yourself, "What was I doing ten years ago, twenty years ago? Would I want to be where I was then?" Of course not! You have moved on to a higher calling. And you are doing just fine, thank you very much!

It is useful to look back, to see how far you've come. If you are a person uneasy about moving forward, say to yourself, "I'll look back and remember how far I've already come. I know I can keep on moving. And ten years from now, this new calling will be a piece of cake!" If you have done it once, you can do it again.

Think of it this way: If ten years ago or twenty years ago God had shown you what you are doing today, maybe you would have felt faint with fear. But you have grown into it. With a little help from upstairs, you are here. With that same help, ten to twenty years from now you will still be moving on, moving up the mountain of Self, expressing an even higher calling.

Darlene's Doodles

Darlene, a talented young woman, had been working as an executive secretary in a publishing firm for several years. She came to see me because she was bored stiff with her job, and she was not making any use of her artistic talent.

As she said to me, "I've settled for a well-paying job, and my creativity has gone down the drain. I go home at night and feel completely depressed. So I flip on the TV and watch some meaningless show until my eyes won't stay open. Then I go to sleep and get up the next day, and repeat. Blah, blah, blah."

"What would you really like to do, Darlene?" I asked.

She was quick to respond, "I know what I would like to do, but it isn't at all practical. My boss, my family and my friends would think I've gone nuts."

I asked her, "What is this 'impractical' idea of yours?"

Darlene laughed. "I want to be an artist and get paid for being an artist. I've been sketching and doodling most of my life, but it's just a hobby. I haven't the slightest idea how I could support myself with it. At one point I looked into art school, but I didn't have the money for it. And I still don't have the money to just quit my job and go to school."

"Would you have to quit your job to do that?" I queried.

She responded, "You do cut right through, don't you? Yes, I suppose I could take art courses on the side, but I don't want to do that. I want to immerse myself completely in art and get out of secretarial work altogether."

"Okay," I responded, "let's brainstorm a bit here. How about voicing every idea you have that's related to what you want to do? And I suggest you write them down as they come to you so you won't lose them."

Darlene came up with quite a long list. Some things were, as she put it, "nutty!" but others looked promising.

I asked her, "Are you willing to follow up this week on these ideas we think might have some promise?"

"Yes," she responded. "I really hadn't put my mind to it seriously before, but I can see there might be some daylight at the end of this tunnel if I do that."

Once this young lady sets her mind to something, she really goes for it. When Darlene came back two weeks later, she had narrowed her list to creating fashion or comic illustrations. She had also put together a portfolio of her drawings, and she was taking an evening art course to refine and broaden her portfolio.

We talked about how she might pursue one or both of those avenues. She said, "I think I could learn fashion illustrating because I love the world of fashion, but I already have quite a few comic drawings that I've done over the years. Maybe at some point I could combine the two, but I think I'd better start with the comic stuff."

Then we talked about possible professional contacts to move her along. She remembered, from several years before, a contact through the publishing firm with an artist who had illustrated several books. And she recalled that one of those books was on humor.

As she said, "Now that I think about it, I remember at the time thinking I ought to talk to him about my interest in comic illustrations. But I said to myself, 'That's way out of my league.'"

I asked, "How are you going to know if it's out of your league if you don't pursue it?"

"You read my mind," she responded. "I'm going to take courage in hand and contact him. The worst he can do is say, 'Get lost!'"

Darlene made the phone call the next day and arranged to interview with that artist. He didn't tell her to get lost. He was actually pleased she had come to him for advice. He asked to see her portfolio. While she fidgeted and mentally planned a quick escape, he looked over her drawings.

After what seemed to Darlene an endless perusal of her sketches, he looked up, smiled and told her, "Your drawings show a lot of promise, young lady. What you need is some professional experience." And he proceeded to give her the names of some illustrators he knew who were so busy they were hiring assistants.

After several months of ups and downs with illustrators who didn't give her the time of day, one of them referred her to someone doing exactly what Darlene wanted to do—comic illustrations in the arena of fashion.

Darlene burst into my office at the end of my client day. "You aren't going to believe this!" she said. "I've got a part-time, evening job as assistant illustrator with the most fabulous artist. When I saw what Gina was doing, I couldn't believe it. She loves to produce comic sketches of high-fashion people, and they are really a stitch! And she's delighted to find an assistant who is interested in combining the two. I just hope I can measure up, but I really think I can do it. If it works out, I'll give notice and leave my secretarial job."

"Terrific!" was my response. I also told Darlene I thought she was smart to keep her secretarial position until she had enough income from illustrating to keep body and soul together.

All of this was a number of years ago. Darlene turned out to be just the assistant Gina was looking for. After a year of proving herself, Darlene accepted Gina's offer to become a full-time partner, combining her secretarial skills with illustrating work.

As she told me when she called to give me an update, "I am getting really proficient at comic fashion illustrating, if I do say so myself. Gina agrees, and our clients are happy with my work. And she is so relieved not to have to do the secretarial aspect of our partnership. That's not her strength. I don't even mind it at this point because it's a necessary aspect of making it all work. We are a great team together."

If reading about Darlene has tuned you into your higher calling, write it down. Make a note about that next rung on your ladder of spiritual initiation or career or relationship—and whatever is one step ahead of where you are now. Think about how to make it happen. Pray about it. And go for it!

Fear of the Future

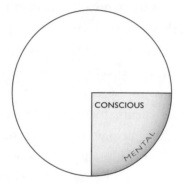

Let's take a look at the second core fear, which exists in the mental quadrant. It's fear of the future, which comes from the cognitive mind—what's going to happen tomorrow?

If you have fear lurking in the folds of your consciousness, you can get so worked up: "What's going to happen to me? What's going to happen to the world? What's going to happen to my community? What's going to happen to my children?" As some people say, "It's a calculated risk to get out of bed in the morning."

Many people tell me they have a fear of the future

since the September 11 terrorist attacks and all that has occurred subsequently. Some of my clients have nightmares about being caught in such an attack. Many fear the possibility of biological or chemical warfare by terrorists, especially since the incidents of anthrax have occurred.

Small children who watched the terrorist-driven planes crashing into the World Trade Center over and over on TV thought it was actually happening over and over. They needed a lot of reassurance from their parents. And what about the families of the thousands killed in those terrorist attacks? They suffered greatly and their future has been impacted, but they can also heal.

Immediately following the terrorist attacks, Tom Farris, psychologist and clinical director of an Alameda, California, firm whose specialty is employee counseling, reported that his clients' focus had shifted dramatically. Instead of asking for help with marriage or family issues, "people are calling because they're afraid their workplace will be the next target," Farris said. "They've never felt this kind of vulnerability."[5]

If we continue to revolve horrendous pictures or fearful thoughts, we can frighten ourselves into feeling totally overcome. Our human mind works that way if we don't call a halt. It's our job to interrupt the horror movie playing in our minds—to turn it off and replace it with a solid determination to live life productively and to hold a vision for a positive future.

We need to give ourselves and each other spiritual inspiration, constructive ideas, emotional support and practical help. And most of all, we need to make daily contact with God through our spiritual practices. As we do so, we can earnestly pray for peace to reign throughout the world and for the future to be bright with promise for all of us.

Take a moment to jot down a few notes about your personal fears of the future. When you face them, you can outwit them. For the most part they are figments of the imagination or leftover images of the past. Therefore, you can change them.

We also do ourselves a favor when we focus on whatever comes our way each day, instead of swamping ourselves with worries about what may never happen. We can choose to handle today's events the best way we know how, with our hand in God's hand and plenty of help from our guardian angels.

We can ask ourselves, "How might Rudy Guiliani or Helen Keller or Winston Churchill handle this?" Think about other steadfast people. What would they do? What would your Higher Self tell you to do? And then follow the example of the hero or heroine of your choice or what your Higher Self or guardian angel is prompting you to do.

When you live each day this way, your heart feels lighter and your soul is at peace.

Live in the Eternal Now

Mrs. Prophet's perspective on the future relates to her remembering past lives. She says:

> Fear of the future has always been around because of all the horrendous things that have happened

on the planet since time began. Whether in this life or past lives, we've been in situations of tremendous jeopardy. We need to tell ourselves, "I'm here, I'm alive, I'm well, I survived."

None of the earth changes, wars or conditions on the planet that caused us harm or death in any previous lifetime has ever been able to stop us. Why fear the future now? When we put things in perspective, we realize we live in the eternal Now.[6]

Even death has no hold over us. We just lay down the body, pick up a new one (a better one if we made good karma) and go on.

When we think about it, we only have the here and now. One second ago is already passed; tomorrow hasn't come yet. So fear of what may happen in the future is connected with past experiences that we project into the future. In our mind we dredge up something unresolved, speculate on it recurring and think, "Isn't that going to be terrible!"

This tendency to bring up ghosts of the past is a part of the human condition. Sometimes we dredge up an old trauma and project it into our future even if it doesn't exactly apply. We act as if we enjoy scaring ourselves, or maybe we're just stuck in a revolving door that we need to move through.

It reminds me of when I was a child. My older sister and her friends thought it was great fun to scare each other—and me. They would spend a whole slumber party telling ghost stories and horror stories, screaming and shuddering and huddling together because they were scared.

They usually succeeded in scaring me, too. But I never could figure it out. What fun was that? I finally realized it was the thrill factor, but I decided I'd rather get my thrills some other way.

Here's my personal prescription for outwitting fear of the future: Take joy in the privilege of helping other people. Honor greatness of character and steadfastness in the face of trouble. Pursue spiritual practices. Avoid preoccupation with horror movies; substitute entertainment that is inspirational and uplifting. Refrain from lengthy conversations about how terrible the world is; instead, pray about it, take a drive and focus on the beauty of nature, or read a good book that heartens and inspires you.

I also know that God will help us through whatever comes our way. He answers our prayers. And when we have faith that God will help us unwrap and handle our karmic package, we don't have to anticipate it and rehearse it ahead of time. If we put our hand in God's hand, we can handle today. And we can handle tomorrow because when tomorrow comes, it will be today.

I believe the most important lesson we can learn from all that has happened since the turn of the new millenium is to remember to turn to God—not only in times of trouble but in times of good fortune and prosperity as well.

When we apply the lessons we have learned, we grow in strength and determination to stand for what we believe. When we uphold our belief in freedom, liberty and justice in our daily lives, we create a positive platform for the future based on the lessons of the past.

As we have seen, when the chips are down, we're a

courageous and caring people. With our hand in God's hand, we will win the victory for our soul and spirit!

Our Future Is What We Make It

Think about Viktor Frankl, who wrote the moving book *Man's Search for Meaning* about his experience in the concentration camps during World War II.[7] He says that people who survived the camps had something to look forward to. It might have been a loved one waiting for them, a destiny they wanted to fulfill or simply the desire to help others.

Frankl kept himself going by envisioning the lectures he would give about what he had endured. He wrote notes on little scraps of paper and hid them in his clothing or wherever he could so he'd be able to tell people what he had learned.

He and others who made it through had created their own meaning in a seemingly meaningless and terribly cruel situation. Their vision of a future was powerful enough to keep them alive.

Our vision of the future needs to be bright enough to move us forward, to keep us reaching for the stars even in the midst of turmoil, to inspire us to realize our highest hopes and dreams.

As has been said, "The future is what you make it" and "What you do today creates your tomorrow." These sayings are apt for us every day. Every day we can choose to create a better tomorrow, a victorious tomorrow.

We set the stage by creating a good day today. When we make a mistake, we decide to learn from it. Each time we get a little smarter! And we are always mindful of that eternal spark of divine light within us, that we are made of the God stuff.

When we put all our good days together, we build a strong pathway to a successful future. We transform our fear of the future into a living pursuit of our destiny.

Ben, a client of mine, was dealing with a very difficult family situation. Yet whenever he came in for a session he had an upbeat approach to whatever was going on. I asked him one time, "How do you manage to be so upbeat in the face of all this?"

He looked at me with a grin and said, "Why not? I don't need to rain on my own parade. Other people are doing that. So I just keep my umbrella up and watch for the sun to come through."

I was curious. "Ben, I sometimes wonder why you come in for therapy. You have a great attitude, and you seem to be handling your life, even with all the furor with the family."

He quickly responded, "I come because I need a cheerleader to cheer me on. You're pretty good at that. It gets kind of too much to do it all by myself. You listen to me, give me pointers, help me think it through, believe in me—all of that helps a lot. And when I think out loud, the answers seem to come."

"I think I'll frame that one," I replied with a smile. "It's great to have a client who does most of the work and thanks me for it!"

We both laughed and finished up for the day. Ben is doing well and doesn't come in often, but I'm happy to be his cheerleader on occasion. He's taken the ball and is running with it, creating a positive future for himself.

That's a real key: taking the ball that's handed to us and running with it, making good things happen today that propel us toward a positive tomorrow.

Fear of Change

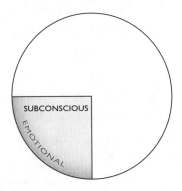

The third core fear is from the emotional quadrant of our being. In that emotional body (also known as the astral, or desire, body), we have to overcome our fear of change.

Change is actually the power of creation, the order of the universe. However, most people have a sense of security in things remaining the same; they don't want anything to change. They shout, "Don't rock the boat!"

Mrs. Prophet says fear of change actually crystallizes like rigor mortis setting in to the emotional body. When we're scared stiff, we find it extremely difficult to welcome any shift in our circumstances. We feel a lot safer sticking with the status quo, whatever that may be.

Yet change is inevitable. And the violet transmuting

flame is a major key in the process. Every time you invoke it, you experience transformation in your four lower bodies—etheric, mental, emotional and physical.

Take a moment to write down your specific fear of change. What kind of change frightens you? You don't have to take long to think about it. Sometimes it's wise to write down the first thing that pops into your mind because that is usually your intuition. What change in your life would you fear most?

The goal is to establish a pattern of recognizing and transforming our fears. When we overcome fear of change, we have a greater storehouse of positive energy to apply to our life and the fulfillment of our mission.

Transforming Pushiness into Diplomacy

One of my clients, Holly, had a job to oversee a group of volunteers who were enthusiastic but slow moving as they sorted clothing and other articles that had been donated for people in need.

Holly was just the opposite. She liked to move fast and move things along quickly. The volunteers were getting exasperated with her because she talked too fast, moved too fast and was annoyed when they couldn't keep up. They decided to go at their own speed, no matter what she said.

At that point, Holly lost her temper, and almost lost her job. She came in to see me with a woebegone expression on her face. "I didn't realize that they couldn't keep up, and I was just awful to them! What am I going to do now?" she asked, tears brimming in her eyes.

"What would you like to do?" I asked.

"I want to tell them I'm sorry and see if they'll give me another chance," she said with a sigh. "But I think I've pretty much alienated the whole crew."

"Why don't you give it a few days and then try again," I suggested. "Maybe they'll respond better than you think. And in the meantime, why don't you give some violet-flame decrees to clear the way?"

That's what Holly did. She decided to concentrate on violet-flame decrees over the next several days to cut through and make changes in the way she related to people. She called to tell me that the violet flame had definitely lifted her spirits and she was going to see if the volunteer organization would give her another try. Would I please pray for her?

I assured her I would, and I did. At the end of the day Holly called, and she was considerably cheered up. "They were pretty nice to me after all," she said. "They're giving me another chance, and I asked them to let me know if I was getting pushy again. They assured me they would!"

It was difficult for Holly because she is a very fast-moving young lady. The next time she called, she said, "I really had to do a bunch of violet flame today because I thought I'd lose my mind with how slow they were moving. But I want you to know I didn't lose my cool."

"Great!" I replied. "Hang in there and keep me posted."

I didn't hear back from Holly for several weeks, and when she did call, it was to tell me the project was going really well. When I asked her, "What are you doing to make it work?" she quickly replied, "I keep doing violet flame and envisioning my pushy self dissolving and transforming into a gentle, diplomatic, accepting person. I'm really happy with my progress. I think I'm going to make it."

When she called me a few months ago, she said, "You know, when you slow down a bit, you appreciate other people a lot more. This has been an important lesson for me. I consider some of these people to be good friends now, and they feel the same way about me. Thanks for your prayers!"

Holly is learning that taking time to "slow down and smell the roses" isn't just a cliché. It is allowing her to make an emotional connection with the other volunteers, something she couldn't do when she was moving so fast.

I have seen people let go of old habits, clear the decks for change and actually enjoy a cycle of change when they are rolling with the violet flame. It's also known as the freedom flame because it can free us from hurtful memories, negative thoughts and emotional distress.

I believe that is exactly what has happened with Holly and many of my other clients who have taken the violet flame seriously. They have freed themselves from old patterns that were holding them back, and they have become calmer, happier and more productive.

So these days I give out that prescription a lot—more violet flame. Here's a decree that several of my clients really like, and it can be sung to the melody of Santa Lucia:

> I AM the violet flame
> In action in me now
> I AM the violet flame
> To light alone I bow

I AM the violet flame
  In mighty cosmic power
I AM the light of God
  Shining every hour
I AM the violet flame
  Blazing like a sun
I AM God's sacred power
  Freeing every one[8]

Change Is Opportunity

Wherever we are on the road of life, if we take what comes our way as a lesson, as an opportunity for new understanding, we will not fear change. And everything that comes to us *is* some kind of lesson and opportunity.

To begin mastering these lessons, welcome whatever comes to you, even when it's painful or distressing and you're not quite sure what to do with it. When you welcome it and realize that every experience is a mirror for something inside of you that you need to celebrate or transform, then change becomes interesting.

Mark Prophet used to tell Yogananda's story of the adept who clucked to the cobra, "Come on, cobra. I'm here, ready to meet you!"[9] Cobras are very poisonous, yet here is the adept inviting the encounter, welcoming change.

Change brings growth, excitement, an opportunity for creativity, new perspective. If it doesn't feel that way when you are going through it, then you may be holding on to the present or to the past.

When it's hard to welcome change, we're usually glued to our old thoughts, old feelings, habitual ways of doing things. If we look forward to every day as an opportunity to learn a new way of doing something, we can greet change with a smile.

Of course, we all need a little stability in our lives. I'm not suggesting we throw everything out and smile at the disarray. But we have a lot more potential for flexibility and growth than we give ourselves credit for.

That's how we can successfully meet change: by cultivating flexibility. And part of being flexible is letting go of the past, letting go of desires that aren't working out. We allow God's desire to be our desire.

Welcome change. Shift your paradigm. Greet change as an opportunity and a lesson—"Hey, what am I going to learn today?" When you do that, it will change your life.

Fear of the Nephilim (Evil)

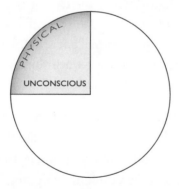

In the last quadrant, the physical quadrant, we have the fear of what the "Nephies," as Mrs. Prophet calls them, are going to do to us.

The Nephies are the Nephilim, the fallen angel archetypes, the forces of darkness that plague us through terrorism, murder, torture, sexual and physical abuse—whatever attempts to destroy people or the good in people. Mrs. Prophet shrinks them down to size, diminishes them and puts them into perspective.

She says:

> So it's, "What are the Nephies going to do to me?" It's a serious fear because it's in the physical octave. And they seem to run the planet.*
>
> Perhaps you speak out, you challenge some policy. Maybe you go on TV and tell the world about it. Pretty soon they are looking down their telescope at you, and they've got your number.
>
> So at that point are you going to speak out or not speak out? Are you going to fear what the Nephies might do to you, or are you going to rise up into that higher calling in God and call a spade a spade?
>
> Jesus told us, "Be ye therefore wise as serpents and harmless as doves."[10] Don't speak until the Holy Spirit moves you to speak, but speak when you're supposed to speak. Be silent when you're supposed to be silent. Outsmart them as Jesus did.

Jesus spoke very little all the way through his trial and crucifixion. He didn't utter a word when they were egging him on and trying to get him to speak, jeering at him, putting the crown of thorns on him, whipping him. Through all of that, he chose to remain silent.

When he was casting the moneychangers out of the temple, the people challenged him for a sign. He said, "Destroy this temple and in three days I will raise it up."[11]

---

*We have seen their modus operandi in the terrorist attacks and the cruelty of groups like the Taliban and al-Qaeda.

Now, that's courage. That's challenging the Nephilim, and it's challenging them through God.

How did he know he was going to rise? Because he knew he was one with the Christ, one with God, and he knew that God was going to handle the physical details. He put his spirit, his soul in God's keeping.

Mrs. Prophet continues:

> Fear of what the Nephilim will do to you is instilled by authority figures—parents, teachers, anyone who's been over you and has threatened you. Maybe you haven't had contact with such individuals in this life and yet you still walk around with fear of the Nephilim and fallen angels. It's ingrained in the planet because they have committed tremendous atrocities against the lightbearers.
>
> That is a fear you can overcome because you know that God is your protection. And nothing can come upon you as long as you are right with God, do his will, have mercy in your heart, hold no ill feelings, grudges, resentments or age-old nonresolution with various individuals, especially with God.[12]

This doesn't mean calamities will never happen to you. It means that nothing can ever destroy you. A determined Viktor Frankl endured through the horrors of the concentration camp. A courageous blind man walked down many flights of stairs in the World Trade Center with his seeing-eye dog while the building was burning. And we continue to see brave American men and women fighting a war against terrorism, a war they have never fought before.

Nothing outside us can destroy our spirit. It was true of those who overcame adversity throughout the ages, and it is true for us today. This is the challenge set before us in the twenty-first century—keeping our spirit alive and well, no matter what.

Ask yourself, "What are my specific fears about the forces of evil? What are my fears about my own dark side? Do my fears keep me from standing up for what I believe in or from giving necessary service to others?"

Jot down what comes to mind and determine to overcome it. God and the angels will help you through. As the Psalmist said, "Yea, though I walk through the valley of the shadow of death, I will fear no evil: for thou art with me; thy rod and thy staff they comfort me."[13]

Lock In to Your Divine Blueprint

Remember the valor of those firemen at the World Trade Center? Even though they lost many of their fellow firefighters, they didn't give up or give in. They didn't faint from fear. They stayed on the job until it was done. Why? Because it was their job, they were brave under fearsome circumstances, and they were dedicated to saving people.

These firemen had a higher calling, and they knew it inwardly. They didn't think twice. They just went for it. We can follow their example and fulfill our own higher calling.

We can lock in to our divine blueprint, our higher calling and enter the circle of God's oneness. When the moment for action comes, we embrace it and run with it.

As Mrs. Prophet says:

> In each case, when we let go of the fear—fear of our higher calling, fear of the future, fear of change and fear of the Nephilim—our four lower bodies become more harmonious.
>
> We express the inner matrix of who we really are. And we displace the fear that says, "I'm this unworthy person. I'm this; I'm that." All of a sudden we wake up one day and say, "I am not these things. Why shouldn't I be whole? I am a son of God. I am a daughter of God."[14]

So where does the fear go? As we turn on the light in the shadowy inner rooms of consciousness, fear is transformed into enlightenment. Many resolute souls have gone before us on that road of fearlessness and enlightenment.

Remember the dramatic example of Shadrach, Meshach and Abednego recorded in the Bible? They walked out of the fiery furnace. And Daniel walked out of the lion's den. Christian teachings say the apostle John was unharmed when he was cast into boiling oil. And Buddhist texts tell us Gautama withstood Mara's fierce assaults and attained enlightenment.

Saints and heroic people throughout history have put their hand in God's hand in order to walk courageously through fearful predicaments. We can, too. And ultimately we will walk right out of our bodies into the arms of the angels and beings of light.

Enoch did. It's recorded in the Bible, both in the Old and New Testaments: "And Enoch walked with God: and he was not; for God took him." "By faith Enoch was translated that he should not see death; and was not found, because God had translated him: for before his translation he had this testimony, that he pleased God."[15]

We don't have to be saints or heroes. We can be ordinary people doing our best, like Dannion Brinkley. He went out of his body and up the tunnel of light into the presence of majestic beings of light.

An acquaintance of mine recommends an affirmation that helps her to be courageous. She says to herself, "The will of God will only take me where the grace of God will sustain me." That is a special concept to remember. It raises your consciousness above the vibration of fear and doubt. It takes you to a place of faith and trust.

Faith and the Healing Process

In my practice I have found that people of faith often move more quickly to psychological resolution. I believe this is because they augment mental, emotional and physical healing techniques with spiritual understanding.

Wayne Muller, therapist and graduate of Harvard Divinity School, poses the question: "How can we reclaim the word *faith,* so that we may use it for our own healing?"

Muller writes,

> [The] antiquated definition of faith taught that if we "had" enough of it, we could change the world around us to make it more to our liking. With enough faith, we could conquer our fears simply by making those things that frightened us miraculously disappear.
>
> If we were poor, faith could bring us more money; if we were sick, faith would make us well; if we were

alone, faith would give us company; and if we were feeling inadequate, our faith could bring us a successful career. An adequate supply of faith would assure us that all would turn out the way we hoped....

Faith is not something that one person "has" and another "doesn't"; faith is not a thing, and so cannot be measured or possessed. Faith is a *way of being*.... It is a place inside ... where we listen to the still, small voices of our heart and soul.

When we are practicing a path of faith, we are in intimate conversation with what is deepest in our mind, heart and spirit.[16]

Muller also notes that the Buddhist word for faith is *sraddha*, which literally means "to put one's heart on." I believe this is key to mobilizing both faith and courage. In order to conquer fear, we center our awareness in the brilliant threefold flame of divine love, wisdom and power in our heart's secret chamber. And we practice heart-centeredness in adverse circumstances.

As we do so, we gradually grow in faith and enlightenment until courage is a part of our very being. We feel it. We are it. It isn't just putting on a garment that we might forget to put on the next day. Over time we experience the heart's coming of age—our heart becomes one with the heart of God.

Such heart-centeredness fosters what Buddhist teachers call equanimity, the capacity to experience life changes while remaining calm, centered and unmoved. A majestic mountain is a symbol of equanimity. Saturated by rain, struck by lightning, covered with snow or sparkling in the sunshine, the mountain remains unwaveringly the mountain.

So may we unwaveringly be who we are created to be —courageous sons and daughters of God, steady as a mountain in our faith and equanimity.

PART TWO

Emotional Mastery:
Tapping Your Hidden Power

5

Mastering the Furies

He that is slow to anger is better than the mighty;
and he that ruleth his spirit than he that taketh a city.

—PROVERBS 16:32

s an old Japanese tale goes, "a belligerent samurai* ...once challenged a Zen master to explain the concept of heaven and hell. But the monk replied with scorn, 'You're nothing but a lout—I can't waste my time with the likes of you.' His very honor attacked, the samurai flew into a rage and, pulling his sword from its scabbard, yelled, 'I could kill you for your impertinence.' 'That,' the monk calmly replied, 'is hell.'

"Startled at seeing the truth in what the master pointed out about the fury that had him in his grip, the

---

*In feudal Japan, a samurai was a warrior or member of a military class. A samurai wore two swords and lived by the code of Bushido, a chivalric code emphasizing loyalty, courage and the preference of death over dishonor.

samurai calmed down, sheathed his sword, and bowed, thanking the monk for his insight. 'And that,' said the monk, 'is heaven.'"[1]

Anger Is a Trap

When we allow ourselves to dissolve into fury, we do damage to our soul and spirit. Elizabeth Clare Prophet gives a poignant example:

> Two individuals, longtime students on the spiritual path, had allowed themselves to become engaged in fits of anger.
>
> One came to me in tears because she had been so profoundly angry, the kind of anger that somehow strips you inside, that she wondered if she had lost her soul.
>
> The other individual, also a woman, had been in a vicious state of anger, pride and condemnation of a family member.
>
> They had both been on the spiritual path for many years. Yet in a moment of someone igniting their pride (a pride perhaps they didn't even know they had), they played Russian roulette with all they had attained.
>
> Anger can come upon you suddenly, like a flash. And you are engaged because it is a trap. It is a trap of the sinister force, the forces of darkness, and it is a trap we lay for ourselves because we don't deliver ourselves from the dweller-on-the-threshold.*
>
> Decrees are one way of dealing with the dweller.

---

*The *dweller-on-the-threshold* is a term used to designate the "anti-self" —the not-self, the antithesis of the Real Self. See also pp. 213–19.

But the will and the determination, the surrender and the consciousness of wrestling with ourselves to get rid of those points of darkness—that's something only we can do.[2]

The Aftermath of an Emotional Bomb

Phil was a young client of mine who, unfortunately, rather liked the charge his anger gave him. He didn't come to me to work on his anger. He wanted to know how to get his friends back.

As he put it, "I've got a couple of buddies and a girl I've known for a long time. I thought we were all friends. But my buddies have started leaving me out of stuff. And my girlfriend is giving me the cold shoulder."

"Do you have any idea why?" I asked.

"No, they won't talk to me about it, and that really gets me. We had kind of a fight awhile back, but I thought it had all blown over." He went into a long tirade about how friends ought to accept each other if they're really friends.

I listened and asked questions. Phil wasn't particularly interested in looking at himself. He wanted to figure out how to get his friends to see things his way.

As he saw it, "If they were real friends they wouldn't dump me just because we don't see things the same way. They don't respect who I am. That's the trouble with them, no respect. I want friends who accept me for who I am."

I asked him, "Why don't you fill me in on the details?"

Phil looked angry. "They wouldn't accept my ideas," he said. "Like we had it all planned out that we were going on this trip, and I knew exactly the right place. They wanted to go somewhere else, but it wouldn't have been anywhere near as good. And I told them so."

"Is that when they rejected you?" I asked.

"Why all these questions? I already told you. I just want to know how to get them to see it my way," Phil answered angrily.

"Phil," I asked, "are you telling me the whole story? It doesn't make sense that they aren't having anything to do with you just because you wanted to go to different places. What happened when you told them where you wanted to go?"

"Okay, okay," he grumbled. "They were being stupid, and I blew my stack at them. But that shouldn't make any difference. Everyone loses his cool sometimes—and this was important to me."

"How did you feel after you blew your stack?" I asked.

"Actually it felt pretty good," Phil responded, "except then they wouldn't have anything to do with me. And now they're planning the trip without me."

I pursued it. "How do you feel about yourself when you get angry and vent it like that? Does it feel masterful on your part?"

Phil grumped back, "Well, it doesn't exactly feel masterful, but at least I'm being honest and it feels good to get it out."

I went on, "How do you feel when people get angry at you? Does it hurt your feelings?"

Phil was beginning to listen. "I guess I don't exactly like being yelled at. Do you really think that's why they won't have anything to do with me? I thought we were better friends than that."

I responded, "Put yourself in their place. You just told me you don't like to be yelled at. Most people don't, because it hurts. And people have different ways of reacting when they feel hurt. I'm wondering if your friends didn't know how to tell you they can't stand being yelled at and ordered around, so they're just giving you the cold shoulder."

Phil was silent, then reacted. "What do you mean I'm ordering them around? I just wanted the best place for our trip!"

I asked, "Phil, how do you feel right now since they are going where they want to go and leaving you out?"

"I don't like it, and it bothers me," Phil sighed. "And I'm beginning to wonder if it's worth it to take a stand like that."

I responded, "I think it may be the 'like that' part that is getting in your way, the part where you got so mad and blew your stack. It's like sticking a knife in someone."

"What?" Phil looked shocked. "I wouldn't do that to my friends."

"It's an emotional knife, Phil," I explained. "It feels just about the same, only it's emotional instead of physical."

Phil pondered what I was saying. "Do you think they really got that hurt when I yelled at them?"

"What do you think, Phil?" was my reply.

He looked a bit chagrined, and I began to catch a glimpse of the real Phil that was somewhere underneath all of his bluster.

"Well," he answered, "I didn't really mean to hurt them. I was just trying to make it the best time ever for all of us."

I didn't respond because I could see that he was beginning to think it through.

He went on, "But they don't see it that way. I guess I've really messed it up. What do you do when you've really hurt someone and you didn't mean to?"

"Apologize," I replied.

He almost got his hackles up again but contained himself. "Why should I apologize? I think they owe me an apology for cutting me out of the trip."

"Who started the fight?" I asked.

"Okay, I did," Phil surrendered. "I can see I've got to learn to control my temper, but it's really hard to do. It just comes out of nowhere."

I smiled at him. "Phil, just the fact that you could calm down and admit this tells me you can do it. I'll be glad to help. And remember this, once you check that quick temper of yours, you're going to discover a huge reservoir of positive power."

Phil decided to go see his friends and apologize. I knew it was hard for him because a part of him still thought he was right and they were wrong. But he did it because he really valued their friendship. They must have been pretty good friends because they accepted the apology. But they didn't give in to his idea, so they all went to the place the friends had picked.

Phil came back in after the trip, looking both pleased and uncomfortable. "Well, we had a great time after all," he said. "It was hard to admit they were right, but it worked out okay."

"Good job!" I responded. "It sounds like you have done a turnaround here. How can I help you?"

Phil relaxed. "Okay, I'm ready to work on that temper of mine," he said. "And also that hint you kept giving me about always wanting my way. My dad always wanted his way, and I didn't like it one bit. I guess it's 'like father, like son.'"

"That doesn't mean you're stuck with it, Phil," I replied. "You've made a good start. Let's get to work on it."

Phil converted his anger, his power energy, into working hard on himself. He came to realize he doesn't like throwing his weight around, especially the aftermath of it. His father did that to him all his growing-up life, but he's no longer accepting that negative hand-me-down. He's aiming to be a powerful guy in a positive way.

Taming the Wild Horse of Anger

We all remember times when we were angry or completely lost our temper. At other times perhaps we were seething with anger, although we didn't express it directly. Clients will sometimes tell me their anger is a good thing, and furthermore, they feel better after they yell it out. They see nothing wrong with venting anger.

Yet when we understand how energy works, we realize that angry vibes (made even more powerful when we yell them) are explosive energy. It's an emotional bomb that disrupts clear reasoning. And the aftermath of negative vibes doesn't just go away. It keeps us in a grumbly mood, pollutes the atmosphere and impacts people around us. Most people don't like those vibes one bit. And they usually forget the point we were trying to make midst the furor.

Think of one of those times in your life when you were seething with anger. Then ask yourself, "What was I angry about? How did I express it?" Now remember a time that you wouldn't say you were angry, but you felt irritated, disgusted, annoyed or frustrated. When you look deeper, you'll discover that those feelings are simply variations of the theme—they all track back to anger.

Have you ever walked into a room where someone has just exploded in anger? How did it feel? Bristly? Agitated? Uncomfortable? Contrast that with entering a room where people have been meditating or having fun together. Think of the difference in the way that room felt. Was it peaceful? Uplifting? Joyful?

The truth is that whatever emotional energy we harbor or give out anytime, anywhere, stays around and combines with energy from other people that vibrates at that same level.

Anger, even when it's just simmering or seething within us, actually creates emotional pollution—in ourselves, our relationships, our home, our neighborhood, the work place and the planet.

What can we do about it?

Checking a runaway temper is like taming a wild horse. If you have ever ridden high-spirited horses, you know that you don't just let them run, especially if they are jumpy or upset. You use the reins to guide them and calm them down by checking them through the bit in the mouth.

We can do the same with anger. We can bridle the beast; we can put the bit in the mouth of that wild horse within us. If we have our mouths closed, we will not misuse our power verbally. If we refuse to strike out with our fists (or feet or whatever), we will not misuse our power physically.

Our anger, though, is not always a reaction to people we're interacting with in our daily life. We might have anger about terrorism or pollution from a chemical plant or trapping dolphins in a tuna catch—all the causes we feel passionate about.

The principle of how we handle our feelings is exactly the same. Whenever we are angry, we need to find a constructive way to approach the situation that is incensing us. For example, we can support our government and our armed forces in the war against terrorism. We can write letters or speak out on pollution or our concerns about the dolphins. We need to seek ways to take constructive action in our own sphere of influence.

Anger is normal—everybody has it, no one is exempt. But how we handle that powerful energy is our choice. If we adjust our perspective, we can take dominion over our passions. When we bridle our temper, we begin to tame that wild horse within. Now we can rein him in, turn him around and head off that display of human volatility.

Take a Quick Time-Out

When someone arouses your wrath, instead of adding fuel to the fire by bursting out with an angry accusation or attempting to control the other person (which is usually pretty futile), take a quick time-out to get back into balance.

Realizing that strategic retreat is often a smart move, excuse yourself for a few moments (a short break, quick phone call, whatever). Once you have calmed down, you will be able to respond in a positive way. This is the same principle as giving a boisterous child a time-out so he can settle down.

In the privacy of your office or another room, take a few slow, deep breaths with your attention centered on the heart. Focus upon mastering your angry thoughts and quieting your unruly tongue. Then envision how you handle yourself at your best and imagine doing that in the immediate situation. In other words, you are centering yourself so you'll be true to your convictions in a positive way.

Once you've shifted your vibration—from bad vibes to good vibes—you are ready to take calm, decisive, effective action. Now you are ready to return to the encounter.

After you come back, do not allow yourself to be set off by anything the other person says or does. Instead, calmly explain your position. Rephrase it as necessary. Listen to the other person's input. Stick to your convictions but look for possible points of agreement or negotiation. No matter how the other person responds, choose to handle yourself in a way you'll feel good about afterwards.

Twentieth-Century Masters

In the twentieth century we had examples of emotional mastery in Hindu leader Mahatma Gandhi, in the devoted Sister of Charity Mother Teresa of Calcutta, and in the freedom fighter Aung San Suu Kyi, who continues her resistance to a tyrannical regime.

As we contemplate the lives of these indomitable ones, we honor their great love for humanity, their strength, fearlessness and compassion. They embraced noble causes, specific missions to fulfill—and lived a life of service.

In the face of tyranny and violence, Gandhi fought for the rights of the people and walked a courageous path of passive resistance to bring about social reform in India. Mother Teresa served the poor and suffering in Calcutta with a prayerful strength, wisdom and compassion that touched the hearts of people throughout the world. Suu Kyi, with gentle determination and confident composure, stands for the rights of the people in the face of the oppressive military government in Burma (Myanmar).

How were these heroic people able to maintain strong, peaceful determination rather than angry reactivity? I believe they understood they would fulfill their destiny only if they lived what they taught. In the heart and soul of such men and women blazes a fierce resolve to demonstrate the path of right choice and not give in to vengeful anger at the wrong choices of others.

To Be or Not to Be

Shakespeare made a dramatic point about the consequences of vengeful anger in his play *Hamlet,* a tragedy of
wrong choices driven by anger and murderous intent. As
you may remember, the backdrop of the play was the
murder of the king of Denmark by his brother, Claudius,
who then became king and married the dead king's
widow.

In the play, the ghost of the dead king visits his son,
Prince Hamlet, to urge him to avenge the murder. And in
the course of the play, Hamlet slowly decides that he
should murder Claudius. In his famous soliloquy, Hamlet
ponders suicide as an escape from his troubles: "To be, or
not to be: that is the question."[3] The play actually ends
with a duel between Hamlet and the courtier Laertes and
death by poison of all the principal characters—Hamlet,
Laertes, Claudius and the Queen.

Thus, vengeful anger always comes full circle. It results
in harm to the soul—whether it be suicide or murder.
Death itself becomes a teacher to the soul. The soul, seeking surcease from pain and trouble on earth, is flung out
of embodiment only to discover that life goes on. Karma
has been created. The soul will revisit a similar circumstance in a future embodiment, perhaps to make a wiser
decision.

Every day we make choices "to be or not to be" who
we really are. I believe that life on earth is a series of lessons, karmic opportunities to learn how to direct energies
creatively to benefit our soul, other people and the earth

itself. In the process, we begin to realize our divine potential—who we really are and who we may become.

Everyone who loves us, challenges us, insults us or endangers us is our teacher. Sometimes the lesson is pleasant and uplifting. Sometimes it's the opposite. But each moment, each circumstance, is a lesson for our soul and spirit. People who trigger our anger are actually instruments of our initiation and our progress on the spiritual path. We just need to see them that way.

Ask yourself, "When I find myself in a scene of peril or injustice (situations that usually tempt us to get angry), how do I usually react?" Jot a note to yourself about that. Now ask yourself, "If I consider the characters in that scenario as my teachers, how would I respond?" Write another note. Contemplate the teaching inherent in your shift of perspective.

Beauty and the Beast

Nearly everyone has read the fairy tale or seen the Walt Disney movie *Beauty and the Beast*. It's a classic tale of emotional mastery, a favorite of young and old that has been told in a variety of ways. It is also an archetypal teaching about the fruits of anger and compassion.

As the story unfolds, we learn that Beast was not always a beast. And therein lies a metaphorical tale of the fate of an angry young man:

Once upon a time, there lived a prince. He was a rather proud and arrogant young man. One day a sorceress, in disguise, came to the door of his castle and offered him a beautiful rose. With obvious disdain, he spurned the gift from the ugly old hag—thereby sealing his fate.

The angry sorceress cast an evil spell on him, turning him into a beast. (A perfect retribution, metaphorically, for the prince had an extremely beastly temper. You could hear him roaring from one end of the castle to the next.)

The prince was doomed to exist as Beast until someone would truly love him despite his beastly ugliness, thereby breaking the spell.

Even in beastly form, the prince still had his tantrums. It seemed almost impossible for him to control his temper. The truth is, he didn't really want to—he could rule everyone in sight or hearing distance by roaring out his rage.

When Beast first met Beauty, his arrogant, beastly behavior frightened her. She really didn't like him. No one else did either. After all, who could put up with someone with such a nasty temper? But Beauty also had a kind heart. She felt sad for Beast because everyone ran away from him, and she could see that underneath his beastliness he was very lonely. In her compassionate nature, she began to feel tenderness toward him.

Beauty decided to reform Beast. She wouldn't give in to his arrogant demands or his temper tantrums. When he tried to control her with rage, she was kind but firm: He must change this behavior because it wasn't going to work with her. She wasn't going to put up with it. She was determined that he reclaim the noble spirit that she sensed was hiding somewhere inside of him.

They had many adventurous go-rounds. Beast tried to control Beauty by yelling and threatening. Beauty wisely ignored his threats. Sometimes that made him even angrier. Yet, no matter how much he ranted and raved, she stood her ground. She countered his outbursts with serenity and loving-kindness.

Now secretly, Beast began to love this beautiful young woman that he couldn't frighten away. He also felt a bit ashamed of himself. So he began to try to behave in a less beastly manner. But it was not an easy task. Only after many fits and starts did Beast eventually let go of his arrogance and learn to control his temper.

Gradually, his true princely nature began to emerge. Even though he still looked like a beast, he was behaving like a prince. Beauty was so happy.

Then came the fateful day when someone would have to love Beast enough to break the spell with a kiss of love, or the prince would live forever in that beastly form. In her compassion, Beauty gave him the kiss of love. And as suddenly as the spell had been cast, it was broken. Before her stood the true prince that he had become.

What changed the nature of Beast? Love. Beauty's inner nature was pure love. Her love broke the spell. Thus Beauty tamed the Beast. And they lived happily ever after.

Taming Our Own Inner Beast

As with many fairy tales, the drama of Beauty and the Beast is all about human nature. It's our own inner drama—the tension between our angry ways and our loving self—and it plays inside each one of us. We sometimes talk about a negative aspect of ourselves (or someone else) by saying, "Well, that's just the nature of the beast!"

All of us have an inner beast. Is there a man or woman

or child who has never been angry or indulged in a fit of temper?

On an energetic level, an unbridled temper tantrum is an outburst of abusive power. Power is a yang, or masculine, energy, whether in a man or woman. In a similar way, love is a yin, or feminine, energy in both men and women.

When we misuse power by roaring with anger, we are coming from our unredeemed, prideful masculine side. Until we recognize and decide to change that beastly potential, we are doomed to act it out. Our prideful masculine side needs taming and redemption through wise understanding and loving restraint—just as Beauty tamed Beast.

Beauty represents our inner feminine, our soul, who has her own lessons to master. She needs to learn compassionate restraint. That is not an easy task. She can get just as angry with that arrogant fellow as he is with her. Instead, she needs to choose to be understanding, loving and forgiving.

It's often difficult to love our angry self—and even more difficult to love the angry self of someone else. Yet life is a great mirror: At some level, the anger of another is a reflection of our own anger. And we often perceive it more clearly when it is mirrored by the other person.

Once we realize the havoc our anger can wreak, we can reclaim it as inner strength. When we do, we generate a powerful force for constructive action.

Do you see yourself clearly? Have you ever been angry with yourself for being prideful, arrogant and ugly? Likely you have, but that just added to the problem, right?

Have you ever been furious with someone else who was behaving in an arrogant, angry way? Do you remember saying or thinking, "I'm not about to put up with that kind of attitude or behavior?" It's a pretty normal reaction. But it is also born of pride. And as the old saying goes, "Pride goeth before destruction, and an haughty spirit before a fall."[4]

Until we master the pride that triggers our anger, we are at the mercy of both of those runaway beasts. Whether we thrust haughty anger at ourselves or at another person, we are in the same no-win situation. Pride and anger are in control of us, not the other way around. And someone always gets hurt.

Even as Beauty in the fairy tale had to win the victory for herself and Beast by loving his inner essence, the same is true for each of us. As she loved him, forgave him, gentled him, we can gentle our own inner beast. As she tamed his beastly temper, we can tame our temper.

Beauty loved the inner self of Beast enough to do it. And he came to love her enough to give up his beastly ways. Will we love ourselves enough to do the same? It's our decision.

Rewrite the Script

How do we do this? We can decide to rewrite our inner script. By being lovingly truthful with our arrogant, angry self, we begin to tame that self. We can trade in our pride for genuine self-esteem, an esteem that comes from identifying with our true self. Through strength of spirit, we can bring out the inner splendor of the prince—our higher, noble masculine side.

But what do we do when we find ourselves totally stuck to the beast with no control whatsoever? First, we decide to face the truth of it. We face our arrogant thoughts, our selfish ways and our habit of trying to control circumstances or people by throwing our weight around. Then we determine to release ourselves from this prison of anger and pride by exercising true inner strength.

We say, "God, please help me! I want to learn my lessons. Show me the truth in this situation. Help me to maintain self-control. I want to honor this other person and love myself through this angry moment. Teach me how to practice the art of loving-kindness in the midst of my soul's adversity."

So we shift our perspective. We strengthen ourselves to remain faithful to our highest convictions. We speak gently and truthfully, yet refrain from impulsive actions we will regret.

Gradually, through the power of a compassionate heart and the process of enlightened self-mastery, we reclaim the harmonious union of our soul and spirit.*

The Equation of Anger and Pain

If we want to stay in the driver's seat of our emotions, we need to continually temper our anger with grace and equanimity. This is talked about in many different ways. As the Old Testament tells us: "He that is slow to anger is better than the mighty. And he that ruleth his spirit

---

*The soul in man or woman is our feminine energy. Our spirit (lower-cased *s*) is our masculine essence.

than he that taketh a city."[5]

When we focus inward and walk a path of self-discovery, we begin to access powerful modes of self-mastery. As we grow in grace and harmony, we are no longer at the mercy of instinctive defensive reactions. We are increasingly able to express the higher nature of our soul and spirit.

We also discover, hidden beneath our anger, the other side of the equation—our sense of painful vulnerability, helplessness and hurt. Francis Bacon's words in the seventeenth century are just as true today as then: "No man is angry who feels not himself hurt."[6] Indeed it is when we feel hurt, vulnerable and helpless that our instinctive reactive anger rises to the surface. We are trying to protect ourselves, but at great cost.

Take the Path of Adeptship

All the adepts have won their victory over pride and anger. It is a major spiritual initiation. We are entrusted with the secrets of the universe only after we have overcome our human reactivity and tendency to misuse power.

Now, we know that Christ Jesus took the whip to the moneychangers in the temple. Was he angry? Yes. Was he indulging in a temper tantrum? No. He was expressing the righteous wrath of God over the defilement of his Father's house.

The adrenaline was surging, but as an adept, he knew what he was doing. He was not out of control. He simply cleared the temple. He upset the tables, wielded the whip and drove the moneychangers out. He was definitely fired up. He was about his Father's business.

So where is the place for righteous wrath? In my opinion, its place is with the angels and the spiritual adepts.

In other words, its place is with those who have united their soul with their Higher Self so there is no risk of misusing power.

Anger can definitely be a misuse of power. Not the emotion itself—everybody has anger. But the unrestrained expression of that anger is a misuse of power.

Because adepts have attained spiritual mastery and self-control, they no longer rage in human pride. They have overcome those underlying weaknesses that would allow raw anger to roar through them. By so doing, they become God's instruments to speak the truth, to deliver a divine rebuke as God gives them direction. And that is exactly what Jesus was doing in the temple.

As you may recall from the scriptures, there were plenty of other times that he could have lost his temper. But he never did. Even in his trial, scourging and crucifixion. Thus he claimed his victory over the seemingly immutable forces of tyranny and death.

We Live at the Level of Our Vibration

Check yourself out. Are you a loving, balanced person who usually keeps your cool under stressful and challenging circumstances? Do you use your inner power to stand for truth and higher principles? Do you send out positive vibes?

You might very well respond, "That's the way I want to be, but I can't always pull it off." Take heart; you're in good company. The apostle Paul felt the same way. As he put it, "For the good that I would, I do not; but the evil which I would not, that I do."[7]

Taking a positive stand isn't any easier in the twenty-first century. How *do* we maintain a loving vibration with hatred and discord and evil running rampant across the planet, sometimes in our own neighborhoods? It isn't easy. But we can do it if we remind ourselves that we are sons and daughters of a loving Father-Mother God and that we want to be true to our divine heritage.

When we pursue higher aspirations, creative ideas, benevolent desires and compassionate behavior, we vibrate at the level of who we really are. When we lower our vibration, we are somewhere else. And when that lower vibration is born of pride and anger, we have put ourselves at the level of those who would defy their Maker, desert honor and truth, and embrace evil. The slide down can be subtle, which is the reason adepts and masters have warned us of the destructive fruits of pride and anger.

El Morya, a great spiritual master known for his dedication to the right use of power, has given profound instruction about anger and what to do with it. He asks us to consider the possibility that we may be angry with God:

> What is anger against God? It could be resentment against God because God has allowed someone in your life to be taken from you, because some event that you wanted to happen in your life did not happen, . . . that the karma you have been dealt is a raw deal and you should have had better.
>
> These elements of anger are often hidden or

suppressed to unconscious levels, because you will not face up to the fact that you have anger against Almighty God. And so, often you transfer that anger. You may transfer it to a spouse, to a child, to your own inner child [i.e., your soul]. Or your unloving inner adult may contain it and unleash it upon just about anyone. . . .

How then does anger manifest?

It manifests in a certain passivity. It manifests as resentment. It manifests as an unwillingness to roll up your sleeves and do what needs to be done. . . .

So, you see, . . . it is not easy to contact this unconscious anger, and your Holy Christ Self [Higher Self] has designed it so. For if you were to open up the "manhole" to your own unconscious and descend into that unconscious, you would have to deal directly with the livid anger of your own dweller-on-the-threshold and you might be totally overcome by it.

This misqualified substance can be in any of the chakras and it can be unleashed when the sacred fire rises from the base to the crown. This is why the raising of the kundalini* is not recommended for those who have not come to their resolution. . . .

There must come a day and date in your life when you decide that you want to . . . be the master of your own psyche, your own soul, and of all the karmic levels and gradations and records of the past. And therefore, . . . this is the hour for absolute resolution with your God.

*The kundalini is the life force that lies coiled at the base-of-the-spine chakra until it is awakened and sent upward through the other chakras to the crown chakra at the head. This sacred fire rises to unite with the descending energy of Spirit, which triggers enlightenment.

When you are ready to proceed, . . . because this is a most serious condition, you will need to do so, whether in a group or individually, with a therapist who can guide you. For once you begin to open up this compartment of the mind, . . . and once you are mindful of suppressed anger and watchful for its subtleties, you will be able to see the specter of anger suddenly come up on the screen of your mind to trigger your emotions.

And this time you will know that it is not directed at you from without, but you will know that it is coming from within. It is coming up out of the unconscious for transmutation. . . .

But, beloved ones, you will not transmute it if you do not let it go. . . . For, you see, . . . this residual anger is based on the very condition of consciousness that will not let go, that does not let go, that does not forgive.

And . . . anger comes out in every manner of physical disease, emotional or psychological problem, the inability to function, the inability to hold down a job. It takes you into alcoholism . . . [and drug] addiction, et cetera. . . .

Failure to deal with anger is an avoidance tactic. It is your soul avoiding . . . to face fair and square that no matter what has ever been done to the soul, it is the soul's responsibility to deal with her own reaction to what has been done. . . .

And if that reaction be anger, anger that is stored, . . . then I say . . . you do have a problem. . . . And this is where the Path will stop for you. . . . If you do not deal with this unconscious anger, it will be with you until you pass from the screen of life and it will be with you on into your next embodiment and the next.[8]

We can begin dealing with unconscious anger by paying attention to our negative motives, thoughts and feelings—and our knee-jerk reactions. We can determine to change them for the better. In our everyday living we can choose to be good-hearted, to be truthful, to give people the benefit of the doubt, to be balanced and thoughtful in our interactions with others.

When we falter, we can pray and ask our Higher Self and the angels to help us. When we fall down, we can get up and try again. El Morya reminds us, "No one ever fails unless he wants to—for one can always get up one more time than he falls down."[9]

6

Masks of the Anger-Dragon

We are so accustomed to disguise ourselves to others,
that in the end we become disguised to ourselves.

—LA ROCHEFOUCAULD
Maxims

When we decide to shift gears and take the high road, we begin the trek upward to higher consciousness. We accelerate even more when we let go of old emotional baggage that weighs us down. And we begin to realize that anger and its companions, including frustration, pride, irritation and annoyance, are a large part of that baggage.

When they mask themselves, they can do the most damage because we have no control over them. We don't even realize they are there. Have you ever been slightly frustrated or annoyed and all of a sudden just completely lost your temper? We've all been there—but it's a big mistake.

Besides polluting the atmosphere, creating karma and

costing us friendships, reactive anger may result in high blood pressure and other kinds of physical problems, even a stroke or heart attack. As a matter of enlightened self-interest, we can decide to master that energy and express it in a constructive way.

Anger is an inner fire. It's a radar signal that tells us all is not well with our inner world. Sometimes the anger is right on the surface and sometimes it is not.

Rage, for example, is very easy to spot. We get red in the face, start fuming, and everyone around us can tell we're mad. This out-of-control anger takes over our entire being. When we are in that state of explosive anger, we cannot even think straight. Most of us do not like being that out of control; it's embarrassing to rage around like an angry bull.

Usually we try to keep rage from emerging. We drive it into the subconscious and ultimately into the unconscious. So now we don't rage openly, only privately, if at all. However, if we don't transform that anger, it will emerge again in one form or another, often when we least expect it.

It may burst out at a moment of hurt or pain, especially if the situation reminds us of a similar experience where we felt pain or anger in the past—even in a past lifetime.

How the Dragon of Anger Disguises Itself

The dragon of anger also has many subtle or not-so-subtle disguises. Sometimes it is just being "nicey-nice." Have you ever been nicey-nice when you were actually seething with anger? Or perhaps you were extraordinarily civil and terribly polite while behind the mask you were all worked up and indignant.

Another thinly veiled disguise of the dragon is passivity. For instance, someone confronts us with something we have left undone. We shrug. We have nothing to say. We do not agree to do anything about it. We exit the scene— leaving the other person furious.

Then, of course, there is the mask of denial. "I don't care if you did tell me three times. I didn't hear you. That's why I didn't do what you told me. Sorry." But we're not really sorry at all.

How about the disguise of procrastination? "I know you asked me to do it. I just haven't been able to get to it." And probably never intended to do it at all.

Depression is often a subtle masking of anger and pain. Although depression can have a biochemical component, it also results from anger turned inward along with what I call "a fall into helplessness." We feel immobilized. Not that we do it on purpose. When anger and pain are ruling the roost from the unconscious, we feel helpless before them.

How about those times when we feel an underlying edginess? Have you ever been pleasant on the surface, or were trying to be, but your so-called pleasant remark came out bristly or edged with irritability? Recognize it for what it is—hidden anger.

Whenever we are aggressive, sarcastic, demanding, controlling, cynical or flippant, some devious form of anger is usually running the show. We can deal with the culprit once we recognize it.

Do you identify with any of these emotional states? Of course, we all do. And we realize that social behavior with anger underlying it usually results in embarrassment or defeat.

Does your anger ever hide behind the mask of humor? Maybe you like to joke. Are they friendly jokes or do they have a barb? Teasing or telling a joke at another's expense has unfortunately become a socially acceptable way of expressing anger in some circles. Yet the vibration and intent are hurtful to whoever is on the receiving end.

Check out your body. Do you have a tense jaw or stiff neck? Do you ever wake up and find yourself with your fists clenched? Do you grind your teeth at night? Do you have frightening or disturbing dreams? These are common indicators of underlying anger, symptoms of subconscious anger that is not being handled at a conscious level. So the anger surfaces as physical tension or as upsetting dreams.[1]

Spiritual and Energetic Law

When we harbor anger, we create problems for other people. We've probably all heard the saying, "Where your attention goes, your energy flows."

This is true whether it is positive or negative energy. When our attention is on someone else and we are happy, they feel buoyed up. When we are angry, they feel the prickles. Our energy impacts their aura and their being in a positive or negative way.

Feng shui practitioners talk about this concept too. They teach us how to choose furnishings and add flowers, plants and fountains in our homes to focalize good energy. And they say if there's an object in our surroundings that we dislike, we're feeding it energy every time we look at it and think, "I don't like this."

In the same vein, Mrs. Prophet explains that it is important to resolve our anger and let go of it in a benign way before going to sleep at night. Instead of allowing our displeasure to wreak nightly havoc on our self and others, we can transform that anger through compassion and forgiveness.

That is the teaching behind the old adage, "Let not the sun go down upon your wrath." Instead of going to sleep angry at another person, we can kneel by our bed and say a simple prayer, such as:

> Beloved Father-Mother God and angels of peace, help me surrender this anger. Help me not to be mad anymore. I know I am, and I do not want to be. Please take it from me. I ask for forgiveness for my angry reaction. I surrender that anger right now. And I ask you to replace it with clear understanding, peaceful strength and compassion for everyone concerned.

We can do a ritual like this before we go to sleep. And we can feel really good about ourselves because we have outwitted that angry dweller-on-the-threshold.

So look for all of the little, almost subterranean, emotional flags. Get acquainted with your style of anger— think about it, write about it, pray about it. And ask God to help you replace it with a strong, positive approach to difficult situations.

Does Venting Anger Resolve It?

Over the years many people have asked me about releasing anger by yelling it out, punching pillows, throwing a tantrum. And there are some therapists who do think this is the way to go. But I do not believe this is the "high" way. It does not uplift us to yell, scream, beat up pillows and do karate chops.

I learned this back in the 1960s before I had any acquaintance with the spiritual teachings of the ascended masters. Those were the days of the hippies and the drug culture. I was teaching at the University of Colorado in Boulder, which at that time was second only to Berkeley as a drug mecca. Young people were having a rough time and a lot of them were angry. This was the time of sit-ins and marching and demonstrating against policies or events the students thought were unfair or inhibiting.

Many therapists were conducting groups where everyone could get their anger out by screaming and yelling and punching pillows. I tried it in my groups. In the first place, I didn't like the noise and mayhem. In the second place, I realized that it did not do what it was supposed to do—resolve the anger.

Of course, if you vent your anger, you instantaneously feel a little better, just as when you sneeze. You have a release of energy and a moment of relaxation, but it doesn't last. A small child having a screaming and crying tantrum has a similar experience when he suddenly relaxes and falls asleep. He's relaxed because he released the energy. But that doesn't make the tantrum a good thing.

I also realized that venting anger was actually training

people to be aggressive in the face of conflict. People were learning to respond aggressively whenever they had an angry feeling. So I stopped that practice in my groups. Instead, we practiced conflict resolution through contacting our inner strength and developing self-mastery.

Many therapists today agree that exploding with anger is not the way to go. It doesn't work in the long run, and it certainly does not enhance our spiritual mastery.

In biblical times, the apostle Paul gave a teaching that is relevant to us today:

> Be ye angry and sin not: let not the sun go down upon your wrath; neither give place to the devil.*

Mark Prophet gave a related teaching. He described how Native American tribes made a circle around the campfire at night. They sat on a log and looked at the fire and said, "O Great Spirit, take now all the things of this day that I have done that are not pleasing unto thee, and let me cast them, one by one, into the fire." Then mentally they threw them into the fire. In this way, they cleared their emotions before sleep and readied themselves to have a better next day.

Paul went on to say,

> Let all bitterness and wrath and anger and clamour and evil speaking be put away from you, with all malice:
>
> And be ye kind one to another, tenderhearted, forgiving one another, even as God for Christ's sake hath forgiven you.[2]

---

*Esoterically, *devil* is defined as "*d*eified *evil*" or "*d*eified *e*nergy *veil*."

This is timeless instruction. We, too, need to redeem inner bitterness and outer clamor. And we initiate that process by opening our hearts to God and each other. As we put away the rancor of pride and anger, we come face-to-face with the underlying pain. Yet when we are gentle, kind and forgiving toward ourselves and others, we begin to heal.

Myths and Fallacies about Anger

Many psychiatrists, psychologists and educators take the position that people do not benefit from venting their anger. In *Anger: The Misunderstood Emotion,* author and social psychologist Carol Tavris discusses the causes of anger and relates three common myths about the emotion.

Myth 1: "Aggression is the instinctive catharsis for anger."

Some people think it's just natural to release anger through aggression, through acting out. Tavris says that aggression is an acquired cathartic habit. In other words, it's a learned reaction practiced by people who think they can get away with behaving that way.

Myth 2: "Talking out anger gets rid of it, or at least makes you feel less angry."

The reality is that overt expression of anger can focus or even intensify the feeling. And that is what happens when we train ourselves to respond aggressively.

I recommend that before you speak out, you evaluate whether you want to stay angry. If you do, then verbalizing your wrath is a good way to do it. It is simply a myth that angry expression will resolve the anger; it just doesn't work that way.

Myth 3: "Tantrums and other childhood rages are healthy expressions of anger that forestall neurosis."

Some inner child therapists encourage people to express their two-year-old self by throwing a temper tantrum. This is not wise or necessary. As Tavris says, tantrums, which tend to peak at two to three years of age, begin to wane by age four unless a child learns to control others through such behavior. Emotions are as subject to the laws of learning as any other behavior.[3]

And that is the truth of the matter. We do not have to wield foam bats or scream out our anger in order to resolve it. In fact, when we do, we are asking for trouble. We open Pandora's box when we indulge in temper tantrums.

"My Old Brain Made Me Do It"

Daniel Goleman, Ph.D., author of the illumining book *Emotional Intelligence,* makes a strong physiological case against venting being the way to resolve anger. In fact, he calls the drama the "ventilation fallacy."[4]

What is usually fueling this kind of emotional catharsis is a sense of being endangered. Danger is a universal trigger for anger, and it is not necessarily from an outright physical threat. It could be a threat to our self-esteem. We might feel we were rudely treated, demeaned or belittled.

If we examine the word *endangered,* we realize it can be divided into the words *end* and *angered.* And that is essentially what happens when we encounter danger—we react physiologically and we end up angered.

How does this happen? When the signal comes into

our brain that something is endangering us, it travels first to the thalamus and then goes to two places—the amygdala and the neocortex.

The first place it goes, in one single synapse, is to the amygdala—the old emotional brain that initiates a fight or flight reaction. The other signal goes through the neocortex, the thinking brain. But that part of our brain mulls the information over and takes it through different levels of brain circuits before it fully perceives and initiates more of a finely tailored response.

The point here is that the amygdala reacts with one quick idea in mind. It is a totally primitive reaction: Is this going to hurt me? Is this something I hate? Is this something I'm scared of? And instantaneously there is a gut reaction.

Once the amygdala reacts, the adrenaline starts surging and you have the primal reaction of fight or flight.

It doesn't really solve the emotional problem to excuse the physiological reaction—"My old brain made me do it!" So what can we do to head it off? The trick is to slow ourselves down enough to consciously decide what to do about the perceived danger. In other words, we allow time for the neocortex, the complex-thinking brain, to kick in before taking action.

So we hold our tongue and remain motionless. We shift to a meditative posture and observe what is going on instead of reacting. In so doing, we take command of ourselves. We aren't allowing that instinctive survival reaction to come out as an angry retort or a physical lashing out.

A Split-Second Opportunity

Mrs. Prophet teaches self-observation of anger as a spiritual practice. She shares her own experience:

> I realized when dealing with anger many years ago that at the point of releasing anger, there is a split second when you have the opportunity to decide not to express it, not to vent it, not to let the anger go into the physical to injure others. And I realized that since I had that choice, if I didn't exercise that choice, I would be making tremendous karma.
>
> And so I began the process of self-observing. When I would see myself about to express anger or irritation or any other similar thing, I realized that I must stop, change gears, and get back in alignment. I must not allow myself to vent whatever it was.
>
> This is one of the greatest liberations we can know—that we are in control of our anger if we want to be, if we are determined. And it's not by forcing ourselves, but it's by internalizing the Word of God. . . .
>
> So every day we have to decide, "Am I going to get annoyed with this person or am I going to rejoice that I can send love to that heart by a beam of the ruby ray* and consume that substance?"
>
> We must prefer Jesus' Sacred Heart to our problems, to our miseries, to our sorrows, to all of the things that beset us as human beings.[5]

What keeps us from doing that? Why do we so often allow that primitive reaction of the amygdala to erupt?

---

*You can visualize sending a beam of light, deep ruby in color, from your heart to the heart of another person as a powerful action of divine love.

First of all, it takes some self-mastery, some self-control. In addition, we may be getting a high from the adrenaline release. If you have serious trouble with your temper, you may be addicted to the adrenaline rush that accompanies the outburst.

Back in the 1960s, Ram Dass used to say, "America is on an adrenaline high." I think that is still true, whether we are talking about the first rush of alcohol or about drugs, sex, TV, rock music, theme park thrill rides, today's extreme sports or speeding along in cars, boats or on motorcycles. All of the thrill experiences that people crave have in common this surge of adrenaline.

That is what happens when anger is aroused. The adrenaline rush starts and we get a high from that surge. That is why people repeat such experiences, because they essentially get a so-called quick fix. People do not necessarily think about it that way. But that's what is happening.

Contrast this kind of reaction with what athletes call being in the zone, a state of equally high alertness. In the case of the athlete, the reaction is channeled into a strong intuitive focus and an on-target outcome.

Seal the Place Where Anger Dwells

My own therapeutic approach to anger management dovetails with Mrs. Prophet's practical spirituality. She says:

> Control your anger by buttoning your lips. That is a stopgap measure. You decide not to open your mouth and say something you will regret, something that will hurt someone, that will cost you karma, that

will be an offense to the living God, your Mighty I AM Presence.* It is better to fume silently than to come out with verbalizations that are costly.

Get to the cause and core of it with therapy. Why are you angry? Is it this life? Is it your parents? Is it the job you didn't get? Is it the opportunity lost, the money you squandered? . . .

We have to exorcise anger with dynamic decrees.† And we have to be determined that we are not going to be dominated or controlled by anger.[6]

So we work on our patterns of anger with conscious awareness, self-restraint, self-examination, prayers and decrees. We decide to seal that place where anger dwells and not to open our mouth or use our fists to let it out. We muzzle the dragon of anger, but we do not stuff our feelings.

With full awareness of how mad we feel, we take a few deep breaths and restrain that dragon. We decide to transform those feelings—changing our pride into self-respect, our anger into constructive action. And we call to the angels to begin the process of healing the wounds that underlie the anger.

A friend of mine told me how she conquered her anger pattern through meditation. Her story highlights the connection of anger with pride and hurt.

She explains,

---

*The Mighty I AM Presence is the individualized Presence of God, the I AM THAT I AM, focused for each one. It is the God-identity of the individual.

†The "Count-to-Nine" decree is an excellent mantra for handling anger. It's a spiritual takeoff on the old saying, "Count to ten." See p. 38.

I used to have a terrible temper, but when I got into meditation, I discovered something that changed me forever.

I had been going to a graduate class in psychology where I met a young man who irritated me quite a bit. He seemed stuck-up and arrogant.

Later in meditation, when I slowed down and observed my thoughts, I saw an instant replay of my first experience with him. He appeared to be rejecting me. I felt hurt, but then I thought, "How dare he!" Then I immediately felt angry, irritated and judgmental toward him.

I realized that pride was the trigger that turned hurt to anger, and I vowed to get rid of pride and be more honest about my feelings of hurt. My whole attitude toward the young man changed, and we became good friends.

From then on, whenever I felt angry toward anyone, I asked myself, "What am I hurt about?" My terrible temper disappeared forever.

We can apply this process to our own patterns of anger. Enter into a meditative state and review your last angry outburst. Replay the episode at slow speed. Look for the hurt and then for the prideful reaction, "How dare you do this to me!" And make a new choice.

In your imagination, give the episode a new ending. Imagine soothing your hurt and speaking up for yourself in a positive way. You will be amazed at what a gift it is to heal the hurt and overcome the propensity to reactive anger.

Liberate Yourself from the Dragon

One time Mrs. Prophet suggested that her students call to Archangel Michael to take their anger and box it up, literally. They were to visualize him sealing that momentum of anger in a box wrapped in shiny blue metallic paper and tied with a blue ribbon. I visualize that box energetically as a blue-fire/white-fire box (for power and purity). And if that angry dragon is really big, it's a really big box.

In my imagery, I ask Archangel Michael to put the dragon in the box and shrink it down to the size of a tiny thimble. And *poof!* That old dragon is shrunk into the nothingness that it really is. When I visualize that scenario, it strikes me funny, and I start laughing and don't feel angry anymore.

You can do it too. Meditation and visualization are benign ways to work at letting go of anger. And they are harmless to yourself and others.

When you begin to get control over your anger, you feel a huge sense of relief. You feel great, because now you can say what you really want to say. Now you can take a stance of positive power. You can make a strong, convincing presentation to someone. You are no longer blowing up outside as you shiver inside.

It is a curious truth that people will hotly deny that they are angry! Anger blinds us. If you ever find yourself hotly denying that you are angry when someone just told you they thought you were, just stop for a minute. Say nothing and ponder how you really feel inside.

If you can't stop yourself from reacting at that moment, say, "Excuse me a minute," and step out of the room. Take a brief walk while you ponder the truth of your feelings and how you want to respond. Then return to the scene.

It is enlightened self-interest not to let the dragon of anger get the best of us. Equally important, we need to understand that that prideful dragon *is* us until we decide it is not. The choice is ours.

"Other People Just Don't Get It!"

A client, Randy, came into therapy to work on his temper. It had cost him jobs and relationships. Finally, when his doctor told him the anger was contributing to high blood pressure, he decided to do something about it.

Now apart from his anger, Randy was a pretty nice guy. He wasn't a vindictive character deliberately using anger to intimidate other people. Yet that is what kept happening because he was constantly on the defensive and had a very short fuse. His various bosses had tried to put up with him because he was so talented. But after a while, it wasn't worth the damage control they had to do with other staff and clients.

Randy was also angry and embarrassed because he couldn't keep a lasting relationship with a woman. Although he didn't physically abuse them, the women in his life simply couldn't take the large doses of his reactive anger. And some of them had been pretty up front with him about it.

As his last girlfriend told him on her way out, "Randy,

I really am fond of you, but I simply can't take your constant anger. It keeps me jumpy because I never know when you are going to react over some little thing. I'm sick and tired of being yelled at!"

Until the medical situation came up, Randy had rationalized all of this as, "Other people just don't get it!"

When I asked him, "What don't they get?" he quickly retorted, "Whatever I try to do. And I'm usually right—they don't get it. They don't get that I'm trying to make something good happen."

I responded, "Do you suppose your anger is speaking so loud they can't hear a word you're saying?"

That stopped him for a minute. With his face darkening, he growled peevishly, "What do you mean by that?"

Since I could now both see and feel his angry vibes, I asked, "Have you ever looked at yourself in the mirror when you are all charged up and trying to get someone to listen to you? Have you ever noticed that you look and sound kind of bristly?"

He immediately went full gear into a reactive mode. "I suppose you agree with my girlfriend. I thought you were supposed to help me, and you're just like all the rest of them." (Meaning all the rest of the women in his life!)

Since he hadn't walked out the door, I thought there was some hope that we could get through this. So I responded humorously, "Really? I think there might be a compliment in there somewhere. Tell me how I'm like all the rest of them."

He actually laughed. "All right, I'll try to disarm. I suppose it's a compliment that I'm trying to impress you with the way people mistreat me, and you're seeing through it."

"Randy," I asked, "what are you feeling right now?"

He paused a moment. "If you really want to know, I'm feeling misunderstood and hurt."

"Okay," I said, "how am I misunderstanding and hurting you? I really don't want to do that. I'm trying to help you."

He sighed. "Okay, I don't like it that you called me bristly."

I responded, "What would you call that reaction you had a minute ago?"

He was thoughtful for a minute, then responded ruefully, "Well, I think you were being cautious with your words. I was actually furious with you."

I laughed. "You're right, Randy. I was being cautious. Now why were you furious with me?"

Randy smiled a bit. "I guess because you didn't sympathize with me. It seemed like you were on their side."

I responded, "I'm on your side. But I'm not sure sympathy would be much help to you. I'm more on the side of taking an honest look at what is happening."

Surprisingly, Randy agreed. "That's why I'm here. If I just wanted someone to sympathize with me, I'd go get drunk with my buddies."

"Okay," I said, "are you ready to take a look at that Mr. Bristly mask?"

He looked puzzled. "What do you mean by mask?"

I explained, "I think it's an emotional mask you put on when you're really hurt or scared underneath. When you're bristly, you're kind of protected. Am I anywhere close?"

Randy sighed. "Yes, you're right on. When I do that, I'm actually feeling upset and hurt inside. And I guess you could say scared, too. Because I don't know what else to do. And I know it's going to be a turnoff to the other person."

I knew Randy was going to make it because he was willing to take an honest look at himself and try to change. This was a gradual process, but Randy began to delve into his defensive mode. It went back to a lot of pain in his youth and childhood. Defensiveness was a habit he had developed to survive emotionally.

When he contacted the pain, he was amazed at how deep it went. I was equally impressed with his willingness to look under that defensive mask and at the courage he mobilized to face that pain and do the emotional release work to let it go.

Gradually he dropped the bristly mask. He put his energy into seeking genuine understanding of himself and others. He watched himself in a mirror as he practiced expressing himself. He could see the difference between his bristly self and his diplomatic self. And as you might expect, his blood pressure normalized.

Randy is a great person without that bristly survival reaction, and he is beginning to believe in himself. He called me about six months ago—a year after he had finished therapy with me. He had recently taken a new job where he was getting the opportunity to express the talented person he really is, minus all the defensive stuff.

As he says, "I'm trusting the good guy I actually am inside. And I'm trusting that other people have a good guy inside too. It's working out great. And you aren't going to believe this, but I'm developing a relationship with a wonderful girl, Nina. We're thinking of getting married. She's kind of like me—really sweet and smart but a bit on the defensive at times. What's neat is that we can talk about it and work things out. It's going great! I thought you might like to know."

I rejoiced with him. "Randy, that's terrific. I knew you could do it. Once you did the work on yourself in therapy, all it was going to take was practice. And you've had the guts to do that. Congratulations! That goes for the job and the girl. Maybe I'll get to meet Nina someday."

Randy asked, "Would you like a picture of us?"

"I sure would," I replied.

Shortly afterward, the picture arrived, and the change is striking. Randy is obviously at peace with himself, and in love. The pain is gone from his eyes. Nina is an attractive young woman who is looking at Randy with such love. I expect that wedding announcement is going to come along sooner rather than later.

7

Pain as an Inner Teacher

Our sincerest laughter
With some pain is fraught;
Our sweetest songs are those
that tell of saddest thought.

—PERCY BYSSHE SHELLEY
"To a Skylark"

All of us experience pain. Not that it is our favorite thing, but it is a part of life. Pain can propel us forward or move us backward depending on how we handle it. And sometimes pain seems to hold us frozen in time and space, not moving anywhere.

Most of us spend a lot of time trying to avoid pain. We try to distract ourselves from disturbing memories, thoughts, feelings or physical sensations. We certainly don't think of pain as a joyful gift or a cosmic lesson. Yet spiritual teachings tell us that at deeper levels of our being this is what pain is all about.

Sufi teacher Pir Vilayat Inayat Khan instructs his students:

> Overcome any bitterness that may have come because you were not up to the magnitude of pain that was entrusted to you. Like the mother of the world who carries the pain of the world in her heart, each one of us is part of her heart, and therefore endowed with a certain measure of cosmic pain. You are sharing in the totality of that pain. You are called upon to meet it in joy instead of self-pity.[1]

We feel pain in our heart and also in our soul. And the awareness of the soul goes vastly beyond this particular lifetime. The joy we feel may very well go all the way back to our soul's memories of the heaven-world. And the pain likely stems from our soul's separation from God when we descended to earth.

Yet there is an end to that mortal pain. The ascended masters teach that the soul has the opportunity to return to God in the ritual of the ascension.* According to right choices made on earth, the soul may live forever. And when we earnestly desire to serve God and God's people and do so in our lives, we may earn that permanence.[2]

If, on the other hand, a soul turns to evil and destructive ways and does not eventually find resolution with God, that consciousness is not allowed to reside in the heaven-world. In God's mercy to all life, any consciousness that does not vibrate at the level of God's love is

---

*The ascension is the culmination of the soul's victorious sojourn in time and space whereby the soul reunites with the Spirit of God. This reunion with God signifies the end of the rounds of karma and rebirth.

ultimately returned to the universe as free energy to be used for new creation.

Our Soul's Departure from Infinite Good

The pain we experience from inner conflict or hurtful events in this life may indeed connect with our soul memories, memories that trace all the way back to our soul's origin in Spirit. When they surface, we become sharply aware of our soul's discomfort in the human predicament. We begin looking for a way out. And we soon realize we can't do this all by ourselves. Thus, we begin our quest for enlightenment.

We ask ourselves, "What is the original source of my pain?" Some think pain begins with birth, which is certainly a physical trauma. In fact, those who remember birth, death and rebirth have said that being born is more painful than dying. After all, here we are swimming around in a warm, comfortable environment, and all of a sudden we're squeezed into a narrow passage and thrust into a glaringly lit, cold, hard world. That's certainly not a pain-free entrance to life.

But the original source of our pain actually stems from our soul's departure from oneness with Infinite Good. The story of the fall from grace has been told over the ages.

Mythological stories relate how Pluto, god of the underworld, abducted Persephone, the daughter of Zeus and Demeter, and took her to his abode in the underworld. She was thereafter allowed to return to earth for only a part of each year. Human beings, as a result, had to experience the desolate cold of winter for some months each year instead of constant summer.

The Bible tells the story of Adam and Eve falling prey to the temptations of the serpent and eating the forbidden fruit. After their fall from grace, they were driven out of the Garden of Eden into the outer world where they had to make their way by the toil of their hands.

Spiritual teachings in the tradition of the Essenes, Theosophists, Rosicrucians and modern mystics tell the story of Lucifer and Satan and the other fallen angels who rebelled against God and were cast into the earth.[3] They have continued their rebellion and have plagued mankind, but their opportunity is limited. One day their time on earth will be up.

Buddhist teachings relate how Gautama Buddha grew up as Prince Siddhartha in the royal household where his father, the king, forbade anyone to bring the young prince into contact with old age, illness or death. Yet during journeys into the countryside, Siddhartha came upon them all: an old person, a sick person, and a lifeless body.

So completely moved was Siddhartha by these experiences that he left his father's palace to seek the antidote to human suffering. First, he tried a stringent path of self-purification, but it didn't bring him what he was seeking. He gave that up, accepted food and garnered strength.

As Gautama sat meditating under the Bodhi tree, Mara, the personification of evil, assaulted him. But Gautama, through his one-pointed attention upon God, withstood those assaults and achieved the enlightenment that all human suffering is caused by desire. He taught his followers to strive for nonattachment to desires through the Four Noble Truths and the Eightfold Path.[4]

In the Bhagavad-gita, Krishna speaks to his friend and devotee Arjuna about the dangers of contamination and entanglement with the material world. Yet, in apparent contradiction, when Arjuna wants to avoid "this ghastly warfare," Krishna advises him that karma-yoga necessitates his fighting in battle as a matter of duty. The point is nonattachment to the things of the world—not renunciation alone, and certainly not avoidance of one's prescribed karmic duty.

All of these ancient teachings depict the challenges of our soul's journey through time and space. Each story reveals a dimension of the cosmic dance of good and evil as it has existed and continues to exist on planet earth. These stories are our story.

Over the course of our journey on earth, in this life and past lives, we have all been subject to the influence of evil. We have been led astray by the infamous behavior of those who have chosen the dark side.

We have suffered pain and confusion. Sometimes we reacted with hatred and vengeance. By so doing, we succumbed to the old saying "if you can't beat 'em, join 'em," which was risky. In our prolonged involvement with good and evil on this planet, many of us eventually no longer knew which was which. That uncertainty added to our pain and confusion.

Pain as Our Initiator

Is there anything good about pain? Yes. Pain becomes a teacher. We hurt as a result of our own or someone else's misbehavior or mishandling of the elements of life. And we learn to avoid whatever caused that painful experience.

It's the same way a toddler learns to stay away from a hot stove—he touches it, cries out because it hurts and learns not to do it again. As we go through life, pain teaches us to eliminate harmful behaviors that result in damage to ourselves and to others.

What would happen if we didn't have pain receptors? I remember hearing about a child who was born without them. This child was continually injuring his body. He was a mass of bruises, burns, injuries of all kinds—all because he did not have sensitivity to physical pain.

Pain also acts as a purifying agent in our life. When we are suffering, we are jarred out of our normal daily routine. We turn our attention to healing, to being gentler with ourselves, to reenergizing our body temple through improving our diet, drinking more water, getting more rest, breathing fresh air, walking or exercising, or simply basking in the warmth of the sun.

Pain is a wake-up call. We stop to consider what we may be doing wrong. We learn to soothe ourselves through the hurt. Physical distress reminds us of our mortality and turns our consciousness inward and upward.

When we are suffering, most of us turn to God and to spiritual practices. We may meditate, fast or pray. And when the intensity of pain keeps us from our usual routine of work and daily living, we have the opportunity to look within to our soul.

If we greet adversity and travail as opportunities—to balance karma, reflect on our consciousness and grow in peaceful nonattachment—we walk the path of the Buddha.

As we appreciate the difficulty of our own burdens, we become more sensitive and tender toward others. We grow in compassion. We understand those who voice their misery in great outpourings of emotion. And we learn the true meaning of inner strength from those who bear their suffering in silence. Once we have been there, we understand. We empathize. We care.

Pain can also draw us closer to our loved ones. In times of anguish and sorrow, we appreciate the comforting, compassionate presence of those who truly understand us. And we learn about false friends who disappear when hardship or calamity strikes.

We begin to understand that pain is a cosmic initiator, an open door to deepening our spirituality, to developing our inner resources and to fulfilling our destiny in this life and beyond.

So we choose to greet hurtful experiences with a steady strength, with our knee bent in reverence to the Creator. And from adversity and pain we learn to open our hearts to God and to one another.

Fear Not to Love or to Be Wounded

Mrs. Prophet explains that pain is a part of the path of adeptship and that closing our hearts to one another in the face of pain is not the way of the initiate. She also talks about what she learned about pain and keeping her heart open:

> As your teacher I don't withhold myself from you.
> I am open to you, and therefore I allow myself to be
> vulnerable to you also. When I open myself to people,
> I allow whatever they are going to send me to come to

me, whether it is anger, whether it is hatred or jealousy. If I should close my heart, then I could not give of myself to you.

I took this example not only from Jesus Christ, Gautama Buddha, Maitreya, Padma Sambhava and Sanat Kumara, but also from our beloved Mark Prophet.

I would see that his heart was also always open; he never closed the door of his heart. And therefore many could avail themselves of the open door. Some would take advantage and use it against him, speak evilly against him. But he still would not close his heart. . . .

Let us never fear to open the door to love and then be wounded. It is all right to be wounded. Your wounds will heal, and you will become a mightier person, a mightier warrior, for the victory of God in your heart.

Jesus said, "Fear not, little flock, for it is your Father's good pleasure to give you the kingdom."[5] He tells us not to fear, not to fear that we will have pain.

Pain is a great teacher. Pain is the means whereby we are softened. We become compassionate; we become lovers of all people. It is wonderful to love our enemies. It is a wonderful life to do that, to keep on loving them and never be disturbed or perturbed at what they may say or do about us. This is the real victory. This is the secret that so many have not discovered, and it is just so very simple.

I remember, though I don't know the year and the date, when the love of Jesus came upon me. This love was so stupendous it transformed me overnight, and I wanted to be with him and walk with him and experience that tenderness so that I could give that

tenderness to others. All of that, of course, is not
without pain. Pain is a joyous fruit of the tree of life.
Let us embrace it with courage.[6]

Embracing the Porcupine

We are told to embrace pain with courage. Yet that is
a somewhat dismaying thought to many of us. It is a bit
like wanting to embrace a porcupine. Who needs it? But
it is very true, psychologically and spiritually, that pain
opens our heart. Pain melts our hardness of heart, hum-
bles us and quickens our awareness of God. Actually, it is
because of pain that many are on a spiritual path today.

Think back. Did you have a spiritual awakening or
take the first step on a spiritual path at a time when you
were hurting? Perhaps you were in the midst of a mental
struggle or some kind of physical or emotional burden.
Many would say, "Yes, that's the way it was for me."

Throughout the ages, adepts have walked the path
of pain and adversity victoriously. They have overcome
vulnerabilities and transformed anger into a prayerful
inner strength. We have the same opportunity. When we
follow their footprints, we gradually become adepts in our
own right.

Even as we seek to harness our anger, we need to heal
the underlying vulnerability that sparks a thorny reaction. That is the real key. Although we can learn ways of
bridling our animosities, the real resolution comes when
we face and address the anguish of our soul.

How do we do this? We acknowledge our feelings. We
tell ourselves the truth, which is simply, "I hurt." If we ask

ourselves what is really going on when we are most angry, we will find our soul saying, "I hurt." But then our pride is saying, "How dare he!" That is the point of choice when our hurt turns to anger. But if we choose against pride, the anger evaporates.

When we begin to heal, we realize that those who have been the instruments of our suffering have their own pain. Through awareness of our own pain, we come to understand theirs. Ultimately we learn to accept the adversary with gratitude—gratitude for the lesson he or she brings us, a lesson we need to learn.

As we do so, we discover that we are better able to temper our reactivity. We begin to take accountability for our part in the hurtful drama. This is a major step forward—and a vital test in becoming adept at handling adversity.

A True Story about a Divine Antidote to Pain

Once we make a turnaround, we are ready to engage in the spiritual process of transmutation and soul transformation. It is a process of discovering and then applying a divine antidote to pain—the violet transmuting flame. The action of that singing, dancing violet fire transforms our soul and spirit.

A friend of mine, Angela, shared with me her remarkable experience with the violet flame. She was traveling with friends, sitting by herself in the backseat and gazing out the window. Suddenly she remembered a really difficult period in her life when, as she put it, "I made a lot of karma."

She had been very lonely at that time and found solace by getting into intimate relationships with various men.

Later she deeply regretted her promiscuity. As she said, "I took on a lot of energy I wished I hadn't. And I got a reputation that took years to live down."

Scene after scene flashed into her memory as the car speeded down the road. So she told her friends, "Don't mind me—I'm going to do some spiritual work back here." And she proceeded to visualize the violet light of forgiveness pouring through those scenes, through herself and everyone she had been involved with while she gave the following mantra over and over.

> I AM forgiveness acting here,
> Casting out all doubt and fear,
> Setting men forever free
> With wings of cosmic victory.
>
> I AM calling in full power,
> For forgiveness every hour;
> To all life in every place
> I flood forth forgiving grace.[7]

Angela kept giving this mantra and other violet-flame affirmations until she felt a sense of relief she hadn't felt in years. As she told me, "I kept it up for almost 2½ hours. My friends didn't mind; they were just driving along, and sometimes they joined in with me. Each memory brought up more guilt and remorse, but I just kept at it.

"I realized that one by one those scenes were kind of dissolving. It was like I couldn't visualize them clearly anymore, and as that happened I felt lighter. I could tell when I was coming down the home stretch because there was just one scene left—one really terrible one I had avoided thinking about for years.

"I prayed for forgiveness and kept on with the violet flame. All of a sudden, I felt a tremendous release. It was like a flood of violet flame that washed away the last dregs of that situation and the bad feelings that went with it. I was so relieved I started to cry.

"My friends were concerned and asked if they could help. I was laughing and crying at the same time as I told them, "Thank you, but I'm really fine now. I'm crying because I'm happy!"

Angela said it was like the angels closed the door on that part of her life. She has never been troubled again by any of those old memories and feels totally at peace. She explained to me, "I knew that God forgave me the first time I prayed for forgiveness several years before this experience on the trip. But it wasn't until I did the violet flame so intensely that I was able to accept God's forgiveness, forgive myself and really let it go."

I rejoiced with Angela and knew what she was talking about because I have had my own experiences with the violet flame. Of all my spiritual practices, the violet flame gives me the most marvelous feeling of exhilaration.

Violet-Flame Mantras and Affirmations

When we invoke the violet fiery light, it begins to saturate our aura, our chakras and our etheric, mental, emotional and physical bodies. The light changes our vibration. It's as if our negative vibes were plunged into a cosmic wash cycle. Those blackened garments are whitened—darkness is transmuted into light, anger into peaceful strength, fear into courage, anxiety into calm resolve.

As we surrender ourselves to this transformational process, the violet fire consumes the burdens of our soul and replaces them with an inner sense of lightness and freedom.

The first violet-flame mantra I learned when I discovered the teachings of the ascended masters is the simple affirmation "I AM a being of violet fire! I AM the purity God desires!" I experienced this beautiful violet light as an aspect of the Holy Spirit.

When I repeated this mantra over and over while visualizing the violet flame, I began to experience joy and reverence. My thinking became startlingly clear; my emotions calmed down and I had a sense of physical exhilaration. I realized that the violet flame could take healing to a whole new level.

I began to teach the mantra to everyone who came to see me for therapy, whether they were religious or not. Some of them felt an immediate uplift, as I had, while others felt it only after they had given the mantra over a period of time. Over the years the violet flame has made all the difference for many of my clients, some of whom I have talked about in this book.

I explain that "I AM" means "God in me is." To affirm "I AM a being of violet fire" is to accept God in us as spiritual transformation, creating beauty and peace. And "I AM the purity God desires" means "I AM who I really am, a pure son or daughter of God."

I also explain that when we give this mantra and visualize shimmering violet light flowing into us, the angels start filling our aura and chakras (our spiritual centers) with that violet light. When we give the mantra a number of times, our aura becomes saturated with it, and we begin to feel a freedom from burden—even physically.

When you give the mantra, visualize the scintillating violet light filling your physical body, your chakras, your aura and all of your surroundings. As you do so, you may begin to feel a sense of relief from your burdens.[8]

When we totally focus and invoke this flame, our emotional distress and reactivity begin to fade away. Why? Because the violet flame sparks a transformational process. As our chakras are saturated with the violet light, burdensome energy is transformed. We feel joyful and crystal-clear in our thinking. When we continue invoking the violet flame over time, we may sense, almost touch, the celestial world.

Greeting Pain with Mindfulness

Buddhist teachings tell us to greet pain with mindfulness, to notice how the pain moves through many phases and to pay attention to the nuances of constriction, pulsation, intensity and the diminishing of intensity.

In mindfulness, we keep our attention focused on these changes even as we experience them. We observe the flow of our thoughts, feelings and sensations. We become explorers of our inner world, and we learn a great deal about ourselves.

As we do so, we gain insight into the cause and core of our karmic condition, our spiritual initiations and the lessons we are meant to learn. We grow in humility, endurance and appreciation for little respites and moments of joy. We expand in courage and acceptance of life's ups and downs. And above all, we become acutely aware that our consciousness transcends the human condition.

In her marvelous book *Emotional Alchemy: How the Mind Can Heal the Heart,* Tara Bennett-Goleman relates how Ram Dass, a close friend of hers, grew in spiritual awareness while incapacitated from a stroke. She writes:

> Ram Dass seems able to use his stroke for his spiritual growth—"stroke yoga," as he calls it—rather than simply letting himself be defined by the new, stark limitations on his body and his mind.
>
> A short while after his stroke, as he was regaining the ability to speak, he told me, with some difficulty, "I feel this illness has been a blessing, because it has erased my superficiality—my sports car, golf, all that." Later he wrote, "From the ego perspective the stroke is no fun—but from a soul perspective, it's been a great learning opportunity."
>
> That the root of liberation from suffering ultimately lies in the mental realm rather than the physical was brought home starkly by a halting comment by Ram Dass. While he was still in the hospital a month or two after the stroke, I asked if he was suffering.
>
> Struggling to find words, he told me, "When I think of who I was, there can be suffering. Or if I think about the future. But when I'm in the present there's no suffering.... The doctors here think that consciousness is in the brain—but my consciousness isn't affected by this illness."[9]

Such a strong spiritual focus carries one safely through the challenges of life, the rigors of debilitation and the death of the body. I have seen stalwart souls greet their transition from this plane to the next with peaceful equanimity. One woman in particular was more and more radiant every time I went to see her. Although she was in pain, her attention was upon God and those who came to tend her. She offered as much love and comfort as she received. And she kept a delightful sense of humor in the process. When she did move on, the intensity of light around her was a blessing to all.

I have noticed that many on the spiritual path grow in grace in the very midst of their final adversity. As their souls move ever closer to leaving the body, these gracious ones become almost translucent. Their peaceful acceptance of the final initiation of life on earth becomes a blessing to all who have known, loved and cared for them.

Be the Buddha under the Bodhi Tree

Whether we are dealing with physical pain, distressing feelings or both, we can train ourselves to respond with peaceful contemplation. Here is an exercise in self-observation that I have found very helpful, spiritually and psychologically. It can help you maintain self-control and peaceful equanimity when facing challenging or changing circumstances. I call it "The Buddha under the Bodhi Tree."

1. Invoke the presence of the Buddha as you sit under the Bodhi tree of higher consciousness. Focus your complete attention upon your heart and the movement of your breath. Stay with that focus for a few minutes.

2. Bring to mind a recent situation where you felt physical pain or uncomfortable emotion. Allow it to well up in you.

3. As you focus on the discomfort, choose to be the Buddha, the divine observer. Keep in mind that as the Buddha under the Bodhi tree, silently observing, you are one step removed from what you are experiencing physically and emotionally.

4. If you begin to get restless, notice that. Observe it. Feel it. Be the Buddha sitting with the restlessness. Whatever happens is okay. Just let it be.

5. Continue to be aware of your emotions. Notice your body's sensations. Observe them. Give this drama space in your consciousness. Sit with it; stay with it. Be the divine observer of whatever arises.

6. If you are distracted from your focus on the emotions and physical sensations, simply notice the distraction, and gently return your attention to the emotions and the body. Notice the ebb and flow of discomfort and ease.

7. Stay with the process for ten to fifteen minutes. Then jot down what you noticed in your imagery, in your emotions, in your body.[10]

Were you able to experience your emotions and bodily sensations and at the same time do this observing technique? Once you are practiced in it, it is one of the most calming and uplifting ways of relieving distress.

What I have learned from using this meditation myself

and with my clients is that when we observe ourselves in a hurtful scene, we first relive the pain of the trauma and after a time we shift to other feelings. We may feel fear, embarrassment, shame, anger, and so forth, and then gradually more uplifting feelings.

As we allow ourselves to stay with the pain, perhaps just saying softly to ourselves, "I hurt," we begin to feel a lessening of that pain. And we feel this with all the other emotions that come along. Ever so gradually we become more peaceful and calm. We may flash on an intuitive insight or a new perspective. By simply sitting with our emotions but not expressing them, the energy flow changes.

Our imaginings, our thoughts, our feelings, are all a matter of vibration and energy flow. As we remain non-attached, simply observing, we allow the energy to change form. We experience the ebb and flow of frustration, anger, pain, calmness, peace and enlightenment—and in the process we become one with the Buddha under the Bodhi tree.

This is an internal posture we need to maintain as we seek to heal our soul not only from the stress and pain of circumstances in this life but also ancient records of past lives that lie unresolved within us. Although such records surface on and off, we do not always recognize them for what they are because they are also connected with present-day happenings. Yet the further we progress on the path of initiation, the more we expand our awareness of other lifetimes. Consequently, whatever we experience becomes a part of our reality—and open to change. That is why we can heal our emotional wounds, even those incurred in past lives.

Death Has No Reality

Ultimately, we come to realize that everything that exists in our awareness is a portion of the eternal Now, and what we label as pain or discomfort is at some level a misuse of divine energy. These energy tangles, including the consciousness of death, dissolve in a state of true enlightenment.

Remember Dan Millman and Socrates in *Way of the Peaceful Warrior?** In addition to instructing Dan on the alchemical transformation of anger, Socrates puts him through the initiation of "death." In this amazing encounter, Dan learns that even death is an illusion to the awakened adept.

Dan describes his experience of dying this way:

> I fell, bouncing, smashing against the rocks, falling down into the bowels of the earth, and then dropping through an opening, I was released by the mountain out into the sunlight, where my shattered body spun downward, finally landing in a heap in a wet green meadow, far, far below....
>
> The seasons changed, and the remains of the body began to dissolve into the soil, enriching it. The frozen snows of winter preserved my bones for a moment in time, but as the seasons flashed by in ever more rapid cycles, even the bones became dust. From the nourishment of my body, flowers and trees grew and died in that meadow. Finally even the meadow disappeared....
>
> ...I saw a white-haired man sitting near me, smiling. Then, from thousands of years away, it all came

*See pp. 39–41.

back, and I felt momentarily saddened by my return
to mortal form. Then I realized that it didn't matter—
nothing could possibly matter!

...I started to laugh. I looked at Socrates; our
eyes gleamed ecstatically. I knew that he knew what
I knew. I leaped forward and hugged him. We danced
around the cavern, laughing wildly at my death."[11]

During this experience, Dan was the conscious observer
of the human predicament and the eternality of Spirit. As
we know, human form is like a speck of dust in time and
space, yet divine consciousness is eternal. Everything in the
matter universe ultimately cycles back into Spirit, including our soul and all we have created in our journey in time
and space.

As the ascended masters have taught, eternal life is
conscious oneness with Spirit—which Dan experienced
momentarily, a little taste of heaven—to which we also
may attain.

The Creator sends avatars, inspires scientists and illu-
mines saints and sages to remind us of the eternal truths
that many of us have forgotten while in embodiment.
Matter itself is intended to be a platform for divine evolution. And God becomes more of God as his progeny
fulfill their potential for oneness with Spirit.

In order to fulfill our own divine potential, we need to
understand something of our soul's cosmic beginnings
and the challenges of the spiritual trek on earth. This is the
story of the mystical journey of the adepts, saints and
sages—and our own journey as adepts-to-be.

PART THREE

Archetypal Influences:
Outwitting the
Dweller-on-the-Threshold

8

Ancient Soul Encounters

But O the ship, the immortal ship!
O ship aboard the ship!
Ship of the body, ship of the soul,
Voyaging, voyaging, voyaging.

—WALT WHITMAN
Leaves of Grass

*W*here did our soul's journey begin? It began in the heaven-world. And where has our journey taken us? We descended to earth and have had many lifetimes of adventures. And all that has transpired during our earthly trek has made an indelible mark upon our soul.

We begin to realize that ancient records and archetypal patterns are a part of our personal, planetary and cosmic history. What is cosmic history? It's the history of the universe as an evolving, orderly, harmonious system—everything that exists in time and space plus dimensions of the spiritual-material universe beyond physical perception.

All of this has an impact on planet earth and on every one of us living on the earth today.

I believe our fascination with science fiction, archaeology, ancient civilizations and space exploration is sparked by the record and memory of ancient history in people's collective and personal unconscious. These are ancient records of the soul. When we are ready to deal with them, psychologically and spiritually, they come to the surface of our awareness.

In many cases, my clients have discovered that they came under the bondage of evil beings through innocence and ignorance—innocence in deciding to interact with them in the first place, ignorance as to the ultimate result of that unfortunate choice. These are the inner burdens of the soul.

A Past-Life Trauma from Ancient Atlantis

A young woman, Amy, came to see me because a terrible memory had surfaced from a past life. She had remembered being a priestess at that time in a sacred temple on Atlantis. She had been trained from childhood to be a priestess and her consciousness was pure and innocent. She loved God and wanted only to serve Him.

One day the high priest called her to him. She hurried to do his bidding. At first all seemed well as they tended the altar together. Suddenly, to her horror, that evil priest demanded she submit to him sexually. Then she blanked out. She hadn't wanted to remember the rest of it until she was in a safe place because she was almost certain he had raped her.

This traumatic memory prompted Amy to begin therapy for post-traumatic stress disorder. She realized that this ancient trauma was likely the root of her fear of sexual violence, which had plagued her throughout her marriage. She had never been able to understand why she would get almost hysterical during marital relations because she had never been raped in this life, and her husband, Terry, was kind and gentle.

We prayed together before working with the trauma, and I made specific spiritual calls for Amy to be sealed in God's light and protection. Then she went into a meditative state and brought the memory back up.

As she focused on the scenes that emerged, she listened through a headset to a neutral tone alternating back and forth between her right and left side. This is a method of bilateral brain stimulation that is used in EMDR therapy.[1]

She began to shake as more and more of the record came up. Tears ran down her cheeks as she reexperienced that horrendous scene with the high priest. He demanded she submit. She was horrified and refused. She tried to escape, but he blocked her way. They struggled, but he was stronger. He raped and killed her. Her last memory was his angry, hate-filled face and a feeling of relief because he had stabbed her in the heart and it was going to be over.

She remembered dying, leaving her body and watching as it was thrown into a fire for sacrifice. As she went through this part of the drama, her breathing evened out and she cried tears of relief. She remembered being met by angels and going with them into brilliant white light. She stayed with that state of bliss until she was ready to open her eyes and talk about it.

When she did so, she smiled and stretched. "What an awful experience and a magnificent relief!" she exclaimed. Then we talked about what she had gone through and what she had learned from it.

She explained, "It really was difficult to go through that whole thing again, but I'm so glad I did it. The last part of it was good because the fire purified all the energy. I'm glad there wasn't anything left of my body because I realize I had taken in that evil priest's darkness. I think the only reason I've continued to carry that record at all is because I was scared it might happen again.

"I'm feeling a sense of relief and peace. And I don't feel scared or sad anymore because I realize I stood up for myself and did what was right. When the memory first came up, I was afraid that maybe I had enticed him or something. But I didn't do anything wrong. I was standing up for myself and for God.

"After I died I was graced with such a loving experience with the angels and the masters. I don't think I'll ever be afraid of dying again—or of making love with my husband. It's a whole different kind of experience when it's about love and union."

Amy felt completely freed from that ancient experience. We had two follow-up sessions just to make sure, one with Amy alone and one with her and her husband. Both sessions went well.

Terry told me, with tears in his eyes, "I'm really proud of Amy for getting to the root of this thing. It's been so hard for her. I'm hoping it makes a difference in our love-making, but even if it doesn't, it's such a relief to understand her panic reaction."

Amy gave him a hug and added, "We're going to keep loving each other and working our way through this. We'll call you if we need some more help."

I was impressed with the maturity of their love. Even though their lovemaking had always been constrained by Amy's unconscious fear and expectation of pain, they had managed to keep the love fires burning for each other.

Amy called me several months later to tell me that she and Terry were beginning to enjoy a loving sexual relationship. She laughed as she exclaimed, "I never thought that making love could be so tender and such fun! It's a second honeymoon—and a new beginning."

Now you might ask, "Why didn't she remember that record before? Why didn't it come up when she was first married?" Amy and I talked about that. She decided she hadn't been ready to face the record until she was totally secure in her husband's love for her. His tenderness helped her feel safe enough to allow the memory to surface.

Once it came to full conscious awareness, she was ready to let it go and to move on. As she put it, "Terry is the antithesis of that terrible priest. What a grace for us to have found each other so that our love could help me heal —and we can go on to have children and pass on a legacy of love instead of fear."

From experience with clients over the years, I have come to realize that there is a certain cosmic timing and inner readiness for such ancient records to surface and healing to take place. That timing is unique for every individual. It's a psychological readiness to face and resolve the inner pain—usually because in some way it is interfering with the person's life.

Sometimes people become so accustomed to that unresolved emotional pain that they unwittingly accept the psychological aftermath of a trauma as part and parcel of "who I am." They carry the pain at subconscious and unconscious levels until some happening, personal or planetary, quickens the record.

Once we consciously remember the old trauma, it is usually a signal that we are mentally, emotionally and physically ready to deal with it. However, we need to honor our own sense of inner timing throughout the healing process.

Why Does God Allow Evil to Exist?

Major catastrophes connected to evil are still with us in modern times—and some of them have both personal and worldwide consequences. The infamous terrorist attacks of September 11 are such an example. This tragedy has created an unforgettable impact upon not only the American people but freedom-loving people throughout the world.

In times of horror and pain, good people cry out, "Why does God allow evil to exist?" It's a sad and complex plight upon this planet, one that theologians and philosophers have sought to understand and explain over the centuries.

The ascended masters teach that the problem of good

and evil comes down to the way people choose to exercise their free will. We are all created in the image of God and given free will. How we spend our allotment of universal energy is our choice. Otherwise we would just be a robot creation controlled by an omnipotent overlord.

We are meant to walk a path of godliness with such fervor and constancy that we achieve a state of ongoing oneness with our God. At the same time, we aspire to keep our individualized consciousness as Susie Q. or John Doe unique and intact.

This is the inner walk with God that adepts, saints and sages have demonstrated over the ages. We have the same opportunity today. What will we choose to do with it?

People who love God usually try to make good choices and pass God's blessings on to others. They feel the prick of conscience when they inadvertently hurt someone, and they want to make it right any way they can.

People who embrace evil do the opposite. Out of malevolence or the desire for personal profit, they choose to be destructive and harmful to others. They often act without conscience or guilt.

When we strive for what Buddhists call right spirit, right mindfulness, right feeling and right action—meaning benevolent motives, positive thinking, compassion and constructive action—we feel good about ourselves.

People who choose to hurt others through malevolent motives, hateful thoughts, raging emotions or destructive actions deny their God-given essence of love. They ultimately become what they express—evil.

When any of us take malevolent action, we create

serious karma and a downward spiraling of consciousness that can lead to our entanglement with evil people—and to a sense of despair. Eventually, we will pay the piper. We all stand accountable for our freewill use of the Creator's energy.

We defeat evil in our own lives by every right choice we make. And ultimately, when enough people make right choices, we will defeat planetary evil and create a golden age, an age of love, peace and prosperity. I believe this is God's dream. Will we make it our own?

Universal Energy Is Neither Good Nor Evil

Both scientists and spiritual teachers tell us that universal energy is neither good nor evil in the human sense of the words. Basically they say energy is neither created nor destroyed but simply undergoes transformation from one form to another.[2]

There is order and patterning within that creative force—the universal intelligence that we call the mind of God. (This is likely why the name *God* has been interpreted esoterically as the "*g*eometry *o*f *d*ivinity.")[3]

Yet that universal intelligence is also understood as a personal God, a loving benefactor of all life. And God's gift to us of free will is what makes us different from animal life. We have the power of thoughtful choice and self-determination.

You might say we get to practice being co-creators with God in our personal lives. At first, all of us make mistakes. But as we mature in the way we use our God-given life energy, we can learn to bless life instead of harming life.

Kuan Yin Riding the Dragon
A Metaphor for Our Soul

Kuan Yin is known in the East as the bodhisattva of compassion. She is the celestial one who "hears the sounds of the world" and rescues people endangered or floundering in perilous situations.

As we see in this portrait on the preceding page, Kuan Yin is serene while she guides the fierce serpent of the deep through tumultuous waves. I see this as a metaphor for the journey of our soul.

We, too, are meant to envision and attain the stance of mastery over turbulent happenings. We are called to tame our own inner dragons when they surface midst the upheavals in our lives.

The rolling waves are a metaphor for those swift-moving ups and downs we go through. We either ride those waves with grace and serenity or tumble into the restless currents. In the face of chaotic circumstances, our choices are determined by our attitude, not by the events themselves. And our outer posture is decided by the inner stance of our soul.

Strength, balance, self-mastery—all these qualities are depicted in Kuan Yin's graceful bearing atop the dragon. She is unmoved by the fierceness of the creature or the swirling of the waves. She is in command of herself, her mode of travel and the forces of nature around her. Will we be equally unmoved?

Some years ago, a store on Ross Alley in San Francisco's Chinatown featured an extraordinary picture of Kuan Yin riding a dragon through billowing clouds. Legend has it that this was a photograph taken by a World War II pilot as he was flying a mission.

That picture of Kuan Yin struck a new chord with me as I was writing this book. I thought her masterful stance so symbolic of the transformational process that I commissioned an artist friend of mine, Roxanne Duke, to create this beautiful painting.

The dragon itself represents primal forces we are in the process of taming. And when they are tamed, they bring good fortune. As we have seen, we have many such dragons—anger, fear, uncertainty, frustration, confusion—add your favorite to the list. How do we tame them? That's what this book is all about!

The ascended master Maitreya describes evil as a veil of energy that separates man from his God—"a forcefield [energy field] of mortal thought and feeling, which mankind weave out of their own discord."

This Eastern master explains that "this energy veil has for centuries effectively deprived him [man] of the truth of his own being and of the Presence of God. Therefore it is man himself who must rend the veil of his own mortal consciousness—of which he alone is the author—ere the wisdom of the law can be imparted."[4]

Maitreya is giving the spiritual explanation that it is our mortal consciousness, our human creation, that blocks us from experiencing oneness with our Christ Self (our Higher Self or Buddha Self) and the Presence of God. It is up to us to rend that veil and seek reunion with God through walking the path of goodness and mercy.

How is it that we have created this veil and entered into a state of illusion and separation from our Real Self? Why have we not remained in the state of goodness and likeness of God that we were graced with in the beginning?

Different religions have different answers to this question, but the one that offers an understanding of the energetic origins of good and evil is from the Kabbalah, the Jewish mystical tradition.

The Kabbalah's Understanding of Creation

Some say the mystical traditions associated with the Kabbalah trace back to the first century B.C. The Kabbalah as a distinct movement emerged around 1200 in Provence, France.

Kabbalists believed that in the beginning, before creation, there was only "divine nothingness," the hidden, transcendent God. They referred to the unmanifest God as *Ein Sof,* meaning "without end" or "the Infinite." Ein Sof was the ultimate reality, unmanifest, incomprehensible and indescribable.

The original creation, they said, came from the vastness of Ein Sof unfolding as a series of ten energy emanations, the *sefirot.* We can think of the sefirot as dimensions of the personality of God, as facets of the jewel of Infinite Being. The Kabbalists understood the sefirot as the divine model for all creation, including the androgynous archetype of man and woman, known as *Adam Kadmon.*

This mystical teaching says that each one of us is patterned after the archetypal sefirot. How do the sefirot relate to us? How do they manifest in our lives?

Keter, the first sefirah to be emanated, is closest in vibration to Ein Sof. It is our divine essence and represents our free will and awareness of God as the Divine Presence.

Hokhmah and *Binah* correspond to the right and left hemispheres of our brain. Hokhmah manifests as genius, inspiration and originality while Binah represents our ability to reason and discriminate.

Hesed manifests as love, mercy, tolerance and unconditional giving while *Gevurah/Din* is discipline, discrimination, justice and true judgment.

Tiferet, at the heart or core of each of us, is our essential nature of inner and outer beauty, harmony, balance and serenity. *Da'at,* sometimes thought of as the quasi sefirah of knowledge, is the ability to express our thoughts.

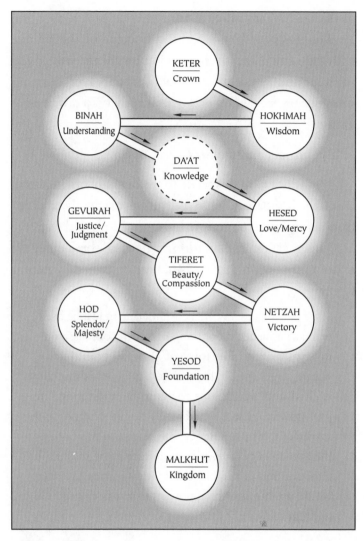

It is also the omniscience and universal consciousness of God.

Netzah and *Hod* govern involuntary and voluntary processes. *Yesod* provides the foundation of spiritual birth, physical procreation and the ego; it is the seat of physical and spiritual pleasure.

Malkhut/Shekhinah is the connector of the Infinite
with the earth plane, the focal point for the meeting of our
spiritual and physical forces. Malkhut/Shekhinah represents our physical body and our receptivity to divine emanations.[5]

Love, Justice and the Origin of Evil

How does all of this relate to the origin of evil? According to the Kabbalists, what we call evil originally emerged
from an upset in the cosmic balance of love and justice.

This mystical explanation is given in the Zohar, the
major text of Jewish mysticism, here described by Arthur
Green:

> The Zohar sees evil as originating in justice itself,
> when that justice is not tempered with compassionate
> loving-kindness. The force of Din [Gevurah, Justice]
> within God has a legitimate role, punishing the
> wicked and setting out to limit the indiscriminate
> love-flow of Hesed, which itself can be destructive if
> not held in proper balance. But once Din has escaped
> the demands of love, it is no longer to be trusted. It
> then becomes a perversion of God's justice, one that
> would use his punishing powers to wreak destruction
> without cause.[6]

Most of us realize that justice without love results in
anger and retribution. We have seen it happen or have
experienced it in our own lives. On a planetary level, it has
often been the justification of those who start "holy" wars
or engage in terrorist activities. It is rampant in warfare,

hatred and violence as the core of what has been called the planetary dweller-on-the-threshold.

The dweller-on-the-threshold is the esoteric name for the conglomerate of the anti-self, the antithesis of our Real Self. It is an inner vortex of negative energy fueled by evil intentions, negative mind-sets, destructive emotions and hurtful behavior. The planetary dweller-on-the-threshold is the planetary momentum of that vortex of evil and destructiveness.

Thus without the balance of love, justice becomes destructive. Think about how you feel when something seems unjust in your life. How loving or merciful do you feel toward the source of that injustice? Most likely you feel somewhat angry or vindictive.

The Zohar goes on to explain how once the balance of love and justice was upset, evil arose from the smoke and fury of anger:

> When the smoke started to come out of the furious anger, the smoke spread farther and farther, anger after anger, one upon another, and one rode upon and dominated the other, like the appearance of male and female, so that all was a furious anger. And when the smoke began to spread it emitted from the anger the emission of a single point, that it might spread. Subsequently, the smoke of the anger spread out in a curling fashion, like the cunning snake, in order to do evil.[7]

The Zohar's concept of "anger after anger" riding upon and dominating the other, like the appearance of male with female, presents an explicit picture of what happens with runaway power. We see the terrible progeny of the union of power and virility without the temperance of love: "furious anger," out of which evil is spread.

We recognize this negative drama in our personal lives—in the warring of the members, as the apostle Paul put it, as hatred for people who treat us unjustly and in our violent imaginings, thoughts, feelings or uncontrolled physical vindictiveness.

Thus, according to the Kabbalah, evil was created when universal energy was misused through the imbalance of love and justice. Instead of continuing to be a pure outpost of the divine, the earth itself became permeated with an energy veil of infamous motives, thoughts, words and deeds.

Archangel Michael and the Dragon

The Christian version of the genesis of evil appears in the twelfth chapter of Revelation:

> And there was war in heaven: Michael and his angels fought against the dragon; and the dragon fought and his angels,
>
> And prevailed not; neither was their place found any more in heaven.
>
> And the great dragon was cast out, that old serpent, called the Devil, and Satan, which deceiveth the whole world: he was cast out into the earth, and his angels were cast out with him.
>
> And I heard a loud voice saying in heaven, Now is come salvation, and strength, and the kingdom of our God, and the power of his Christ: for the accuser of our brethren is cast down, which accused them

before our God day and night.

And they overcame him by the blood of the Lamb, and by the word of their testimony; and they loved not their lives unto the death.

Therefore rejoice, ye heavens, and ye that dwell in them. Woe to the inhabiters of the earth and of the sea! for the devil is come down unto you, having great wrath, because he knoweth that he hath but a short time.

And when the dragon saw that he was cast unto the earth, he persecuted the woman which brought forth the man child.

And to the woman were given two wings of a great eagle, that she might fly into the wilderness, into her place, where she is nourished for a time, and times, and half a time, from the face of the serpent.

And the serpent cast out of his mouth water as a flood after the woman, that he might cause her to be carried away of the flood.

And the earth helped the woman, and the earth opened her mouth, and swallowed up the flood which the dragon cast out of his mouth.

And the dragon was wroth with the woman, and went to make war with the remnant of her seed, which keep the commandments of God, and have the testimony of Jesus Christ.[8]

Various religious traditions tell the story differently, but the essence of it is the same—the entrance of evil into the earth plane and the consequent darkness and confusion that came upon God's people.

The Pride and Trickery of the Fallen Angels

According to esoteric teachings, the original fall from grace began with the rebel angels who refused to honor the sons and daughters of God. In their pride, anger and sense of injustice, these rebellious ones challenged their Maker: "We were created first. Why should we bow down to them?"[9]

Thus they forfeited their opportunity to live in the heaven-world—the ethereal plane of eternal existence. They were cast out and descended to the planes of matter, where they remain until their energy is spent. And no longer do they have access to the Creator's pure divine energy.

Over time they will use up their reservoir of energy; they will be no more—unless they bend the knee to their Creator and begin the process of balancing the karma they have made. For the most part, in their pride and arrogance, they refuse to do so.

Spiritually, we understand that God extends mercy and opportunity to all, even fallen angels. But ultimately, God cancels out the identity and consciousness of evil and returns that energy to its original, pure state. Thus, evil is never permanent. Fallen angels have limited time and space. Only God-good ultimately endures.

I believe this is the esoteric meaning of the "lake of fire" in Revelation.[10] It consumes all that is not God-good.

Those fallen angels might have spent their energy long ago had it not been for the energy of God's light they steal to keep themselves going. How do they do that? They get it from the children of God who believe their lies and deception and give themselves over to these haughty beings.

We have all been there. We have been deceived, betrayed and violated by fallen angels and their cohorts. We have lived lives of quiet desperation. Sometimes we even joined those fallen ones because we forgot to pray and didn't know what else to do. In the darkest of the dark ages, we forgot that there was any other way to live.

A Tale of Woe on Earth

This is the ancient story of the soul—your soul, my soul. According to esoteric teachings, the original evolutions of God on earth were called root races. Each root race was a group of souls who shared a unique archetypal pattern, divine plan and divine mission to fulfill on earth. When they fulfilled that mission, they won their immortal freedom. They were free from the wheel of rebirth.

The first three root races lived in purity and innocence upon earth in three golden ages.* Through obedience to cosmic law and total identification with the Real Self, these three root races ascended from the earth plane to oneness with God.

During the time of the fourth root race, on the ancient continent of Lemuria, the rebellion of the fallen angels took place in the heaven-world. Once they were cast into the earth plane, they preyed upon the people. These rebellious fallen angels used serpentine spinal energies to beguile the soul (feminine principle) and the spirit (masculine principle).

Thus, at the time of the fourth root race, people began

---

*These were periods in earth's history where enlightenment, peace and prosperity were paramount.

to misuse their free will to create negative instead of positive spirals of consciousness. They made wrong choices and indulged in actions that were destructive to life. As they increasingly misused divine energy, they more and more identified with the energy veil, the veil of misqualified energy.

Through dishonoring the universal laws of the Creator, their vibration and consciousness cycled downward. They no longer felt connected with the higher consciousness of divine love. In the end, they didn't believe they had any purpose on earth other than survival and propagation of the species.[11]

The Coming of Sanat Kumara, the Ancient of Days

And this brings us to the story of the magnificent ascended master who many aeons ago looked with divine pity upon the plight of the evolutions on earth.

After the fallen angels descended to earth and conveyed their rebellious ways to the fourth root race, the cosmic councils faced a momentous decision—whether the planet should continue to exist or simply be dissolved into undifferentiated universal energy. The future did not look hopeful for the planet or her people.

Enter Sanat Kumara, known to many as the Ancient of Days. He volunteered to come to the rescue of the people of earth.[12] Inspired by his example, legions of angels and beings of light determined he would not come alone.

Many of us were among the rescuers and have a soul memory of these events. We came to earth so joyous and determined to bring our fellow lightbearers home to God. It was difficult to imagine the tremendous challenges we would face when we actually arrived. The vibrations of the earth were dark and heavy, and the people living here seemed numbed to them, some even completely identifying with that darkness.

Frequently the lightbearers already on earth (even those we had known in the etheric realm) didn't recognize or trust us and wanted us to go away. And we also had to deal with the treachery of the fallen angels and try to maintain our attunement to God in the presence of entrenched evil.

As we sought to fulfill our rescue mission, we became separated from one another and lost our bearings. In the course of time and confusing events, we also fell prey to the lies and deception of the fallen angels and their cohorts.

We may have become curious about the ways of the world or succumbed to the trickery of the fallen angels or reacted angrily to their abuse of earth's people—suffering pain and disillusionment in the process.

One way or another, we lost sight of our rescue mission and lowered our vibration after we left the higher octaves of light. And we made the karma that tied us to continuing rounds of rebirth on earth.

The Karmic Predicament of the Rescuers

For many of us, this was the beginning a deep momentum of pain and anger—anger at the fallen angels who were creating the suffering, anger at our own predicament. Some of us even became angry with God. Why?

Because in our suffering at the hands of the fallen angels, we no longer remembered that we had chosen this mission of mercy.

In the midst of our turmoil and pain, we forgot that God's gift of free will reigns supreme on the earth. We decided that God didn't care about us anymore—a major mistake.

Over many years, perhaps lifetimes, we tried to handle our suffering. When it didn't stop, we tried to make ourselves immune to pain by hardening our heart and soul. In the process, we became more and more dense. We no longer remembered to call to God for guidance, strength and mercy.

In time we became so distraught that we either gave up or became angry and vengeful. By so doing, we inflicted pain on ourselves and on the very people we were trying to help. All of us eventually got caught in a web of karmic circumstances that necessitated our cycles of rebirth, lifetime after lifetime.

Yet God continued to love all of us and to try to help us remember that we are his sons and daughters, that we bear the light of God within our hearts. So he sent avatars, prophets, saints, sages and teachers to remind us of our mission.

These have been the enlightened ones. They have demonstrated how to greet and overcome the negative influences on earth that have been such driving forces in our lives. They have taught the inner mysteries and the path of initiation and redemption that restores the soul's original divine nature and returns her to the heart of God.

By word and example, these spiritual adepts have sought to fulfill their divine mission. They have shepherded the lifewaves of earth and reminded the rescuers of their destiny to do the same.

All of the emissaries of God have brought one central redemptive message: "God loves you." And they offer a corollary teaching: "You can make it all the way Home if you fulfill your destiny as sons and daughters of God." How? By walking the path of divine love, embracing divine wisdom and invoking divine power to create God-good on earth and among her people.

Thus we are called to remember our destiny to hold the balance of divine light in the midst of planetary darkness—and to help the lightbearers on earth remember their divine origin. We, too, are meant to leave our footprints in the sands of time so all of God's children may find their way. And we are meant to return home to God with our mission accomplished.

Why Am I Still Here?

Yet here we are on earth today, still stuck in some aspect of the human condition. So we ask ourselves, "What am I doing wrong? Why is it so difficult to walk the spiritual path the adepts have demonstrated? Why does the earth itself seem to be getting darker instead of lighter? Why can't I live in the place of my dreams, a beautiful place where it's easy to practice divine love, wisdom and power?"

The answer lies in our reaction to the antics of the fallen angels and what we have internalized from them.

These energy patterns not only reside in the collective unconscious of the planet, they also reside in the depths of our personal unconscious. These planetary and personal patterns of darkness interact and play themselves out in our daily lives—until we completely transmute and transform the dark magnets we carry within ourselves.

Remember what happened once the rebellious fallen angels entered the earth? Those prideful ones absolutely refused to honor the children of God evolving on earth. Instead, they found subtle ways to deceive those innocent ones, to steal their light, their spiritual energy, and to get them to embrace evil.

Under the charisma and influence of these angels of darkness, both the children of God and the well-intentioned rescuers began to indulge in desires and behaviors that were incongruent with their divine nature.

They internalized and reacted to the lies and misdeeds of the fallen angels; they began to create their personal dweller-on-the-threshold. This negative consciousness has been passed on from generation to generation.

We are those people. And the dragon of the misuse of the sacred fire of God is still active today, warring upon the inhabitants of the earth.

This negative dilemma is the spiritual challenge for us today. We have the opportunity to choose good over evil. But in order to do so, we must recognize evil when it appears, not only at its worst but also at the subtle levels that invade our personal lives.

9

The Dance of Good and Evil

Yea, though I walk through the valley
of the shadow of death,
I will fear no evil: for thou art with me.

—PSALM 23:4

How do we recognize and outwit the powers of darkness, especially when they are subtle or hide behind a benign surface? And how do we come to terms with our own dark side?

Evil reveals itself in every act of brutality and atrocity. It is behind every calculated lie, every intentional act of violence, degradation, murder and mayhem. Evil lurked behind the hatred and treachery that led to two world wars and all the other wars not as widespread but just as deadly. Evil is behind the merciless killings by terrorists throughout the world today.

It appears in movies or on our TV screen as we watch

with horror the calculated cruelty of archetypes of core evil—archetypes such as the raging terrorists in the movie *Air Force One* or the Emperor in the *Star Wars* trilogy. Evil appears in our cities and neighborhoods in the form of crime and violence.

As was the case with Amy, I have clients who specifically come into therapy to explore their own ancient records and memories, particularly those of being on the receiving end of evil. Such memories from an individual's unconscious usually come up as flashes of awareness or dreams of experiences in ancient civilizations or unfamiliar settings.

When we first explore these memories, people rarely believe there's a direct connection between that past life and their present situations. Yet during the process of the therapy we usually find that the experiences do relate. Once the past-life drama is understood, they often see a similar lesson in their current life.

When the memory is from a recent past life, the client can sometimes fill in important details from people still living who were part of that past life. Often this information completes the picture and brings into focus the lesson for the soul. Many times that lesson is about how we handle ourselves when we come face-to-face with evil.

Judith's Victory over Guilt and Self-Punishment

A young woman, Judith, came to see me because she had a history of guilt and self-punishment that she had experienced for as long as she could remember. She continually deprived herself or gave in to other people out of a sense that she owed it to them—even people she'd never met before. She didn't want to marry out of a sense of obligation, nor did she want to pass her self-denigrating attitude on to her children.

Judith's distress related to a childhood incident where she had wandered off from her mother during a shopping trip and her mother had been extremely frightened and angry when she finally found her. She tried to tell her mother she just went to look at the pretty jewelry, but her mother was so upset that she punished her severely. Judith decided she was a really bad girl.

As she was working on the emotional residue of this incident in therapy, she suddenly flashed to a memory of her past life as a little Jewish girl in Germany during World War II. What she remembered was Nazi soldiers dragging her father out of their home for interrogation. He never returned to his family and their inquiries were ignored.

Judith felt it had all been her fault. As the memories came back, she tearfully recounted how she and a number of other children had overturned a garbage pail in the path of some Nazi soldiers. They all ran away and didn't think anyone had followed them. But her mother had scolded her when she found out what they had done. And the next day the soldiers came and took her father away. Judith had been so frightened that she hid in the closet until they were gone.

The family was later told that the father had been executed for underground activities and treason against the Führer. But Judith was certain she had been the cause of it and never forgave herself. Fortunately, through friends in the underground, the family was able to escape before undergoing the terrible fate of the gas chambers. Many of their friends were not so fortunate.

Whether or not the children's prank was responsible for the father's incarceration and death, Judith would never know. It was likely the Nazis were already tracking him because of his involvement in the underground. But even though her mother tried to reassure her, she was convinced in her own mind that she was responsible.

As Judith was remembering this terrible event, we prayed for the souls of her family and the six million Jews who suffered and perished during that horrendous Holocaust. We both realized she had had an encounter with evil personified.

Judith, a Christian in this life, asked God for forgiveness and accepted that God loved and forgave her. She also wrote a letter to the soul of her father and burned it, asking the angels to take it to him. She told him how much she loved him and that she prayed for the fulfillment of his mission of championing freedom and goodness.

Judith was able to track down records of her older sister in that previous life, the only family member still living. Her sister later revealed that Judith herself had died at the age of thirty-four in a single car accident. Out of guilt and self-recrimination she had never married. (Judith was reborn into her present life two years later.)

Her sister, although skeptical about Judith really being her sister reembodied, completely verified what Judith remembered. She also told her she was quite certain her father had been killed because of his connection with the underground and that her little sister had nothing to do with it.

With a huge sigh of relief, Judith realized it was point-less to hold on to a sense of guilt that went back to this past life. She worked hard in therapy to release her feelings and gradually the cloud of guilt began to lift. As she told me, "It feels like I've been released from prison. I am so grateful!"

Judith began to celebrate the fact that she is alive and well today and that she has a right to enjoy life. She also realized her guilt in this life was a combination of pain, anger and self-reproach for what she had done in her past life, but even then she had only indulged in a childish prank. The twists and turns in her own consciousness had condemned her.

The incident of Judith's mother punishing her severely for running off to look at the pretty jewelry had quickened the past-life memory. But it was not until she was an adult that she was ready to face and overcome what happened in that past life. Once she did that, she was ready to heal and move on.

A few years later she called to tell me she was married and had given birth to a baby boy. She said, "You know, I still feel a sense of sadness about what happened in that life, but I also feel a sense of joy and hope. I have such a wonderful husband. And I feel so close to our baby. It's like we already know each other. I wonder if he could be my father reembodied. Wouldn't that be neat?

"I must have done something right to earn the life I am

living now—and I am grateful. God has been good to me. And I have a right to be good to myself and to my family. I am so grateful that we have all been born in America this time. I wish everyone knew what a gift that is. I know I will always champion the blessing of freedom of religion. Truly America is God's country, and wherever there is goodness instead of evil, I know that is God's country too."

"People of the Lie"

We see the modus operandi of core evil in individuals whom author and psychiatrist M. Scott Peck has described as "people of the lie."[1] These are people who consciously choose to hurt, defile and destroy others.

In psychology and psychiatry, we used to call such people *psychopaths.** This is accurate terminology because psychopaths have no conscience or sense of guilt about their murderous ways.

As evil increasingly infiltrated our society, we began to dilute the essence of the problem by calling these people *sociopaths.*† As time went on, society became so numbed to evil that we simply labeled them *antisocial personalities.*

In reality, evil is much more than these labels. We have seen the face of evil in Mafia mobsters, Nazi storm troopers, hooded members of the Ku Klux Klan and today's terrorist network. Such morally depraved people make deliberate and deadly choices to inflict pain and anguish upon others. They have become evil personified.

---

*The term *psycho* comes from *psyche*, Greek for "soul"; *path* is a short form of *pathology*, meaning the "conditions, processes or results of a disease."

†From *socio*, relating to social behavior, and *path*, referring to *pathology*.

Evil is a growing cancer upon the earth. Yet through the unity of God-fearing, freedom-loving people, evil can and will be overcome. President George Bush said it well in his address to a joint session of Congress on September 20, 2001:

> These terrorists kill not merely to end lives but to disrupt and end a way of life. With every atrocity, they hope that America grows fearful, retreating from the world and forsaking [her] friends. They stand against us, because we stand in their way....
>
> We have seen their kind before. They are the heirs of all the murderous ideologies of the twentieth century. By sacrificing human life to serve their radical visions—by abandoning every value except the will to power—they follow in the path of fascism and Nazism and totalitarianism. And they will follow that path all the way to where it ends: in history's unmarked grave of discarded lies....
>
> This is the world's fight. This is civilization's fight. This is the fight of all who believe in progress and pluralism, tolerance and freedom....
>
> Some speak of an age of terror. I know there are struggles ahead and dangers to face. But this country will define our times, not be defined by them. As long as the United States of America is determined and strong, this will not be an age of terror; this will be an age of liberty, here and across the world.
>
> Great harm has been done to us. We have suffered great loss. And in our grief and anger we have found our mission and our moment. Freedom and fear are at war. The advance of human freedom—the great

achievement of our time, and the great hope of every time—now depends on us.

Our nation—this generation—will lift the dark threat of violence from our people and our future. We will rally the world to this cause by our efforts, by our courage. We will not tire, we will not falter, and we will not fail. . . .

The course of this conflict is not known, yet its outcome is certain. Freedom and fear, justice and cruelty, have always been at war, and we know that God is not neutral between them.

Fellow citizens, we'll meet violence with patient justice—assured of the rightness of our cause, and confident of the victories to come. In all that lies before us, may God grant us wisdom, and may He watch over the United States of America.[2]

Freedom-loving people everywhere echo President Bush's courageous words. We realize that the forces of evil are active across the planet, challenging our nations and each of us personally. I believe our personal challenge is to ask ourselves if we are harboring evil in any way, actively or passively.

We need to uproot seeds of evil that may have been planted in our consciousness as a result of our reaction to evildoers. How can we recognize these embryonic spores? They come to light when we observe our own enmity or ill will when we are displeased with someone else's behavior.

When we indulge in vengeful fantasies, hostile thoughts, reactive hatred or violent behavior, we vibrate at the same level as evil. We entangle ourselves with evil. The more entangled we become, the less we recognize evil for what it is—and the more we compromise our innate goodness. Malicious intentions, hostile thinking, hateful emotions and destructive behavior generate more of that dark, shadowy energy that we call evil.

M. Scott Peck describes evil as murder, whether of the body or the spirit:

> It is a reflection of the enormous mystery of the subject that we do not have a generally accepted definition of evil. Yet in our hearts I think we all have some understanding of its nature. For the moment I can do no better than to heed my son, who, with the characteristic vision of eight-year-olds, explained simply, "Why, Daddy, evil is 'live' spelled backward."
>
> Evil is in opposition to life. It is that which opposes the life force. It has, in short, to do with killing. Specifically it has to do with murder—namely, unnecessary killing, killing that is not required for biological survival.
>
> Let us not forget this. There are some who have written about evil so intellectually that it comes out sounding abstract to the point of irrelevancy. Murder is not abstract. . . .
>
> When I say that evil has to do with killing, I do not mean to restrict myself to corporeal murder. Evil is also that which kills spirit. . . .
>
> Evil, then, for the moment, is that force, residing either inside or outside of human beings, that seeks to kill life or liveliness. And goodness is its opposite. Goodness is that which promotes life and liveliness.[3]

Peck's statement is powerful and succinct. How can we deal with the virulent force of evil? Basically, the antidote is God-good. It is claiming within ourselves all that is sacred and life-giving, all that is good and uplifting, all that is true and loving, all that brings joy and vitality.

A Personal Encounter with the Face of Evil

I will never forget a client I saw briefly a number of years ago, one of the few truly evil people I have ever seen in my practice.

This man told me, with a malicious glint in his eye, "I've been in prison for murder. I'm out now. And I've got a mental list of people that don't deserve to live. I'm going to see to it that they don't. What do you think about that?"

"Why are you telling me?" I asked. "Surely you know I'll report this to the police."

He seemed unmoved by that. "It doesn't matter. There's no evidence. And besides, I'm going to the second death anyway."

"What do you mean by that?" I responded. Only later did I realize he was talking about the disintegration of his soul.

"You know what I mean," he said.

There was no reaching this man. His eyes were empty. He was a walking bomb of hatred and malice.

My supervisor and I called the police and related his threat. But the police said that unless he made a direct threat toward an individual they could do nothing about it. I never saw him again. But I had a very clear sense that God had shown me the face of evil so that I would never forget it.

Later I learned that the second death means the dissolving of the soul's individuality back into universal energy.

Mark and Elizabeth Prophet teach that every soul who loves God has the opportunity to return to God in the victory of the ascension. But fallen angels (who have sworn enmity with God and God's people) and those who join forces with them eventually come to the end of their opportunity in time and space. If they have not turned from their evil ways, their identity is canceled out and the energy reclaimed for new creation.

Truly we are living in a time of judgment of the fallen angels and those who align themselves with absolute evil. They can be judged when they make their moves against the light and God's people.[4] Terrorist attacks are such a move.

The Story of Our Personal Dweller-on-the-Threshold

Our own dark side, our personal dweller-on-the-threshold, was born of our misuse of divine love linked with our soul's pain, frustration and demands for justice and retribution. Sometimes the dweller evolved out of our confusion and fear. Every time we misused the light of God in some way, we made more karma, dug ourselves deeper into our karmic predicament—and strengthened our dweller.

To this murky brew was added the energy we took in from the fallen angels. Any time we interact with someone, there is an energy exchange; that's just how it works. In the case of our interaction with the vengeful fallen angels, they took our light and we took in their patterns of darkness. We began to think like them, feel like them, act like them.

After awhile, we didn't recognize the difference between our dweller and our soul. All we knew was that we were not happy, and we were making others unhappy too. We felt ashamed and disheartened every time we hurt the people we loved.

Our dweller, then, is the conglomerate of all the negative qualities, motives, thoughts, feelings and habit patterns we harbor within ourselves. And the dragon of angry reactions and vicious words is a very proud part of that dweller.

On an energetic level, the dweller is made up of tangles of our incorrect use of universal energy—or those tangles we have taken in from others. These dissonant patterns circulate in the unconscious and subconscious, hidden from our outer awareness.

Yet they can suddenly emerge when triggered by pain, confusion or frustration. When they burst out as hostility, anger, resentment and retaliation, the eruption can be of volcanic intensity. It's like the lash of a hidden dragon's tail.

The fact is, no matter how much we love God, the dweller we have created doesn't. It lives on within us, burdening our heart and soul, until we transform it.

The spiritual teachings on the dweller-on-the-threshold relate to the apostle Paul's statement on the dangers of people's carnal nature, meaning their tendency to indulge in sensual pleasures or worldly concerns at the expense of the soul. Paul understood the strife between the carnal nature of people versus the spiritual nature of the soul.

Using himself as an example, he wrote:

> The good that I would, I do not; but the evil which I would not, that I do.
>
> Now if I do that I would not, it is no more I that do it, but sin that dwelleth in me.
>
> I find then a law, that, when I would do good, evil is present with me.
>
> For I delight in the law of God after the inward man:
>
> But I see another law in my members, warring against the law of my mind, and bringing me into captivity to the law of sin which is in my members.

Thus Paul taught that carnal-mindedness (spiritually, an aspect of the dweller) is inner captivity. He also spoke of it as enmity with God:

> For to be carnally minded is death; but to be spiritually minded is life and peace.
>
> Because the carnal mind is enmity against God, for it is not subject to the law of God, neither indeed can be.[5]

Truly this is the case. Either we outwit that carnal mind or we are in conflict with our soul and our God. This is a dilemma we can face and do something about.

These five steps can help you set your consciousness in the right direction:

1. Realize and affirm that you are a son or daughter of God with a divine destiny to fulfill.

2. Determine that your dweller will not rule your motives, thoughts, words or actions.

3. Ask God and the angels to amplify the divine light that you carry in every cell and atom of your being.

4. Choose to be strong and steady within yourself, wise and compassionate toward yourself, your family, your friends—and your adversaries.

5. Make your decisions for the highest good and take the high road in every situation.

Each day as you strive to maintain the stance of a true son or daughter of God, you are reclaiming your rightful heritage as a bearer of God's light to the earth. This is the path that adepts, saints and sages have walked. You have the same divine potential.

You can begin to actualize it when you rid yourself of pride, anger and their fellow travelers, for thereby you dismantle and redeem the core of the dweller consciousness. You take another mighty step forward when you claim your courage, honor and integrity. And you take a giant stride toward victory when you affirm your faith and allegiance to Almighty God and follow the guidance of the angels and your own Higher Self.

Star Wars and the Dweller-on-the-Threshold

A film clip from the *Star Wars* trilogy illustrates the confrontation with the dweller-on-the-threshold. In it Luke is running through the forest with Yoda on his shoulder—Yoda, the guru, the teacher. When he comes to a certain spot, Yoda tells him to go into an underground opening.

Luke asks, "What am I going to find there?"

Yoda replies, "Only that which you take with you."

Then Luke asks if he should take his weapon with him.

Yoda says, in a most disarming manner, "Oh, no."

That was a Zen test. Does a true warrior ever lay down his weapon in the face of the unknown? No. So Luke straps his weapon on and descends into the depths of a cavern. All of a sudden he hears the *whoosh! whoosh!* of someone approaching.

Out of the darkness comes Darth Vader—a huge, hulking black-helmeted figure, who draws his light sword. So Luke turns on his own light sword and they duel.

Suddenly Luke's sword of light cuts off Darth Vader's head. It falls to the floor with the helmet still on. When the visor flies up, Luke is staring down into his own face.

Here is the psychological symbolism of this drama: Luke has to go underground into the subconscious, into the unconscious, to slay his own dweller-on-the-threshold, his counterpart of the darkness that Darth Vader represents.

Think of Darth Vader as the soul following untoward desires into the mists of maya. He turns from the path of the Jedi Knight to serve his own dark side and eventually finds himself serving absolute darkness in the person of the Emperor.

Now Luke, deep in the caverns of his own unconscious, comes face-to-face with that darkness in himself. This remarkable scene depicts what the spiritual path is all about—slaying the dweller, our own Darth Vader, that hides in the depths of our subconscious and unconscious.

When we confront and banish that inner darkness, we move forward in spiritual adeptship. That is why spiritual work such as calling to the angels to bind the dweller and replace it with the power of light is so important. When we center ourselves in the light of God, darkness has no lasting power.

Luke's underground encounter with the Darth-Vader figure was key. He needed to understand that the Darth Vader he slew was the personification of his own repressed dark side. He needed to be stronger than his own dark side, to slay the evil within himself before he could successfully confront what Darth Vader had embraced—the absolute evil of the Emperor.

In the dramatic final scene between the Emperor, Darth Vader and Luke, Luke functions with such valor that he inspires a major change in Darth Vader (who turns out to be Luke's father). Luke wins a "Jedi Knight" victory. He is also the instrument of Darth Vader's turnaround and the defeat of the absolute wickedness of the Emperor.

Of course, movies do not match reality. At the end of this episode, Darth Vader is in a transcendent state that resembles the ascension.[6] This is unrealistic. Even though he may have been an adept before defecting to the evil Emperor, he would have to balance the negative karma he'd made before he could ascend.

In real life, a person like Darth Vader would reembody in order to redeem the energies of evil he had assimilated and acted out. He would go through additional cycles of rebirth—however many lifetimes it would take—to balance the karma, rebuild a momentum of light and win the ultimate victory of the ascension.

Our Greatest Stumbling Block on the Path

The ascended master Jesus Christ warns of the personal danger inherent in our failure to recognize evil incarnate. He says:

> From our perspective, one of the factors that is destroying Western civilization is the denial on the part of some that there is anything wrong with the current downward trends or that there are any wrongdoers systematically focusing on the dismantling of society and its ultimate destruction.
>
> If you have not come to grips with the reality that evil can work through anyone, well-intentioned or not (including yourself), in an unguarded moment, then you have missed a vital point of the Path....
>
> A large percentage of the people evolving on the planet cannot and will not believe that evil is a force to be reckoned with. They do not want to know that evil, in the form of the dweller-on-the-threshold, lurks in their own unconscious mind until they wage war against the not-self. And only when they completely vanquish the not-self are they able to discern light and darkness, good and evil....
>
> People who have an evil intent are usually bent upon self-destruction, but their persona is beguiling. It is calculated to "deceive the very elect." If you have not knowingly encountered such people, beware! For I have sent you [the lightbearers] into the world to analyze and then to challenge those individuals whom one of your modern authors calls "the people of the lie."
>
> You must understand evil so that you might get the victory over evil and so that, through you, the

world itself might get the victory over evil.

Therefore, lament not that you have been burdened by the circumstances of your life or been persecuted or been in dysfunctional homes. You had lessons to learn and karmas to pay, and many of you are still paying them. Praise God for the opportunity to be in embodiment and make the most of life's journey.

The major lesson that you came into embodiment to learn is what is evil and what is its modus operandi. Indeed, you came to learn how it is possible that souls of light can be duped again and again by the forces of evil. . . .

I lay this subject on your heart. Ponder it well, for your failure to recognize evil incarnate in the fallen angels in your midst is your greatest stumbling block on the spiritual path. It is the major test that light-bearers fail again and again. And until they pass that test, not only will they be vulnerable to the forces of evil but the evolutions of earth who follow their lead will also be vulnerable to the forces of evil.

When you understand this equation, you will gain your personal victory over death and hell. When you no longer allow the fallen angels to manipulate you, for you see through them and their ploys from A to Z, you will then be of the utmost assistance to the Darjeeling Council.* And one day you may even receive the mantle of conquering hero or heroine for meritorious service in exposing the seed of the Wicked One.

Therefore be wise as serpents and harmless as

---

*The Darjeeling Council is a council of ascended masters and unascended devotees. Its objective is to train souls for world service in government, the economy, international relations and the realization of the inner Christ in all.

doves. Do not whitewash the deeds of the seed of the Wicked One. Do not sympathize with the sorrows of Satan or his cohorts. But meditate upon the wondrous love of God and contemplate his wisdom. Go to the altar and let God tell you, through your Mighty I AM Presence, what is truth, what is error, what is real, what is unreal."[7]

Make a Conscious Choice to Disengage from Evil

Where do we begin? I believe we can take a step forward by recognizing our own inner magnets of darkness —magnets we have taken in from our interactions with the dark forces.

We need to comprehend how these magnets attract and mesh us with evil. Then we can consciously disconnect from them, surrender that dark power and transform it into the power of light.

To accomplish this, we need to ask for divine help— to call upon our Higher Self and the angels to light the way. As the Master Jesus tells us, "Come unto me, all ye that labour and are heavy laden, and I will give you rest. ... For my yoke is easy, and my burden is light."[8]

We can embrace Gautama Buddha's Middle Way.* We can choose the way of the Tao. Mystics from all of the world's major religions teach the inner path that raises the soul out of darkness into the light of God's kingdom.

When we make the choice to uphold the light, we do an about-face and gradually begin to extricate ourselves from the snares of darkness. Of course, it's easier said than

*See p. 345, n. 4.

done. We tend to underestimate the powers of darkness that still inhabit the earth.

Yet that darkness has no *permanent* reality, and our destiny is to affirm the light. Two mantras that will help you affirm the light are "Evil is not real and its appearance has no power!" and "The light of God never fails, the light of God never fails, the light of God never fails. And the beloved Mighty I AM Presence is that light!"

God Does Not Leave His Children Bereft

The ascended masters teach that the Father-Mother God envisions the redemption of all of the lightbearers on earth. The ascended master Sanat Kumara holds that higher vision for our victory. Avatars have been sent. Mystery schools have been founded so that those who remember or sense their divine origin can find their way. The masters who sponsor the mystery schools teach the eternal truths to all who are earnestly seeking their way home to God.

Some of the rescuers have returned to the heaven-world. Those who are still serving here continue to receive the help of the ascended masters and the angels. At night many attend classes in etheric universities, even though they don't always remember those experiences. They are tutored from within, which is how many of us have redis-covered our spiritual path.

What is the foremost spiritual lesson for each of us? I believe it is to become consciously aware of our own pockets of darkness, those inner magnets and our personal dweller-on-the-threshold. Only then can we take the stance of the adept to understand, challenge and redeem that darkness—and do so with divine love and grace. Those valiant lightbearers who have gone before us have done this. They have shown us the way.

How does this relate to us today? In the face of the evil of terrorism, we have a choice to make: Will we stand strong in our faith in God and choose the path of enlightened, heroic action? Or will we allow our own dark side to emerge?

I believe that the real heroes of history have been God-fearing people, whether they outwardly acknowledged this or not. When they went to war against forces of evil, they maintained their higher principles. In the throes of war, they were courageous and inspiring leaders. They proved themselves valiant in battle and compassionate in victory.

Two Million Right Decisions

Why doesn't God simply reach down and rescue us? Because as sons and daughters of the Father-Mother God, our most precious heritage is our gift of free will—we can decide to be good or do otherwise. We are not little robot people and windup toys who are good because God makes us be good.

We can elect to fulfill our divine mission, balance our karma and return home to God—mission accomplished. God intends us to do just that. Or we can decide to do the opposite. It's our choice.

If we choose to return home to the heaven-world, we need to walk the path of divine love, pass our initiations and balance our karma. Ultimately, when our energy accelerates and vibrates in complete consonance with divine love, wisdom and power (the qualities of the divine spark within us), we too can return to union with God.

As we walk the spiritual path toward this goal, our Higher Self continues to be our special guardian angel, who is just a prayer away. And God will send troops of all kinds of special angels to walk with us, to guide us along the rocky path of our returning karma. We just need to surrender our human resistance and trust in God's timing and divine plan.

When we pray for guidance and help, God hears our call and answers. We can then go on to make the good karma of right decisions. The ascended master Saint Germain says he made his ascension by making two million right decisions (over many embodiments). We can do the same.

As we've learned, every decision we make results in either good karma or not-so-good karma. Furthermore, that karmic energy becomes who we are at all levels of our being. As Mrs. Prophet said one time, we *are* our karma, right down to the freckle on the end of our nose.

Our job today is to balance that karma. It's up to us to remember our divine origin, to remember our loving Father-Mother God. And it's our redemptive task to take accountability for our circumstances and to see God in the reality of divine love—instead of through the veil of pain and anger.

Understanding Leads to Enlightenment

We all have our own way of understanding the Father-Mother God. When I was a little child I thought of the Father as a kindly, wise, protective grandfather who really loved me. And Mother Mary represented the loving Mother, with all of the mystery, beauty, serenity, peace and nurturing I could imagine.

Later, when I discovered Eastern teachings, I also thought of Gautama Buddha as representing the Father. His vibration of peace, enlightenment and love have been a comfort to my soul. All the Buddhas, with their gentle peace and nonattachment, can help us remain calm, even in the most trying circumstances. We can learn from the Buddhas how to be nonattached to our opinions or possessions or to having our own way. And we can learn not to become angry when challenged by someone else but instead hold fast to our peace.

When Gautama experienced the fierce attack of Mara, the emissary of evil, he remained in peaceful meditation, nonattached and awake, and achieved enlightenment. We can ask him to help us do the same.

I also look to Kuan Yin, the bodhisattva of compassion, the one who "hears the cries of the world."* She reminds us to offer mercy and forgiveness to all, including those who hurt us.

In the artist's depiction facing page 188, Kuan Yin is riding a dragon, guiding that serpent force with total equanimity and peace. The waters are roaring, the dragon is fierce and she is standing on his back taking a smooth ride. Each of us can strive to be as the peaceful Kuan Yin midst the waves of emotion that come up inside of us.

---

*In Eastern teachings, Kuan Yin is a feminine form of the bodhisattva of compassion. In masculine form the bodhisattva is known as Avalokiteś-vara. (A bodhisattva is a Buddha-to-be.)

The Power of Bending the Knee

Instead of battling with our human emotions, we can ask our Higher Self and the angels to help us take care of the drama.

We can call upon Archangel Michael, a mighty being often portrayed with his foot on a fallen angel or devil. We can ask Archangel Michael to deal with fallen-angel types —and our own dweller. We can ask the merciful Kuan Yin to help us transmute our patterns of hurt, pride, anger and resentment.

So we humble ourselves. We pray and talk to God and call upon the hosts of the LORD. And we do not take aggressive action, for in our human reactivity we are too likely to misuse our power.

We don't have to yell and scream at anyone; we don't have to punch anybody out. Our role is to make the call to our Higher Self and the angels and then listen inwardly for the response. And often the answer comes as an intuition, a shift in perspective or a creative idea about how to handle the situation.

An example of this is the New Testament story about the angry crowd that was going to stone the woman taken in adultery. (The punishment for adultery at that time was to be stoned to death.) So they brought the woman to Jesus and asked him how he would handle it. What did Jesus do? He "stooped down and with his finger wrote on the ground, as though he heard them not." Then, with the wisdom of the Christ mind, he said, "He that is without sin among you, let him first cast a stone at her."[9]

Can you imagine the power of that challenge from Jesus? None of them could in good conscience cast that first stone. So they went their way and the woman was unharmed. And Jesus said to her, "Neither do I condemn thee; go, and sin no more."

We also have the example of Jesus in the Garden of Gethsemane. Think of all that he had done to fulfill his mission on earth. Yet there he was, facing betrayal and death. A disciple and friend would betray him, and he would die on the cross, a very painful way to go.

How did Jesus handle his feelings? Instead of being angry or despondent, he knelt in prayer. He knelt in the garden and talked to God about it: "Father, if thou be willing, remove this cup from me: nevertheless not my will, but thine, be done."[10] He surrendered to his destiny. He had not forgotten his mission to show God's people the way to their own Christhood.

In contrast, the disciple Peter, who was impetuous and lost his temper, grabbed his sword and cut off the ear of one of the soldiers arresting Jesus. What did Jesus do? He told Peter to put his sword away and proceeded to place the ear back on the soldier and heal him.

This is the "high road" walked by saints, sages and avatars. They are unmoved by evil, their attention focused one-pointedly upon their mission for good.

Mahatma Gandhi, for instance, walked the way of peaceful nonresistance as an example to his nation and to the world. He lived for peace. He died for peace. May his spirit live forever in our hearts.

And as a vignette of the founding of America, we have

that wonderful painting of George Washington kneeling in prayer in the snow beside his horse. It's a magnificent depiction of a valiant commander praying for guidance and strength. He offered supplication to his Maker for his troops on numerous occasions throughout the Revolutionary War, even as today President Bush bows his head in prayer as he leads the nation in the war against terrorism.

In the new millennium, freedom-loving peoples throughout the world are bending the knee to God to pray for the victory of divine love over hatred, fanaticism and terrorism.

May we always remember the power of prayer, of bending the knee. This is a tremendous key to overcoming anger because it mobilizes divine power and dismantles human pride—our "they can't do this to me!" attitude. When we are in a prayerful mode, we can ask God for inner strength and guidance so we can be in the right vibration at the right time and place to take right action.

The Alchemy of Transmutation

Let's look at the alchemy of transmutation that prepares us to return home to God. What is transmutation? It is an inner process of refinement of our personal energies and consciousness. It gradually restores us to oneness with the Divine and prepares us to return Home.

As we've seen, every one of us, somewhere along the way, departed from our original state of innocence and grace. We misused divine power through pride, reactive anger and trying to control others. We misused divine wisdom through the never-ending labyrinth of human reasoning. We misused divine love through hardness of heart, emotional density and hatred toward those who harmed us.

By our misuses of energy, we ended up hurting ourselves, as well as others. The negative karma we made still ties us to the earth and the cycles of rebirth.

But God loves us anyway—the Infinite One forgives our human errors when we are truly sorry, ask forgiveness for our misdeeds and extend forgiveness to those who have hurt us. We speed up the process of refinement and transmutation when we invoke the violet flame through mantras, prayers or affirmations.[11]

As the violet fire is invoked, it causes a step-up in our vibration. It not only accelerates our emotional, mental and etheric energy fields, it also accelerates the millions of electrons whirling in our physical body. As the electrons whirl faster and faster in their tiny orbits, the impurities are spun off into the violet flame, which transforms that impure substance into its original divine vibration.

In this way, we actually re-create ourselves, energetically, at all levels of our being. Through the action of the violet flame, we are gradually refined and restored to oneness with our original divine blueprint. Thus, we reclaim our identity as sons and daughters of God.

The Trek Upward Is Worth the Inconvenience

By choosing the high road, embracing our initiations and invoking the violet transmuting flame over the years, we heal our soul, balance our karma and fulfill our mission on earth. Our chakras begin to whirl and spin just as the fire of God within us is spinning, and we gradually become one with that white fire. We become one with our

Higher Self, one with the Christ and the Buddha.

Our goal is to ascend to oneness with our God, our soul's ultimate victory. As the ascended master El Morya says, "The trek upward is worth the inconvenience!" Even as Elijah was taken up in a whirlwind and chariot of fire, so can we be enfolded in the fiery coil of ascension's light.

In the initiatic process of the transfiguration, resurrection and ascension, our consciousness spirals upward from the base-of-the-spine through the seat-of-the-soul, solar-plexus, heart, throat, third-eye and crown chakras—ascending to God.

One with our Higher Self and enveloped in brilliant, pulsating, fiery white light, we ascend to the highest level of universal being, the Great I AM, the I AM Presence. Having fulfilled our individualization of the God flame, we become one with the Infinite—our unique individuality intact.

10

Keys to Enlightened Self-Mastery

To dry one's eyes and laugh at a fall,
And baffled, get up and begin again.

—ROBERT BROWNING
"Life in a Love"

Would you like to take a major step forward on the path of initiation and adeptship? If so, you will go a long way by transforming anger, fear and pain into positive action, courage and forgiveness.

How do we do that? It is a process of gradual enlightenment that takes determination and self-mastery. Once we understand the need to heal the wounded aspects of our consciousness, we can transform emotional pain and reactivity. We can convert them into balanced, illumined action. And our soul will heave a sigh of relief!

Every time we take a firm stand without losing our cool, we heal the fear and pain of our soul. We begin to build a momentum on courage. And forgiving the aggressor blesses and frees us as well as the other person.

Embark on a Journey of Transformation

People ask me, "How can I change my emotional reactions? They seem to come out of nowhere." The process of transforming our emotions begins with paying attention when they do surface. Once we are fully aware of our painful feelings and the accompanying urge to react, we can choose to master ourselves. Then we can take positive action.

Here is a five-step process of self-analysis and emotional mastery, which can result in remarkable self-transformation:

1. Admit it when you have angry feelings. Understand that they stem from unresolved fear and pain, from past or present hurts, from feeling endangered.

2. Determine to harness that anger and create what I call a stop reflex. This is something that signals you to stop, to shift into neutral. I had to do that many years ago when I was learning to handle my own anger. I would literally visualize a stop sign or a red light. And at that moment I would zip the lip and do nothing.

3. Make a call to your Higher Self or your guardian angel to take command and help you master your propensity to react angrily. Or follow that homely wisdom your parents or grandparents may have taught you: Silently and slowly, count to ten (or twenty or whatever it takes) to cool down.* Consciously surrender the anger while you are doing this.

*For the "Count-to-Nine Decree," see p. 38.

4. Remove yourself from the situation that is triggering your anger. Just walk right out of it. Don't worry about having the last word. Simply leave the field.

5. Give yourself emotional first aid. Take a walk. Make it a point to look at the flowers, look at the clouds, look at the trees. You might want to do some yoga or pushups, or take a run around the block.

Or do this breathing exercise: Focus your full attention on the breath, inhaling through your nose, filling your abdomen, diaphragm and chest. Exhale slowly through the mouth—the slower, the better. Breathe in deeply through your nostrils with your attention totally on the breath. Then exhale slowly through your mouth. Try mentally counting to ten or twenty while exhaling.

All of this is part of a process of observing, harnessing and mastering your emotional reactions and thereby beginning to heal your fear and pain. You can do the same with frustration, irritation, annoyance and all of anger's other "kissing cousins." Once you are back in control of yourself, you can choose to think about the lesson and how you prefer to respond to the situation.

Make it a point to practice self-mastery every time you find yourself in a difficult or provoking situation. Focus on enlightened self-mastery instead of emotional reactivity. Gradually, you will begin to experience the positive charge that comes with handling your emotions in a masterful way.

When Have I Felt This Way Before?

Sometimes our emotional reactivity is so ingrained that we don't recognize it. For example, a friend or family member tells us they wish we would stop being so angry, and we go into denial—"Who me, angry?"

When we do take the comment seriously, we blame ourselves for being angry and feel bad about our flare-up. Pretty soon we feel like a victim. You know, the "I can't help it—people just don't understand me" kind of reaction.

In the process we tend to get defensive and indignant—"It's not fair!" Here comes the emotional reactivity again. But instead of allowing our emotions to rule us, we can decide to work with ourselves; we can become survivors.

We know our feelings were hurt, and maybe we're scared we can't lick the anger—but that friend or family member did us a favor. It takes a true friend to tell us an unpleasant truth. And being confronted with the hurtful impact of our anger can become a powerful wake-up call and motivator for transformation. We can change the way we handle feelings of vulnerability and powerlessness.

A good way to begin is to examine the kinds of experiences that you realize incite an emotional reaction. When you feel cornered or find your dander up, say to yourself, "What's usually happening when I feel this way?" You might remember some recent upsetting event or a trauma from much earlier in your life. You may remember a series of times when underlying pain or fear triggered combative feelings, whether or not you expressed them.

I suggest you jot down major times you remember being frightened, frustrated or angry—with yourself, someone else or some event on the world scene. When you examine what you have written, you will likely see a pattern to your reactions—and to the kinds of situations or people that tend to trigger them.

Jim and the Boss

Perhaps your pattern is similar to one that Jim, a client of mine, successfully outwitted. When he first came to see me, Jim said, "I realize I have a problem with my anger. The other day I just lost it with my boss. And I can't afford to do that. He put me on notice."

I responded, "That must have been unnerving."

Jim nodded. "It sure was, and still is. I'd like to work with it, but I don't know where to start. That outburst came out of nowhere."

I could see he was ready to deal with the anger, so I began to help him probe the roots of it: "Okay, I want you to remember that moment of losing it with your boss and tune in to how you felt when that happened. Now, when have you ever felt that way before? Perhaps as a child or a teenager or a young adult just starting out on your own? When do you remember feeling that way earlier in your life?"

Jim thought for a few minutes and then replied, "I think I felt that way a lot as a kid when my parents would blame me for doing something wrong. I usually didn't even know it was wrong. I'd feel really bad, and I didn't know how to fix whatever I was doing wrong.

"It got worse in my teens because just about every friend I made or new activity I wanted to try was 'wrong.' I got disgusted because they always wanted to scrutinize my friends, and they never wanted me to try anything that wasn't in the family tradition. I remember being really mad about that, but I tried not to let them know it because that would have just gotten me into more trouble.

"So I sneaked around with my friends and did a bunch of rebellious stuff I didn't even like doing. But it felt pretty good to be my own man."

I asked him, "Did you always get away with it?"

He sighed. "Almost, but not quite. One time I borrowed the family car just for the fun of it. I thought I could get it back before my dad got home, but my buddies and I were having such a good time, we didn't make it. Boy, was my dad mad! I thought he was going to punch me out.

"That time I knew I had stepped over the bounds, so I wasn't so much mad at him as I was at myself for being stupid. It cost me a lot because my dad never really trusted me again. To this day he holds it over my head. And that makes me mad. You would think the guy could drop the grudge after twenty years.

"In a way he's just like my boss. One mistake and you've had it. It's never forgotten."

That was an important insight. So I asked Jim, "Do you think your angry reaction to your boss could be a carryover from the way you react to your dad?"

Jim reflected and then nodded. "I hadn't thought about it that way, but I can see the correlation. I feel like they both want to run my life. I realize when I'm around the boss I have a chip on my shoulder, but he always manages to set me off."

"Look at it this way, Jim," I remarked. "Maybe the universe is conspiring to help you resolve that chip you've been carrying around. Either you do that in some way, or you could be out of a job. Right?"

Jim smiled ruefully. "Right. But what do you suggest when he sets me off by being so unreasonable?"

I replied, "Well, what could you do at that moment that would be constructive rather than reactive?"

Jim answered, "I probably should just keep my mouth shut. He's the boss. But then I feel like I'm just a kid again being ordered around."

"Okay," I said, "what else could you do instead of just keeping your mouth shut?"

Jim began to think. "I suppose I could consider his point of view. I get so mad that I don't really do that. I just want him to give me a chance to give some input. I've got some really good ideas that could help the business."

I asked, "How could you give input in a way your boss might feel good about?"

Jim brightened up. "You know, I hadn't thought of this before, but I think I'm not giving him my input in the way he likes to see that kind of thing. He wants all the facts and figures and the reasoning behind it. And I can do that. I think I've just been avoiding it because if I do, my ideas will be on the line."

I asked, "Do you feel ready to try it at this point?"

Jim responded, thoughtfully, "I don't have a lot of choice. If I don't start producing instead of reacting, he's eventually going to fire me."

I replied, "Okay, why don't you get your material together and rehearse it with someone. You could run it by one of your business associates before you try it out on the boss."

And that's exactly what Jim did. He put his presentation together and rehearsed it with one of his co-workers. In the process of working on it and talking it over, he came up with more creative ideas that were in line with the boss's business plan. When he came in to see me after he went over his ideas with the boss, he was really happy with himself.

He exclaimed, "I actually did it! And it just about blew the boss away. After he got over his shock about me coming up with a really good approach to marketing this new product, he and I brainstormed awhile. We came up with a top-notch plan. He took me off notice and congratulated me. How about that?"

"Great, Jim!" I replied. "It's like you came of age with yourself, if you know what I mean."

Jim laughed. "I know exactly what you mean. I've been acting like a retard carrying that chip around instead of allowing my creative brain to give some well-designed input. And I realize that's what my boss has been looking for, some real productivity on my part.

"Another thing, since I've been thinking about all of this after my breakthrough with the boss, I realize that I actually feel less resentful toward my dad. I suppose in his own way he was just trying to raise me the best way he could."

"That's a good insight, Jim," I said. "Most parents make mistakes but really want to be good parents. And the important thing about what you did with your boss is you claimed who you are as your own person. Plus, you did it in a constructive, creative way instead of getting caught in that old reactive pattern."

"Yes," replied Jim, "I understand that. And it feels

good. It's a real breakthrough for me."

"One more question, Jim," I said. "How's your inner teenager doing?"

Jim was quick to respond, "He's doing great. As I was walking out of the boss's office after all this, I heard a big 'yahoo!' inside of myself. That was him, celebrating."

A Shift from Reactivity to Enlightened Response

As a follow-through to Jim's story, take a moment to think about the most recent time you felt threatened or reacted angrily. Feel it. Be there again. Make a few notes to yourself about it.

Explore the painful roots of that emotional reaction in similar situations—particularly in childhood, youth or young adulthood. Write about what happened or dialogue with the younger parts of yourself. Remember how you looked and felt at their age and what was going on that sparked your upset emotions. See if you can make a connection between those earlier dramas in your life and your tendency toward a bristly response today.

Once you have a handle on that carryover reaction, ask yourself, "What would I rather do in a problematic situation instead of getting all worked up?" Practice it by playacting with yourself. And proceed accordingly the next time it comes up.

The trick is to make the shift from the old negative, knee-jerk reaction to a well thought-out, positive action plan. In the process, you stop being a victim of your reactions to challenging circumstances. Instead, you consciously and actively overcome the obstacles.

Sometimes this is an outer process that you plan and think through, and sometimes it's more of an inner drama —a shift in consciousness from emotional reactivity to enlightened response. Once we overcome our inner propensity to react unthinkingly, we can address outer scenarios constructively. And this directly relates to redeeming our personal dweller-on-the-threshold.

Redeeming the Dweller

A close friend of mine shared her experience of a difficult work situation that initiated an amazing redemptive process with her dweller-on-the-threshold. She relates her personal story:

> I was working as a counselor in a runaway shelter where the tension between the needs of the kids and the rules and regulations imposed by the government was very high. The person in the job before me had started crying without being able to stop and had become emotionally unable to continue the work.
>
> We had just spent three days and nights hashing out a set of rules we thought we could live with. An administrator who had not been part of our deliberations came in and picked apart what we had so carefully created. I felt that I could explain to him how he was not understanding the process we had gone through, and I spent a couple of days trying to see him and get him together with another administrator with whom he was at odds.
>
> The whole organization was about to split down the middle because of the split between these two top

people, and our set of rules was at the core of the dispute. Their argument was very like that of two parents who don't see that their positions are complementary.

After several days, I was at a maximum peak of frustration, staying at the house of one of the other counselors. When a girl walked in with a sympathetic face, I burst into tears and couldn't stop crying. I felt as if I were seven years old, in my bed, listening to my parents argue in the next room about how to discipline the children. I was biting my fingernails and saying to myself, "They'll never agree."

After I finally stopped crying, I was extremely exhausted, and the other counselor suggested I go to sleep in her bed. When I lay down, I noticed a book on her bedside table. It was Alice Bailey's classic, *Glamour: A World Problem*. I picked it up and opened it at random.

There I read a page near the end of the book about the initiations of the dweller-on-the-threshold. She wrote that this was a set of inner initiations requiring that the soul cross a "burning ground" three times. I immediately thought of the lake of fire spoken of in the Book of Revelation. I closed the book, snuggled down in the covers and went immediately into the first initiation.

I was in my body yet not in my body—aware of my breathing but in another place altogether. I saw myself standing on the lake of fire, and the lake was burning up a false persona that my father had created in me.

I realized that it was the "little princess" persona that many fathers create in their daughters. All full of feminine wiles, the little princess wraps her father around her little finger and manipulates him because he wants to be manipulated in that way. When that persona was totally burned up, I became a jeweled, multicolored dragon and the experience ended. For weeks after, I could just think of it and feel myself turning into the dragon.

I now know that the dragon was my dweller-on-the-threshold, and I had to identify with it in order to be completely honest with myself. I also had to realize that the dweller was utterly lost and needed to be redeemed.

My next experience was a couple of months later when I went spontaneously into the second initiation. This time, I was the dragon again, but I was sinking into the lake of fire. I called to Jesus to save me, and he pulled me out.

The third and final initiation happened two or three months later. I had become a being of light, and I flew across the lake of fire to a crystalline city that was made of pure, goldlike, polished glass, just like the New Jerusalem as it is described in the Book of Revelation. I may still have a dweller, but my soul has been forgiven, and I know myself now as a being of light.

Now this doesn't mean that this soul of light will never have another initiation with her dweller. But it does mean that she has had an inner victory of light and redemption. When we pass such an initiation on inner planes, we garner light. This increases our spiritual attainment and ability to handle life's challenges constructively.

Exasperating Circumstances Are a Gift

What about situations where we feel stretched to the limits of our patience and self-mastery? How about welcoming the opportunity to develop limitless patience and to increase our mastery of negative thoughts and testy emotions?

I'm not pretending that difficult situations are easy, but I have found that setbacks and defeats in my own life push me to reevaluate my goals, my strategies, my mindsets and my levels of expertise. They prod me to reassess my direction and rethink how I want to get from here to there. In the process I have to make room for new concepts and better methods of doing whatever it is I am doing. Through it all, I learn and grow.

I believe that situations that stretch our limits force our growth by shaking us loose from the daily treadmill. Even as deadly a situation as a terrorist attack can not only sharpen our awareness of evil but also intensify our determination to pursue the cause of good. Blatant evil presents an opportunity for us to examine our own lives and the motives of our hearts. We can pray for justice and renew our resolve to live in a way that blesses others.

Each life situation brings us new challenges and opportunities. When we face adversity with the God-determination to take right action, our character is honed and refined. As we meet challenge after challenge, we move forward to new vistas of opportunity. We win victory after victory over our lower self until we become one with our Higher Self. Ultimately, just over the horizon, we will see ascension flags waving.

Bundles of returning karma are tremendous gifts when we choose to look at them that way. Not only do we add to the positive side of our karmic equation, but we also become more adept in handling life's challenges with grace and poise. Gradually we gain such a momentum of patience and self-mastery that we are absolutely unflappable. That's a remarkable quality—unflappability!

Nineteenth-century writer Robert Louis Stevenson expressed a similar philosophy in his personal creed:

1. Make up your mind to be happy. Learn to find pleasure in simple things.

2. Make the best of your circumstances. No one has everything, and everyone has something of sorrow intermingled with the gladness of life. The trick is to make the laughter outweigh the tears.

3. Don't take yourself too seriously. Don't think that somehow you should be protected from misfortunes that befall others.

4. You can't please everybody. Don't let criticism worry you.

5. Don't let your neighbor set your standards. Be yourself.

6. Do the things you enjoy doing, but stay out of debt.

7. Don't borrow trouble. Imaginary things are harder to bear than the actual ones.

8. Since hate poisons the soul, do not cherish enmities, grudges. Avoid people who make you unhappy.

9. Have many interests. If you can't travel, read about new places.

10. Don't hold postmortems. Don't spend your life brooding over sorrows and mistakes. Don't be one who never gets over things.

11. Do what you can for those less fortunate than yourself.

12. Keep busy at something. A very busy person never has time to be unhappy.[1]

We Can Create Positive Change in Ourselves

All of us can create positive change in ourselves and in our way of meeting difficult situations. We are the stage manager of our day and of our attitude toward daily challenges. One practical way to get a head start on this is to create positive thoughts and feelings at the beginning of each day. We might even want to write up our personal philosophy in the form of a creed, as Robert Louis Stevenson did, and follow it on a daily basis.

Let's say you wake up in the morning feeling good. You had a nice dream, the sun is shining, the birds are singing. You are thinking, "What a beautiful day! I am going to get a lot done and I am looking forward to my meeting because I have some new ideas. I want to see what the others have come up with." What follows? Good feelings and an inner set for positive action. You have set the stage for having a good day.

But what if you wake up thinking, "My alarm didn't go off, I'm running late, I didn't get a good night's sleep. I do *not* want to go to work today. And I especially do not want to go to that meeting with so and so, who always goes out of his way to push my buttons. What right does he have to do that to me?"

Now there is an entirely different set of feelings you

just churned up: frustration, irritation and indignation. It is a perfect set-up for an uncomfortable interaction. And you are not likely to have a good day or a good meeting.

Remember, whatever somebody has already done to you is in the past. What you are dealing with is the aftermath inside of yourself. Happily, that is an inner drama you can change. You can choose to be the observer of the drama. When you are in command of yourself, you can decide to create a good day no matter what happens.

If you shift your perspective and mind-set into a creative, constructive direction, then your feelings and bodily reactions will follow suit. But in order to do that, you need to stop, take time out, breathe and center yourself in a more positive mode.

Here's a four-step exercise to prepare yourself for handling a difficult meeting or any other kind of challenging situation:

1. Take several minutes to breathe deeply, breathing in brilliant white light. Envision the light filling your mind and heart with clarity and peace. Breathe in the light. Breathe out the distress. Breathing quietly, stay with it until you feel your energy lightening up.

2. Envision your emotions flowing smoothly, like the sparkling currents of a mountain river. See the sunlight dancing along the water and peeking through the forest. Stay with that image for one to two minutes. If your thoughts wander, gently bring them back.

3. Focus on your physical heartbeat. Imagine your physical body radiating with the light and vigor that flows through your heart. Stay with that awareness for a minute or two.

4. Ask your Higher Self three questions, and write down what comes to mind in response to each one:
   - What is my primary goal in this meeting (or encounter or dialogue, etc.)?
   - How do I want to conduct myself so that I feel good about myself, no matter what happens?
   - How will I handle myself if other people disagree with me?

Once you have made a positive shift within yourself, you are ready to head for the office. Whatever happens in your meeting (or encounters with other people), handle yourself so you feel good about you. If the outcome is positive for everyone, you've made a major contribution. If it doesn't turn out quite the way you hoped, you know you gave it your best shot. In either case, you win.

Self-Mastery as a Path to Emotional Maturity

Learning to handle our emotions in a positive way is a big step toward maturing emotionally. In fact, emotional maturity is the result of our ongoing striving for self-mastery.

I particularly like the criteria for emotional maturity that the Menninger Clinic put out several years ago:

1. The ability to deal constructively with reality
2. The capacity to adapt to change

3. A relative freedom from symptoms that are pro-
   duced by tensions and anxieties
4. The capacity to find more satisfaction in giving
   than receiving
5. The capacity to relate to other people in a consistent
   manner with mutual satisfaction and helpfulness
6. The capacity to sublimate, to direct one's instinctive
   hostile energy into creative and constructive outlets
7. The capacity to love[2]

Looking at the sixth criterion, you might be wondering,
"How do I sublimate instinctive hostility?" It's no different
than any other kind of energy. Basically, when you sublimate
something, you take one kind of energy and redirect it into
a different outlet. So instead of allowing hostile energy to
rule your life, you turn it into a positive show of strength.

Perhaps you decide to do something creative with it.
Maybe you draw a hostile picture to express it. But then
you turn it into a cartoon. Pretty soon you're laughing,
laughing at yourself, and you feel better. Your creative
power has taken the place of the hostility.

Take a moment to rate yourself on a scale of 1 to 10
for each of these points of emotional maturity. Top score
would be 70, 10 for each of the seven criteria.

Releasing Anger, Frustration and Hurt in a Healthy Way

Let's complete our practice with anger-processing by
considering some additional healthy ways to release anger
and the frustration and hurt that are often the under-

pinnings of anger. Here are five basic steps:

First, sit down with a trusted friend, someone who can be neutral and supportive. Share your frustration and anger. Talk through your hurt. Ideally this would be someone with whom you feel really free to share your feelings, to cry if you feel like it, to vehemently express your indignation if you feel like it.

If you do not have someone you feel comfortable doing this with, talk it through with yourself or write a long letter to yourself about it. Include all of your thoughts and feelings—the hurt, the frustration and the fury.

Second, write a letter to the person who hurt you— and then burn it instead of sending it. Fully express your pain and anger. Write it out with all the excruciating details you can remember. Then as you burn the letter, ask the Higher Self of the person you are sending it to, to deliver it to the soul at a point that it will be of benefit.

That message to the soul helps people understand the painful outcome of their hurtful words or actions. Often people don't understand the pain they have caused others until they end up being on the receiving end of the same treatment. Sometimes they don't get it until they go through the life review.[3]

Third, sit in your easy chair and take a guided imagery trip. Close your eyes and go within. Make a call to God to guide you, and ask your Higher Self to overshadow you. Then bring to mind the person who triggered your hurt, your frustration and your anger.

Now imagine going for a walk with that person. Tell him or her your feelings. Imagine that person listening, acknowledging your feelings, coming to understand your point of view and apologizing for hurting you. Imagine the two of you talking it over, working through the difficulty. Imagine coming to a point of mutual understanding and appreciation of each other, coming to terms about your differences through love and empathy.

Fourth, exercise strenuously and visualize working out the anger, the frustration and the pain. You can do this through jogging, running, swimming or any other kind of active physical movement that suits you. Exercise is an excellent way to release tension.

When you begin to feel better, celebrate your good feelings through some kind of physical movement or dance. It is a wonderful healing method.

Fifth, write down your thoughts and feelings about the hurtful incident. You might write it as a dialogue between yourself and the other person. As you write out this dialogue, you are creating a play, and you are detaching yourself.

So you write out this little play. You review it. You decide to learn from it. And when you have let go of the anger, learned from your frustration and come to resolution of your hurt, celebrate! It's important to celebrate your victories.

Postscript: Once you have reached a resolution inwardly, ask yourself, "Am I content to take comfort in my own inner resolution? Or would it be best to go to the other person and say, 'What happened between us? It really hurt my feelings. Could we talk about it?'" Whatever you decide to do, do it in a spirit of compassion—for yourself and for the other person.

PART FOUR

Forging Your Destiny
in a Troubled World

11

Experience Your Inner Joy

Awake my soul! stretch every nerve,
And press with vigor on;
A heavenly race demands thy zeal,
And an immortal crown.

—PHILIP DODDRIDGE
Hymns

We live in troubled times, times that propel us to seek resolution deep within ourselves. We seek respite from anxiety about world crises and personal dilemmas. And we also desire to resolve residue of the past that burdens our soul and spirit.

We have lived many times on this earth, and every challenge has been an initiation to propel us upward. Our soul is absolutely intent on mastering her earthly lessons so that she can return to the higher octaves of light.

Thus, we instinctively seek out encounters that afford us opportunity to grow. And we are inwardly stirred to reflect on those experiences until we grasp the lessons. As we review difficult situations, we gradually discover that painful memories, thoughts and feelings can be replaced with insight, understanding and a reverence for the initiatic process.

Once we understand and pass the initiation, our soul is ready to let go of the experience and move on. And we feel a burst of joy!

Intertwining of Past and Present Lives

When we don't feel a sense of joy, it may or may not be a current situation that is at issue. Obstacles often arise from unresolved circumstances or traumas of the past.

Such traumas can be resolved spiritually, mentally, emotionally and physically. In the course of trauma-release therapy,[1] the traumatic memory dissipates, negative emotions are neutralized, painful thoughts shift to a positive point of view and physical symptoms are relieved. Through what becomes a truly transformational process, the individual reclaims a sense of inner joy and peace.

Many of my clients seek this kind of therapy because a dilemma in their life is clouding their joy. For example, Sandy came to see me because her relationship with her children was growing more and more stormy. Rarely a day went by that they didn't have some kind of major argument. And getting the children to do their share of the chores was becoming, as she put it, a nightmare.

Sandy was a divorced mom, and she was feeling the weight of that. And although she and her ex-husband were on reasonably good terms, she had the children on a daily basis and he only on the weekends. Thus, she was the one enforcing daily discipline.

As we explored the family dynamics, Sandy told me that this was particularly upsetting because she had recently had a nightmare about a similar situation in a previous life. In that life she and her husband had a farm in Ireland, and he was always busy with the outside work. He left the raising of the children to her, and she was expected to discipline them. They were difficult to handle, and she was often at her wit's end trying to get them to do their chores.

In her dream, which she realized was actually the surfacing of a past-life memory, she remembered in excruciating detail the day the children got completely out of hand. She sent them out to the fields to work with their father. And only at the end of the day, when he came home, did she find out they never got there.

They and their neighbors searched the countryside and finally came upon the bodies of the children. A renegade band of robbers had violated and killed them. The couple never got over it. And Sandy carried her deep pain and guilt into this lifetime.

She told me she knew her children in this life were the same children and that they had been born to her because she owed them life. She also thought her husband was the same husband in both lifetimes and that this unresolved trauma was the unconscious root of their marital problems and eventual divorce.

As Sandy talked about her dream, she broke down completely, sobbing, "I can't go through it again. I have to take care of them. And I don't know how to do it."

We did trauma-release work on the dream, which was very difficult for Sandy. However, she stuck with it, and the pain of the past-life trauma came full-blown to the surface. As she moved through and released her anguish, the dream images began to fade.

When we made spiritual calls to the angels, she saw light around the children's bodies. Then, amazingly, she saw the children leave their bodies and go with the angels. The entire scene was bathed in light, and Sandy gave a deep sigh of relief.

As we talked about this tragedy, Sandy said she believed she agreed to give birth to these children again in order to balance her karma with them. And because she and her husband both had a close soul connection with the children, they were married. As she said, "I always felt that we were married to bring in children. But what I'm having trouble with is that he's checked out again, and here I am with the major responsibility of raising the children."

"What do you mean, 'checked out'?" I asked.

She replied, "He doesn't have the day-to-day responsibility for them anymore. When he sees them, it's fun time for them all. I'm still the one who has to do all the discipline. I'd like to send them to him and see what happens when he has to deal with their daily shenanigans over chores and homework!"

And then she stopped, shocked at what she had just said in light of the past-life trauma she had just gone through.

"Oh, my God," she said, "I'm doing it all over again. I'm trying to push the responsibility onto him instead of figuring out how to handle it myself."

This was clearly a major wake-up call. She realized she was called to put on the mantle of disciplinarian that she had evaded in the past life, to her deep sorrow and the detriment to her soul and the souls of her children. And she also realized how much she loves her children.

Sandy and I had several more sessions where she talked through the relation of the past life to this one and went through a forgiveness ritual, asking God and the souls of her husband and children to forgive her. It took some time for her to accept the return current of forgiveness, even though she felt it spiritually.

The hardest step of all was forgiving herself. Yet she gradually accepted the fact that she had not sent those children to their death in any conscious way. It was a dreadful happening but not her fault.

She realized that her lesson, in the past life and the present, has been to shoulder the responsibility of disciplining her children with love—and "to keep on keeping on," even when she feels like quitting the job of mother.

The corollary was to realize with an increasing sense of joy that she really loves her children. As she told me, "I guess every mother gets exasperated with her children at times, and I really love them so much. I just need to show it more. I am working on my exasperation. What I'm doing is giving it to God every time it comes up."

It was a different Sandy who came in several months later for a follow-up session. She said, "I feel like a different person. If you would believe it, I'm getting along great with the kids. If I didn't know better, I'd think some magician had done some work on all of us. But what I do know is that I have had a complete change of heart.

"I'm asking instead of telling, helping instead of ordering, making it fun instead of drudgery—and the kids are lapping it up. I certainly haven't told them about my dream, but it's as if their souls realize I've had a change of heart. I mean they aren't perfect, of course, but they really are making an effort to cooperate. And I love them so much that I want to make it easy for them. Can you believe they even agreed to come into another life with me as their mother?"

"Sandy," I responded, "obviously they love you too. And their souls have likely been longing for the resolution that is happening right now. Whether or not they ever remember what happened in that past life, their souls are at peace because they know you love them and you're doing the best you can."

Sandy was thoughtful. "I wonder if Ben has any memory of this whole drama that's so clear to me now. That's the last piece of this. Forgiving myself was first, caring for the children next and now it's making it right with Ben."

Life isn't a fairy tale. They didn't get back together and live happily ever after—human nature doesn't change that instantly. But they did begin to communicate in positive ways about the children. And the children have blossomed from having good times with both of them.

Sandy has realized a great truth: *Unconditional love opens the door to peace in heart and soul.* She now views her former tribulations as a blessing in disguise. And she and Ben are more at ease with one another. They may never remarry, but they are recapturing friendship and mutual respect.

The Gift of the Developed Heart

Sandy's revitalized relationship with her children and ex-husband is a touching example of the transformational power of love and forgiveness. When we love and forgive, we progress, spiritually, and become a blessing to others. As Mrs. Prophet says:

> The developed heart is truly a gift because love and loving-kindness will take you a long way on the spiritual path....
>
> Like Mother Teresa, those who embody the living flame of love are transformers. That means that each of us is capable of transforming ourselves, our country, our relationship with our children, our role in society.... No matter who we are, no matter what our calling, if we so choose, we can be a living transformer of love.

Many things can prevent us from connecting with others and giving and receiving love. We may be afraid to open our heart because we were deeply hurt by someone in this life or a past life. We may lack self-esteem and therefore fear being rejected.

Perhaps we have hidden anger and resentment against others, or against God himself. We may have a sense of guilt and think we don't deserve love or to be love in action. As a result, we build up layers of defenses that we don't even know we have.

How do we heal the heart so that we can give and receive more love and help others to be healed? ...

There is nothing more important than increasing our *capacity* to love. The apostle John wrote, "This is the message that ye heard from the beginning, that we should love one another. ... He that loveth not knoweth not God, for God is love."[2]

Gautama Buddha essentially taught the same thing when he was asked by a disciple, "Would it be true to say that a part of our training is for the development of love and compassion?"

Gautama replied, "No, it would not be true to say this. It would be true to say that the whole of our training is for the development of love and compassion."...

Love isn't really love unless it is practical. The first step on this path of practical love is forgiveness. First, last and always, forgive. If you haven't forgiven someone, go and find him and implore his forgiveness.

You can't expand the power of your heart if you hold on to anger. It's amazing when we realize how much anger is in the world and how determined some people are to hang on to that anger.

When we refuse to forgive a friend or an enemy who has wronged us, we tie ourselves not only to that person but to his anger. ... We create negative karma with that person, and we are not truly free of that person until we resolve the anger and balance the karma.

People go to their graves without making peace with their enemies. This is indeed a tragedy, for they carry their resentments and their desire for revenge into their next life. What a great pity when in the course of the very same embodiment, they could reach ultimately to the stars and surrender their life to absolute God-victory. Yet lifetime after lifetime they may hold on to their resentment and revenge, with no letup in sight.

Our beloved Jesus was a prophet of love. Maybe you have heard his words on love and forgiveness so many times that you don't stop to think about what they really say. To me they are one of the most practical guides to spirituality you could ask for.

Peter asked Jesus, "How oft shall my brother sin against me, and I forgive him? till seven times?" Jesus replied, "Not...seven times, but until seventy times seven."[3]

On another occasion Jesus said, "Ye have heard that it hath been said, Thou shalt love thy neighbour and hate thine enemy. But I say unto you, Love your enemies...and pray for them which despitefully use you, that ye may be the children of your Father which is in heaven....

"For if ye love them which love you, what reward have ye? Do not even the publicans [tax collectors, who were very unpopular people in Jesus' day] do the same? And if ye salute your brethren only, what do ye more than others?...Be ye therefore perfect, even as your Father which is in heaven is perfect."[4]

A few years ago my Holy Christ Self [Higher Self] awakened me in the depth of this teaching. One morning when I had just awakened, I heard my Holy Christ Self forgive the person I thought was my greatest enemy. My Holy Christ Self was setting the example for me. He was showing me: This is how you must love your enemies.

Now this is easier said than done, as we all know. It is not easy to forgive when you have to forgive those who have committed crimes against the soul, the mind, the body.

So what is the appropriate response of a spiritual seeker to evil and the evildoer?

I once asked the ascended master El Morya this question after a woman poured out her heart to me in a letter. "Try as hard as I can," she wrote, "I cannot forgive my former husband for molesting my daughters. They have suffered all their lives as a result of this. They have problems in their marriages, they have not been able to work through the trauma of it all, and I cannot forgive him. What shall I do?"

Beloved El Morya came to my heart and said that resolution is a two-step process. The first step is to invoke the law of divine mercy for the forgiveness of the soul of the evildoer. We forgive the soul, and we ask God to forgive the soul.

The second step is to invoke the law of divine justice for the judgment of the not-self of the evildoer. The not-self is our dark side, the side of us that impels the soul to disobey the laws of God.

What El Morya is saying is we can feel free to forgive the soul of anyone. And we can feel free to ask God to bind up the forces of evil that hold the soul in their grip. We can ask God to give that soul the opportunity to repent of her evil deeds, to strengthen herself so she can resist the call of evil when it knocks again at her door.

To the woman who wrote the letter, this teaching was the healing of a lifetime. At last she had found resolution because she knew that God would dispense both his mercy and his divine justice, and she could let go of the situation.[5]

The Joy of Inner Resolution

Thus, spiritual teachers remind us that there is great joy in healing work with the soul. When we invite God to be our partner, we gain an increment of spiritual enlightenment and we shift our perspective. Although we continue our daily routine, our inner world is different. We find ourselves adopting a positive attitude, looking forward to what we may learn and experiencing a sense of peace.

Buddhist psychiatrist Mark Epstein, in his insightful book *Going to Pieces without Falling Apart,* tells a Zen story about an old Chinese monk who had spent many years in spiritual practice without coming to the deeper realization he sought. He asked permission of his master to retreat into a mountain cave to seek enlightenment.

After the master granted his request, the monk set out on foot for the neighboring mountains, taking only his robes, his begging bowl and a few possessions. As he was climbing in the mountains, he encountered an old man carrying a huge bundle on his back coming down the path toward him. As the story goes, this man was actually the bodhisattva Manjushri, who appears to people at the moment of enlightenment.

Manjushri asked the monk where he was going. And

the monk responded that he was going up to the highest mountains to find a cave and meditate until he either died or realized awakening. He then looked more closely at the old man who stood before him and asked, "Do you know anything of this enlightenment I am seeking?"

The old man simply dropped his bundle onto the ground. And at that very moment the monk was enlightened but also a bit confused. So he asked Manjushri, "Now what?"

The bodhisattva simply smiled, silently picked up his bundle and continued down the path.[6]

For the monk, everything in his inner world had changed but nothing outward was altered. Thus we see that enlightenment means inner freedom rather than forsaking the world in which we live. We continue to live in the world but are no longer deceived by or reactive to appearances. It's a turning of the dial of consciousness. As the spiritual adage goes, "Be ye in the world, but not of it."

Which Horse Are You?

In one of the Buddha's teachings, he talked about human nature as four types of horses: the excellent horse, the good horse, the poor horse and the really bad horse. In her book *Awakening Loving-Kindness,* Pema Chödrön describes this teaching:

> The excellent horse, according to the sutra, moves before the whip even touches its back; just the shadow of the whip or the slightest sound from the driver is enough to make the horse move. The good horse runs

at the lightest touch of the whip on its back. The poor horse doesn't go until it feels pain, and the very bad horse doesn't budge until the pain penetrates to the marrow of its bones.[7]

We would all like to think of ourselves as the excellent horse, which means to me that we move through life with instant attunement and a perfect response to whatever is going on around us. We all may have moments like that, but few of us could honestly say we are that attuned all the time.

Some of the time we may be the good horse, meaning we immediately take enlightened action once we get a physical prompting. But my guess is that the majority of us spend much more time as the poor horse, being obedient to our higher calling only at moments when pain is our wake-up call. And we can all think of plenty of times that we have been the bad horse, immobilized out of fear or stubbornness, refusing to take a step forward until pain forced the issue.

Now, it really doesn't matter which of these horses we think we are because all of us at times are the excellent, good, poor or bad horse in our lives. When we are intuitively and instantly obedient to the gentle guidance of our Higher Self on a daily basis, we have become Buddha's "excellent horse."

Go to Nature for Respite

Even the excellent horse needs a rest from time to time, and our soul needs occasional surcease from painful circumstances. When we look for respite from the cares of yesterday, today and anticipated tomorrows, we discover that nature can be wonderfully healing to the soul.

I view Mother Nature as God's healing partner on earth. Focusing on nature's majesty lifts our consciousness above the cares of the day and the clamor of the world. When your heart and soul need peace and inspiration, take a nature retreat or try a visualization exercise:

- When you are out on a walk, look around you and notice the natural beauty of the scenery. Or visit an art gallery that specializes in paintings of nature. You might prefer to sit in your easy chair and look at pictures of beautiful natural panoramas. Or simply close your eyes and remember scenes of natural splendor that have impressed themselves upon your consciousness.

    Notice the beauty and peace of the scene and project yourself into it. Allow yourself to feel the essence of the Holy Spirit that flows through nature.

- Imagine you are a swan, symbol of the soul, gliding along in the water—peaceful, serene, calm. Or see yourself as a water lily, another symbol of the soul, floating on the water.

- Envision yourself sitting near a beautiful waterfall. Feel the mist. Relax into it. (Rushing water emits negative ions that are restorative. That is one of the reasons we feel so good when we're near a waterfall.)

- See yourself walking along a trail in a beautiful forest. Feel the presence of the angels and nature spirits (the elementals)[8] all around you. Notice a bush of wild roses—pink roses, like the roses of love in your heart, budding, sprinkled with the dew. Or perhaps they are yellow roses—roses of wisdom and illumination, the gentle peace that you feel when you meditate upon the Buddha.

See each delicate bud blossoming into a fragrant flower as a love note from the Creator. See the angels and elementals tending the flowers. And reflect on how each one of us is both a mighty being and at the same time a delicate flower. Be gentle with yourself, with others and with elemental life.

- Envision yourself in the high mountains of Tibet or India, surrounded by the grandeur of nature and the presence of God. Or see yourself at the Teton Mountains, experiencing a sense of ethereal uplift and clarity of mind. (The high vibration at the Tetons actually emanates from a spiritual retreat in a different dimension connected with those magnificent mountains.)

  Think of the mountains as the eternal Father. As you imagine climbing the highest peak, envision the climb as a spiritual ascent. Stand at the top, victorious, as you touch the hem of the garment of the Infinite One.

- Imagine you are on a ship in the ocean. Sunlight is streaming through the clouds, reminding you that the light ultimately penetrates through. Feel the power and vastness of the waters stretching to the horizon in every direction.

As you come closer to land, enjoy the sunlight reflecting off the shining waves. Watch for schools of fish and humpback whales, and see the white-topped waves cresting and crashing against the rocky shore. Observe the sea gulls circling overhead, swooping down to feed in the ocean and then soaring up in the sky.

• Imagine yourself as a sea gull, partaking of the gifts of earth and sea, then taking flight to enter the heavenly octaves.

When we go to nature for respite, the quiet beauty and invigorating energy give us surcease from the burdens of our karma and the complex puzzle of human existence. Mother Nature restores our spiritual awareness and uplifts our soul.

Meditation and Loving-Kindness Practice

Here is a meditative practice for healing emotional discomfort or tensions you may be harboring in your heart and soul and body.

1. Position yourself in meditation to be the divine observer of your discomfort. Choose a quiet place and put on some beautiful, uplifting music. Close your eyes and simply notice that discomfort as you sit quietly under your Bodhi tree (Higher Self).

2. Center in your heart and focus on your breathing as if the breath were moving through your heart. Meditate upon the divine energy of God that

emanates through the breath and as the flow of spiritual light in your chakras.

3. Gently ready yourself to become fully aware of whatever is upsetting you. Observe the drama. Feel those ripples of emotion moving through you. Stay with them. Give those feelings space in your consciousness. Simply allow them to be. Stay in touch with your heart as you sit with your discomfort, with your emotional reaction, feeling it, observing it.

4. Capture the moment of that reaction earlier in life. You might even become aware of a related experience in a past life.

5. Focus your attention on your loving, wise, strong adult self in the likeness of your Higher Self. As the loving adult, love and comfort your soul, that younger part of yourself who is carrying the pain of that disturbing drama of the past. Your younger self who needs healing at this moment may be in utero, just born, three years old, twelve years old, twenty-one, forty, fifty, sixty-five—any age up to a minute ago.

6. As you meditate and send love to this younger part of yourself, remember that this younger self is also your ancient soul, wise in many ways yet dealing with necessary lessons and patterns of unresolved karma from past lives. Relate the uncomfortable feelings of today to the possible yesterdays of your soul. Love yourself through the pain. Give your soul a voice, a hug, a blessing.

7. Mobilize the divine antidote to your discomfort. Decide that you will be calm and confident as you revisit the trauma that comes to mind and that you will be able to take positive action. If you don't feel calm and confident, visualize and meditate on yourself feeling that way. Gradually your meditative reverie will bring it about. As you experience qualities in meditation, you prepare yourself to express them in your life encounters.

8. See yourself taking wise action in the situation that aroused your discomfort in the first place. Give it your best effort. Do the best you can. Call it good. And surrender the outcome to God.

9. Invoke the beautiful violet flame* to transmute everything in your being that is the antithesis of the real you. Focus on transforming that not-self into who you really are.

10. Ask God to forgive you for your part in the upsetting drama. And consciously accept God's loving forgiveness. Now extend forgiveness to yourself and to the person you perceive as the adversary. This is one of the most powerful techniques I know for soul healing—asking for and extending forgiveness to oneself and to the adversary.

11. As an ongoing practice, you may wish to send metta, loving-kindness, to yourself and others. This is the inner nature of the Buddha Maitreya. In fact, metta (*maitri* in Sanskrit) is also the inner meaning

---

*See pp. 87, 103–4, 169, 171, 331–32.

of his name. He is known as the Buddha of loving-
kindness, who offers his loving-kindness to all.

In the practice of metta, you visualize sending
loving-kindness to yourself, to your benefactors, to
your friends, to your family, to a neutral person,
and ultimately to the adversary.* Sending metta to
the adversary may take some practice, but what a
victory for love when you achieve it!

12. Return frequently to your meditative posture as an
objective observer under your Bodhi tree. Whenever an uncomfortable situation comes up and you
want to claim a victory (or learn from a defeat so
next time you'll have a victory), know that the victory comes about from your oneness with your
Real Self.

When you find yourself burdened by distressing emotions and go through these twelve steps, you are chipping
away at old emotional habit patterns. They are gradually
transformed into positive emotions and insights.

Joy Is the Motor of Life

We gain a sense of freedom as we come to an inner
understanding of our karmic patterns, limiting thoughts,
emotional blocks and untoward physical reactions—and
realize we are able to redeem them. When we are free
from painful memories and the hurtful words or actions of
the past, our joy blossoms.

Each increment of transformation and attainment
_____
*For the classic statements to use, see p. 47.

brings joy to the soul. Joy is like a spring rain that re-freshes the soul, allows us to lighten up, to enjoy life and to move onward and upward to our victory.

Thus, we can celebrate our soul's inner joy as we make our way through every challenging circumstance. This is the way to forge victory after victory—and make it all the way home to God.

Saint Germain, sponsor of the Aquarian age and lumi-nary of the twenty-first century, tells us, "Joy is indeed the motor of life."[9] Have you ever thought about it that way? When we feel joyful, everything seems to fall into place—and we move along the road of life with a triumphant sense of overcoming.

Sustaining Joy in the Middle of Turmoil

Through their attunement and loving obedience to the will of God, masters, saints and sages have shown us how to greet adverse circumstances. Their inner strength, wisdom and love are the fruit of their soul's union with the Higher Self. As we follow in their footprints, we, too, may grow in divine perfection and move ever closer to our own soul's victory.

Saint Germain has given timeless instruction that is applicable to those pursuing the spiritual path today. He offers us, as adepts-to-be, a higher vision, a glimpse of cos-mic consciousness. He reminds us of our soul's journey and dream of the ages—a trek upward that transcends the turmoil of the world and the jangling clash of human per-sonalities.

He says:

It is not necessary for you to take all of perfection and manifest it at once. You can take increments of perfection and manifest them as you are able right where you are.... Drops of beauty are also drops of wholeness, and they sing within you as they touch the altar stone of the heart....

The song they sing within you is: I AM life! I AM life! I AM life beating within you, singing within you and drawing you closer to the strands of heavenly sunshine... crowning all of life with God-direction, perceiving in all the summoning of the elect, yea, from the four winds of the earth into the domain of heaven's beauty.

O beloved children of the light, let nothing whatsoever stop in you the manifestation of God that speaks and thunders at the same time that he speaks.

Long ago, as he spake unto Moses saying, "I AM THAT I AM,"... it was the echo of the foundation of the world speaking unto him. It was the lightning and the thunder.... It was the power of God that always dwells within man.

Man seeks for this plan, for the unfoldment thereof and perceives it not. But those who pursue it relentlessly,... pursue it with determination,... pursue it in the face of the young child as in those of age, ... pursue it in the emerging consciousness within themselves—they shall find.

For that which thunders within them... will also fill the cup of life until the cup of life runneth over. And the joy of God and the dream thereof are sung as a new song, yea, a song of hope and peace which shall be to all people.

The message . . . that long ago rang over the plains of Bethlehem, . . . the infinite clothed within the finite . . . the drama of the young child, emerges still in the world and is the stirring of renewed hope in many hearts. It is a song that must not be stilled.

We must move, beloved ones, toward a crescendo. We must not be satisfied with that which has been. We must move toward the crescendo of the lightning and the thunder. We must move toward the song and the joy. We must move to the eclipse of human wonder, and to that fragile gift of God without alloy.[10]

12

The Fount of Mercy and Forgiveness

Teach me to feel another's woe,
To hide the fault I see;
That mercy I to others show,
That mercy show to me.

—ALEXANDER POPE
"The Universal Prayer"

We may understand that the gentle gifts of mercy and forgiveness bless and heal—and that evildoers eventually receive divine justice. But our soul's desire to love and forgive becomes clouded over when we are convinced that someone else is doing something terribly wrong. What do we do when we expect human justice, and we don't think it's right to forgive?

The answer lies in plumbing the depths of our own heart and soul. Let's meditate upon the gentle wisdom of the ascended lady master Kuan Yin:

I would speak to you of mercy and mercy's flame. Will you not before twelve o'clock this night go before your altar or walk in a quiet place and make your peace with anyone and everyone? Let forgiveness flow from the fount of a magnanimous heart. Open up your heart. Do not delay it. Do not be found wanting, beloved, but give and give love again and again and again.

Let joy spring forth from your chakras. Let joy be multiplied by the vast geometry of a cosmos. Let joy know forgiveness. For many it is hard to forgive. ... But, beloved, unless and until you forgive, you have lost contact with the Supreme Being, with the saints of heaven. Waste no time, beloved, but run to the altar of God and acknowledge that you would be his servant forever and forever.

Call to the archangels and the ascended hosts of light. Ask that you might serve with them also, that you might also be taken to the retreats, to the Royal Teton* and other retreats in the heaven-world, known as the etheric plane.

I am Kuan Yin. I am the mother of mercy. I move with Portia, consort of Saint Germain. She does come with divine justice. You have heard again and again, "Vengeance [justice] is mine; I will repay, saith the Lord."[1]

Give amply of forgiveness. Give gratitude, beloved. For you will never know how many times God has forgiven you, loved ones have forgiven you.

Enter into the rejoicing of the heart, where your heart is no longer a stone but may be softened through

---

*The spiritual focus known as the Royal Teton Retreat is congruent with the Grand Teton Mountain, Jackson Hole, Wyoming.

my heart and its alchemy this night, that you might know that the open door to all fulfillment, opportunity, self-transcendence and the entering in to the planes of the heaven-world must come with the forgiveness of all life.

Ponder these teachings, beloved; ponder in your heart. Have you left a stone there that is hardened? Go after it. Cast it out. Restore that place with the fullness of the elixir of mercy. Blessed ones, mercy is the first step on the path of return to the Godhead. Know this and reach for it.

If you should pass from the screen of life on . . . the morrow, six months from now or twenty years, I should hope, beloved, that you would not have left a stone unturned, that you would have long ago cast into the sacred fire the nonmerciful heart.

May you, then, remember these words: "I AM forgiveness acting here, casting out all doubt and fear, setting men forever free with wings of cosmic victory." May your life, then, be one of fulfillment, for you have left behind all the stones of stumbling, and today you can proclaim to the Lord, "I AM my brother's keeper." . . .

May you give to all the understanding that there is forgiveness, that reincarnation is true. It is the mercy of God as well as the justice of God. Thus shout it from the housetops.

Let the world know that God has given again and again and again dispensations of mercy toward those who have committed great crimes. God has forgiven, but he has also given assignments to those who have moved against his little ones. And those assignments are to balance that karma, to serve those whom they have wronged.

There is no injustice anywhere in the universe. Therefore count on God to deliver that premise. And let mercy and justice forever and forever abide within you. Keep a pad next to your nightstand and write down those that come to mind whom you have not forgiven. Find them. Ask for forgiveness. And if you have not kept in touch with them, then go to the altar and make things right.

I speak simply. I speak fully. Become who you are by the living fount of justice and mercy.[2]

In honor of the gracious ascended lady master Kuan Yin, in compassion for our own soul and all souls we have encountered in this or past lives, let us remember the blessing we receive when we forgive. Let us choose to forgive, to let go and move on.

Unconditional Love and Forgiveness

So what specifically do we do when someone deliberately wounds us and shows no remorse? We call to Archangel Michael to bind the evil working through that person, but we forgive the soul that has erred because we too have erred and wounded other people. As Alexander Pope so aptly put it, "To err is human, to forgive divine."[3]

So we forgive. And we commend the dweller, that conglomerate of evil that prompts all of us to take harmful actions, to Almighty God for adjudication.

Sometimes, though, we may harden our hearts when we come to an impasse or breach in a relationship with another person. This typically happens when we expect something we don't get or our demand isn't met in the way we think it should be met.

Our expectations and demands represent the way our human self thinks others should behave. When our expectations aren't met, we may refuse to extend ourselves and may even withdraw friendship until the other person meets our demands. This is not divine love; it is conditional love. We are essentially saying we refuse to love unless our expectations, demands or conditions are heeded.

But God teaches unconditional love. The sun and stars shine on both the good and the not-so-good. The rain refreshes the proud and the humble. Nature's wealth is bestowed on all who visit her kingdom. And the avatars have taught and walked among saints and sinners alike, demonstrating the higher path of unconditional love and forgiveness.

It is interesting to note that in the Aramaic language the word *forgiveness* means "to cancel." What is it that we are canceling when we choose to forgive?

We are not canceling the wrongdoing. We can't cancel or recall energy that has already gone out into time and space. The deed has already been done. Even forgiveness is not a pardon that wipes out or redeems our wrongdoings or the wrongs of other people. The karma of wrong action remains to be balanced.

The good news is that we can cancel the wrong motives or attitudes behind our own misdeeds—and refrain from repeating them. And we can do the spiritual work to transform the negative energy and try to make up for our errors.

Thus, when we are in the wrong, we admit it—to ourselves, to God and to whomever we have wronged. We pray for forgiveness and accept the return current of that forgiveness. And we ask those we have hurt to forgive us. If they don't, we simply forgive them.

Even if we believe they started the whole thing, we pray for them. And we ask God to bind all of our dwellers and keep us from harming one another again. Then, to transmute the negative energy that may still be troubling us, we invoke the violet flame.

Although we may not immediately forget a wrong, the cosmic eraser of the violet flame can actually lift the burden once we are ready for it. Sometimes we need to remember what happened to protect ourselves or others in the future.

However, we can hold our remembrance in a state of loving nonattachment. We can be as the Buddha where we stand and observe with loving-kindness everyone involved, including ourselves. And we can allow the remembrance to fade as we gain in attainment and self-mastery.

Viewing Preferences
through the Window of Divine Love

In order to forgive completely, we need to change our focus. How? By not dwelling upon a wrong we think has been done and our feelings about it. By turning the dial of consciousness and realizing that we reacted because we wanted the other person to "do it our way."

Our preference actually blocks us from seeing the good in the other person's action or way of thinking. By making room for differences of opinion, by surrendering our fixed position, our preference, we begin to resolve the inharmony.

When we choose to love others regardless of their attitudes or the particular stand they take, we love them unconditionally. We honor their virtues even when their human weaknesses are at play.

Through the window of divine love, then, we begin to look at our disappointments differently. We feel compassion for other people's dilemmas, as well as our own.

As our consciousness shifts to unconditional love, we break through our impasse with others. As we negotiate our preferences, we often come up with creative solutions that are mutually acceptable.

We begin to understand more deeply the wisdom of Gautama Buddha's teaching on nonattachment to human desires.* Attachment to our desires blocks the flow of universal love. It's like standing on the hose while we're trying to water the garden.

When our love-flow stops, only we can remove that block. How do we do it? By choosing to see and love the good in ourselves and in others—and by suspending judgment when someone else's way is not our way.

When we identify with unconditional love, we enter in to a genuine love relationship with God and with other people. Now we can let go of those expectations, demands and rigorous conditions that we have inflicted upon ourselves and others.

We have the power to change. We can let them go. In the spirit of divine love, we can express our opinions as

*See p. 345, n. 4.

preferences, instead of mandates. We can adopt a posture of compassion—the compassion of the Christ, the Buddha, Krishna, Kuan Yin. And our soul will rejoice.

Thus we forgive for our own good and for the good of everyone we encounter. We forgive for the higher purpose of each soul's progress in passing earthly initiations and realizing oneness with God.

When we truly forgive, we bring harmony to ourselves and to our relationships. As we open the door to the flow of unconditional love from our Creator, we take a giant step forward on our quest for higher consciousness.

Forgiveness Frees the Soul to Move Ahead

God's forgiveness is a grace. It sets aside the karmic burden for a period of time, freeing the soul to move ahead. Forgiveness accelerates the healing of our soul and sparks the awakening of true self-esteem.

Charlie, a middle-aged businessman, came to see me because he was harboring resentment toward a boss he had worked for several years before. Even though he no longer worked for that boss, he was still angry about the way he had been treated.

As he said, "Every time I remember the way that guy dealt with me and the other guys who worked with me, I get upset and angry all over again. I still think he ought to be straightened out. I can't seem to let it go."

"Have you thought of filing a grievance?" I asked.

"I'd like to," he replied, "but I've waited so long that it wouldn't carry any weight."

"Have you considered putting your grievance in

writing, even if it can't be formally filed?" I asked.

"No, he'd just pitch it in the waste basket," he said. "I know it wouldn't do any good."

"Would it help you to put it on paper for yourself, just to evaluate it from a more objective stance?" I asked.

He considered that. "Maybe, but I think it might actually fuel my anger even more. I could write a dozen pages on his mistreatment of employees."

I responded, "Sometimes it helps to write out the way you see a situation and your feelings about it—as many pages as it takes—even if the other person isn't going to read it. When you do that, you get it out of your head and onto the paper. And then you at least stop revolving it in your own mind. Would you be willing to try it?"

Charlie thought for minute. "I don't know. Maybe. I'm still angry even though I know it's useless."

"Okay, let's look at that. What would help you get rid of your anger?" I asked.

"To punch him out!" he said forcefully.

"Usually that just fuels the fire," I said mildly.

Charlie said, "Okay, okay, I know I'm not going to do that. But I would like to see some retribution. He's probably ruined a few other guys since I left there."

"Do you really think he's ruined you?" I asked.

That stopped him.

"Not exactly," he said. "But when I get to thinking about that whole disaster—and I still do—I'm not as efficient as I could be on the job I have now. I'm afraid I'll sabotage myself if I can't let go of this."

"Okay," I said, "now we're getting somewhere. It

really would be to your advantage to let this whole thing
go, no matter how much of a jerk your old boss was. Isn't
that right?"

"Right," he responded. "But how do you let something go when it's out-and-out wrong?"

"It's enlightened self-interest," I answered. "You'll feel
better, and you won't be sabotaging the job you have now."

After a long silence, Charlie's mouth twitched into a
smile. "You don't have any magic answers?"

"Nope," I said, "I'm fresh out of magic today."

"Well, neither do I," he said. "I guess I was hoping
you would come up with something I hadn't thought of.
What I hear you saying is that it's my problem now."

"Yes, that is what it looks like to me," I replied,
"because you're being held back by not letting this go."

"I suppose that's true," he answered. "But every time
I think about that whole situation, I get this hard feeling
in my heart and stomach. Maybe I don't want to let it go."

"Why not?" I queried.

Charlie was thoughtful. "That kind of came out of
nowhere, but I think it's true. I'm concerned that I might
get into the same kind of situation again. If I stay angry,
I'm on guard and I won't let that happen."

"It looks like you're paying a big price to stay on
guard," I remarked.

"I suppose that's true," Charlie responded.

"What could you do instead?" I asked.

He pondered for a minute. "I guess I could try to let it
go and chalk it up to experience. Actually, a lot of that
guy's bluster and micromanaging has to do with insecurity

on his part. He thinks he has to be a tough guy to get everyone working to the max so he won't get in trouble with upper management."

I replied, "If that's true, it doesn't sound like it's your problem. He's his own worst enemy. Sounds like he's the victim of his own insecurity rather than being a totally out-to-get-you kind of person. What do you think?"

Charlie was thoughtful for a few minutes. "I hadn't even considered that kind of thing, but it's a definite possibility."

"If that were true, would it make it any easier to let it go?" I asked.

"Maybe," he said.

"Let's look at it this way—who is paying the price for your anger?" I asked.

"I suppose I am," Charlie admitted.

I asked, "Is it worth it to you to stay angry at a guy that's not handling his own insecurities?"

There was a long pause before Charlie finally came to the realization that he was hurting himself.

He sighed. "I guess I hadn't thought much about the reasons for his high-handedness, and I hadn't realized how much my anger is getting in my own way. I don't like the angry part of me very much. And I know I make karma when I give into it."

I could see he was turning around, so I said, "Charlie, one of the best ways I know to let go of anger is to surrender it to God. And then ask the angels to transform that anger into positive power, the inner strength to do the right thing. Then you can draw on that positive power to forgive and forget your ex-boss and to forgive yourself for getting so angry. Are you ready to do that?"

It took Charlie some time, but he finally decided to try it. First he wrote out all the grievances in a letter to God. Then we went through a meditation in which he asked God to help him surrender all of it and let go of the anger. He envisioned himself surrendering it, claiming his positive power and forgiving the old boss. That took real effort but he was visibly cheered up as he went through the process. The final step was to forgive himself for hanging on to it so long and to consciously let it go.

Afterwards, he remarked, "That's amazing. It feels great not to have that knot in my stomach anymore. I feel freed up. You know, I really don't like being angry and vengeful. I'd rather get the lesson and move on. And I'm beginning to realize the lesson here is not to nurse grudges, no matter how justified they might be. It's been damaging to me to do that, and it didn't change the situation."

It is enlightened self-interest to forgive those who have wronged us. We know that nursing a grudge simply adds to the pain in our own heart and soul—and to the pain of the world. And it can also contribute to emotional problems, physical stress, even heart disease.

Forgiveness is the divine antidote to pain we experience from difficult interactions. And when we ask for it, God extends the grace of forgiveness that we need to resolve karmic encounters. As we surrender our vengeance and choose to forgive, our soul wins a powerful victory.

We make our way upward by good works and by grace. We do our part by keeping our mind and heart stayed on God and by learning the lessons our karmic circumstances teach us. When we do our best to do the right thing, God's divine grace makes up the difference.

The Antidote to Hatred in the Heart

But what do we do when we tell ourselves all of this and realize we actually hate the person who has hurt us? Most of us do not like to admit to hating anyone, yet if we earnestly search our heart and soul, we may be able to admit it to ourselves. What do we do then?

The Dalai Lama offers excellent advice:

> The antidote to hatred in the heart, the source of violence, is tolerance. Tolerance is an important virtue of bodhisattvas (enlightened heroes and heroines)—it enables you to refrain from reacting angrily to the harm inflicted on you by others.
>
> You could call this practice "inner disarmament," in that a well-developed tolerance makes you free from the compulsion to counterattack. For the same reason, we also call tolerance the "best armor," since it protects you from being conquered by hatred itself.[4]

Tolerance does not mean agreement with the aggressor. It means understanding the situation from a merciful heart and choosing to be unmoved by the aggressor's attack. It means quieting our angry thoughts and feelings and tempering our physical actions.

All of us can appreciate the wisdom of this approach. We eventually discover that it does not help anyone to be screamed at or beaten down for an infraction. Heavy-handed action may temporarily control unruly behavior, but at what cost? It also teaches fear, resentment and aggression, which may very well reinforce the offensive behavior rather than correcting it.

What, then, does help? Loving tolerance and balanced action. We've looked at tolerance, but what does balanced action look like? It combines a nonjudgmental attitude with wise understanding, calm explanation and loving discipline. And it's the posture we need to take when hatred tries to creep into our heart and soul.

We can practice inner disarmament; we can disarm hatred, anger and the desire for vengeance. We can notice but not act upon thoughts, feelings or actions that could hurt people. In their stead, we can send loving-kindness, metta, to ourselves and others. This process brings us solace.

We can seek inner peace by cultivating mindfulness, the state of being "awake" to the present moment. When we are mindful, we are aware of our body, feelings and thoughts. We are aware of our ups and downs, the travels of our consciousness. We notice the coming and going of physical sensations, feelings and attitudes.

We are not removed or detached. Awareness does not mean separating ourselves from our experience in the moment; it means allowing it and sensing it fully. When our attention strays, as it inevitably will, we gently bring it back to experiencing the moment. This is active mindfulness—and a practice that brings the fruit of peace. Such mindfulness is tolerance at its best.

Mindfulness is also cultivated through meditation. Psychologist and meditation master Jack Kornfield tells us that meditation can be thought of as the art of awakening. And that it takes steadiness of attention. He describes it in an amusing way:

> Meditation is very much like training a puppy. You put the puppy down and say, "Stay." Does the puppy listen? It gets up and it runs away. You sit the puppy back down again. "Stay." And the puppy runs away over and over again.
>
> Sometimes the puppy jumps up, runs over, and pees in the corner or makes some other mess. Our minds are much the same as the puppy, only they create even bigger messes. In training the mind, or the puppy, we have to start over and over again. . . .
>
> Steadiness is nourished by the degree of interest with which we focus our meditation. . . . Concentration combines full interest with delicacy of attention.[5]

But what do we do if we practice mindfulness and try our level best, and we still can't let go of our anger toward those who have committed great wrongs? What about terrorists, murderers, warmongers, child abusers, those who violate and rape life? How can we handle ourselves in the face of such abominable behavior?

A Capstone to Tolerance

Accepting the need for forgiveness of the soul is a capstone to the teachings on tolerance. Mrs. Prophet teaches that it may be very difficult "to forgive the murderer, the rapist, the one who sets fire to your house or destroys your business." But we need to understand that it is the soul we are forgiving, not the dweller-on-the-threshold.

She advises us:

> You can make fierce calls for the binding and judgment of the dweller—the portion of the self that is evil, that is not of God and that is not to be forgiven. Then turn your attention to the soul.
>
> The soul may be impure and have all sorts of imperfections, but it still has the potential to one day realize God. Therefore, no matter how bad a person's deeds are, you can call upon the law of forgiveness for the soul. You can call for the soul to be liberated from her negative momentums of psychology and past records that have caused her to sin. Ask for the soul to be cut free by the angels, to be taught by God, to be taken into the retreats in the heaven-world to be tutored.
>
> Give the violet flame and calls for forgiveness. Pray for this soul to make a turnaround, to be converted by the Holy Spirit and to come into the service of God. But also call for the binding of that individual's dweller-on-the-threshold, specifically the momentum that caused the crime. Do this for a certain period of time, such as fourteen days. Then turn over the soul to Archangel Michael and the will of God....
>
> When your inner work is done, you can know with absolute certainty that justice will be meted out and the soul will be assisted in God's own time and way.[6]

When you call for the binding of the dweller-on-the-threshold of someone who has wronged you but forgive the soul, both divine justice and mercy are satisfied and you yourself can be cut free from any sense of injustice or anger that would tie you to that one.

Stages of Trauma, Healing and Forgiveness

When we experience a major upheaval, loss or set-back, we need to heal emotionally. Let's look at the typical stages we go through during the healing process.

Shock and Denial

- Initially we experience the shock of the trauma and simultaneously try to avoid the impact of the painful experience. We bury our thoughts and feelings and deny that we are upset. Everything is okay. Only we're really not.

  What helps? Give yourself time. Be kind to yourself. It's okay to accept an impact gradually.

Fear and Anger

- Once the shock begins to pass (in a few hours or days), we register the trauma. Fear begins to surface: What will come next? Will we fall apart? And we begin to get angry. We want to hold someone responsible for the injury or injustice, even if it's ourselves. In our minds, we go over and over what happened and revisit similar situations.

  What helps? Love yourself through the fear. Take some kind of positive action. And turn the outcome over to God.

Pain and Depression

- We begin to feel the depths of our pain. It often feels intolerable. We may feel so overwhelmed that we begin to slide into depression, to have that sinking feeling that nothing is ever going to be all right again. We find it difficult to get out of bed or to do the necessary self-care like eating, bathing, cleaning up around us. We feel a foreboding that nothing can help us feel any better. We may have moments of total despair.

What helps? Open the window; turn your face to the sun. Be kind to yourself. Do one of your favorite things. Get professional help if you need it. And remind yourself, "This, too, shall pass." For indeed it will.

Vulnerability and Loneliness

- We experience our vulnerability and a deep sense of loneliness. Sometimes it happens when no one else is around and we feel we can really let down. Sometimes it occurs because someone perseveres with such caring that we drop our defenses. Sometimes we simply reach a point where we can't hold it in any longer.

   What helps? Remember that God loves you. Do little things for yourself that you would do for a lonely child. Give yourself a hug. And open your heart to a friend.

Mourning Our Losses

- Once we allow ourselves to be fully aware of our loss, we finally dissolve into tears. As we cry, we express the pain, release the tension and begin the healing process. Sometimes it's easier to do alone; sometimes it's easier to have a loving friend close at hand. And somehow, even in the depths of despair, we feel a sense of relief in expressing our pain and gradually letting it go.

What helps? Let yourself cry. Put your arms around yourself and rock yourself gently. Pour your heart out to God.

Surviving
- Finally, in a few days, weeks or months, the light comes on. We realize that although we have been deeply wounded, we have, in fact, survived. Our painful experience has stripped us of things we valued but taught us quite a bit in the process. We become aware of an inner strength that has carried us through.

  What helps? Remind yourself that you have survived, and renew your hope and vision for the future. Focus on the positive lessons you have learned, and accent your strengths. Be your own best friend.

Coming to Life Again
- We welcome the return of an interest in something besides our own pain. We begin to feel compassion for other people who may have been hurt. We take comfort in realizing that, all things considered, we probably did the best we could. We clean up our house and eat real meals, we go for walks or a drive, and we begin to take an interest in friends or neighbors.

  What helps? Champion yourself, nurture yourself, reach out to others. Do simple activities that make you feel good.

Learning from the Experience

- Ultimately, we learn from the experience. We turn over to God those who have intentionally hurt us. We begin to realize that those who have hurt us may have been doing the best they could. If we are more than our wounds, then perhaps they are more than the inflicters of those wounds. We begin to release ourselves from the prison of negative thinking and reclaim the poisoned darts we have sent to others. We start to put the past in perspective and to get on with our lives.

  What helps? Focus on the here and now. Think positively. Take constructive action.

Forgiveness

- We begin the process of forgiveness. And we become more than simply our mental and emotional reactions. In truth, we are bearers of cups of divine mercy and forgiveness for the soul—our soul and the souls of all we meet along life's way. When we forgive, we release ourselves from the prison of negative emotions. Forgiveness itself becomes an act of mercy. It frees our soul to move on.

  What helps? Open your heart. Pray for everyone involved. Do a ritual of forgiveness where you write a letter asking God to forgive you and those who hurt you or didn't come to your rescue. Burn the letter, and open your heart to the return current of God's loving forgiveness.[7]

Healing the Pain of Grief and Bitterness

I want to share with you a profoundly moving story, told in more detail in *Forgiveness: How to Make Peace with Your Past and Get On with Your Life,* by Dr. Sidney B. Simon and Suzanne Simon.

Suzanne's personal story offers a deeper understanding of how taking courage to face a seemingly bottomless pit of pain begins the healing of soul and spirit. And how gentle waters of forgiveness can wash away grief and bitterness and allow us to get on with our lives. She writes:

> We stood around the casket, my brother, my sister, and I, gazing down at what remained of the man whom we had always loved but sometimes hated.... He barely resembled the formidable giant who wielded so much power over us when we were children....
>
> I was thinking about the man who had been a skilled craftsman, an imaginative storyteller, an avid reader, and an exceptional gardener.... "I thought we could bury these with Dad," I said, reaching into my pocket to retrieve a gift I tearfully bought soon after receiving the news of his death. Both my brother and my sister laughed out loud when they saw what I held, a half-dozen packets of seeds, the very same kind our dad planted each spring for as far back as any of us could remember....
>
> Sharing a joyful moment in the midst of an otherwise solemn occasion, we smiled affectionately and chuckled as we whispered to each other about visiting our father's grave and finding a magnificent garden growing on it.

> We did not defame this man who was our father.
> We celebrated him. . . . It was a tribute to the healing
> his children had done during the years preceding his
> death.[8]

The author explains that their father had sexually molested his children and had lashed out at them in explosive bursts of rage and frustration. As she said, had he died a few years earlier they would likely not have acknowledged that he was anything more than his abusive ways. They would still have been victims of the abuser.

Instead, each of these three adults standing around the coffin had reached a point of peace with their father and themselves. How? They had forgiven him because they needed their own pain to go away. Each of them, in his or her own way, had worked through the pain and allowed it to be washed away in the redemptive waters of forgiveness.

That did not mean they had forgotten or condoned their father's actions. It means that these courageous people had truly come of age. They had reached a point where they no longer needed to make the father pay for the unconscionable things he had done to them as children.

How did they get there? They chose to take responsibility for their own lives. They worked through their anger, fear and pain. They no longer brooded over the wrongs the father had perpetrated in their childhood. When they let go of their reactive emotions and healed the pain of the soul, they came to a point of resolution where they were able to forgive the unforgivable.

The Internal Process of Surrender and Forgiveness

Is there someone you still need to forgive? A very simple way to do this is to kneel down by your bed at night and ask God to forgive you for all you have done to hurt anyone and to forgive everybody who has ever hurt you.

Surrender your hurt feelings to God. Pray for those you have hurt or who have hurt you. Accept the gentle return of loving forgiveness from the heart of the Almighty One.

When you practice this ritual every night over a period of time, it gradually becomes a natural and joyous communion. And you will be amazed at how infrequently you react angrily or fearfully or take offense at someone's behavior.

This internal process of surrender and forgiveness is communion with God, with our soul and with the soul of another. And it is a by-product of our willingness to face our anger and resentment. When we surrender and forgive, we open the door of our heart and love ourselves. It is easier to love others because we understand that we all have thorns in the flesh. Through forgiveness comes renewed compassion for ourselves and those who have been the instruments of our pain.

Seven Life-Enhancing Strategies

Once you have successfully forgiven, you are ready to move on. I recommend the following life-enhancing strategies because they have helped many of my clients:

- Practice empathy for others. Imagine what it would be like to be in the other person's position.

- Give yourself and other people the benefit of the doubt. Remember we all have our hurts, bruises and defensive reactions.

- Choose to be tolerant and forgiving of yourself and of others, even when they hurt you.

- Center in your heart and assert yourself positively —or not at all.

- If you feel yourself getting too tense in a difficult situation, simply excuse yourself. Gracefully retire from the scene.

- Keep your energy moving by engaging in activities you enjoy: Do deep breathing, run, dance, swim, shoot baskets, take nature walks, play the piano or guitar, write a poem, paint a picture—any creative activity of your choice.

- Learn to laugh at yourself. When you are able to do that, you stick a pin in that huge balloon of pain, fear, anger and resentment. And *pop!* it deflates.

The master El Morya is the source of that last piece of advice. He knows the positive power of joyful laughter. He advises his chelas, "A twinkle of mirth is needed on earth." Try it and watch your life lighten up!

13

Claiming Your Soul's Victory

The windows of my soul I throw
Wide open to the sun.

—JOHN GREENLEAF WHITTIER
"My Psalm"

When the Dalai Lama spoke for the first time on his initial visit to the United States, he gave a simple but profound teaching: "All beings are seeking happiness. It is the purpose of life."[1]

The Dalai Lama repeated this teaching many times. He was attempting to awaken his listeners to the understanding that the search for happiness through accumulating material goods or ideal relationships or even by perfecting the human self doesn't bring happiness. Happiness arises when we surrender our desires for accumulation or human perfection.

To me the happiness the Dalai Lama is talking about is the exhilarating process of realizing who we are and who we may become. This is a process that occurs when we let go of our fervor for material acquisition or human perfection—and pursue our soul's highest hopes and dreams. It is rediscovering and building upon our divine blueprint, our unique God-given essence. We are called to expand our awareness of *being* instead of focusing so much on *doing*.

Our Search for Higher Union

We all have our own vision of what lies beyond this mortal realm. Christians look forward to being received by Jesus in heaven. Buddhists look forward to nirvana. Hindus look forward to reunion with Brahman. Mystics look forward to experiencing oneness with the Infinite. And we have a wealth of information from people who have visited the heaven-world in near-death experiences.

We all have moments in our lives when we taste a little bit of heaven—uplifting moments when we transcend our earthly consciousness to touch the hem of the garment of God. Sometimes it's a mystical experience; at other times it's a beautiful relationship, the exhilaration of being "in the zone" or a breathtaking view of a snow-covered mountain peak.

Actually, all of these are mountaintop experiences. What do they have in common? It's the transcendence to a higher state of consciousness as the bliss of the divine is quickened in us.

When we understand that we are more than our physical body, our mind, our feelings and our memory, we ask, "Who am I beyond my humanness?" On a spiritual level, you are who you are, no matter who you may think you are. You are a spark of light, a son or daughter of God. You are a child of the universe, born from the consciousness of the Creator. You are a cosmic being in embryo, growing, expanding and becoming a unique individualization of the great God flame.

Within each of us burns a spark of the divine that beats our heart and nourishes our body, mind and soul. It is the hidden Presence of God, our inner source of enlightenment and higher consciousness, which connects our human self with what we intuitively recognize as the divine.

Esoteric tradition teaches that it is this inner spark of light that allowed Bernadette of Lourdes and others to see the Blessed Mother, that allowed a simple shepherd boy to compose the Psalms and an apostle of Christ to comprehend the mysteries of divine revelation.

It is this flame of the divine within that gives courage to resolute souls such as Sir Thomas More. In the face of execution by order of King Henry VIII of England, he pronounced that he died "the king's good servant, but God's first."

I AM THAT I AM

How do we understand this cosmic dimension of ourselves, and how do we correlate it with our human consciousness?

Mark and Elizabeth Prophet have given profound teaching on this subject in their book *Climb the Highest Mountain: The Path of the Higher Self:*

When man understands that he lives and moves and has his being in God, he can joyously affirm, "Where I AM, there God is!" or "Where God is, there I AM!" and thus establish a reference point for the flowering of his divine potential....

Man need not manufacture an illusion to establish the existence of God within his consciousness; the very fact that man is conscious is indicative of the inner presence of the Higher Mind. It is, then, through the consciousness of God in man—through God's awareness of himself *in* and *as* man—that man becomes aware of the Self *in* and *as* God....

If, therefore, man is to find the living God, he must look within himself. And if man is to find this God within himself, he must realize that God, life, and consciousness are synonymous terms for the vibrant forcefield of cosmic energy that sustains his being....

Have you ever asked yourself the question, Where am I located in my physical body? Where is the seat of my identity?

Most people cannot establish the exact location of the self in form. Some say that the seat of consciousness is in the heart. Others are convinced that man's individuality is in his thoughts and that the center of being is in the brain. Still others go so far as to say that the consciousness of man is located in all parts of the body through the nervous system, while some believe that the seat of the soul is in the belly....

The four lower bodies are the soul's vehicles of expression in the world of material form. As the musician uses his instrument to draw forth harmonies unheard and unseen without his magic touch, the soul gives utterance to the music of the spheres through its "four-stringed lute," focalizing in the four lower bodies the designs of cosmos and the creative energies of the universe.

Although each of the four planes corresponding to the four bodies has a unique atomic frequency, providing the opportunity for a unique expression of the soul's potential, the four lower bodies interpenetrate one another and are connected through the etheric chakras anchored in the physical body through the central nervous system and the endocrine system.

In this way the bodies function as a unit; and thought, feeling and memory patterns passing through the physical body create ripples of vibration simultaneously on the mental, emotional, and etheric planes.

Thus the chakras are the receiving stations for the flow of light-energy that descends from the [God] Presence and Christ Self through the heart flame to the physical, mental, emotional and memory vehicles. Serving as step-down transformers, these centers focus the light from on high and transform it, making it practical for distribution to each of the four lower bodies.

Without these centers . . . God's individuality as man's individuality would remain unexpressed on the four lower planes of consciousness. . . .

The Real Self, or the immortal Spirit—the animating principle of all *man*ifestation—exists independently of the four lower bodies. As the temporal manifestation of the Spirit, the soul must evolve through the four sheaths in order to become immortal. Thus the soul can be lost, the Spirit of the I AM THAT I AM* can never die.

---

*I AM THAT I AM, the name of God (Exod. 3:13–15).

When embodied on the physical plane, the soul is anchored in all four bodies and its perceptions are grounded in the physical world. The physical orientation of the consciousness precludes its perception of the Higher Self, the invisible world, and the spiritual side of life until the soul anchors enough spiritual substance, or light, in the physical body to form a bridge between the material and the spiritual planes....

This process of filling the bodies with light is the means whereby the transition is made from the human to the Divine. The progressive unfoldment of the soul's potential is therefore realized through the thinning of the veils of the four lower bodies.

The LORD God who declared before the worlds were framed, "I AM where I AM!" hides behind the screen of individual identity in man and Nature....

In order to experience the God who dwells in him, man must first appropriate His light. Then the light that he invokes from on high will release the light that lies dormant within as the sleeping giant of his True Self.

Just as man's outer consciousness enables him to establish the relationship of his identity to his environment, so God's indwelling light focused in the microcosm enables man to relate to God in the Macrocosm and to become one with Him—as Above, so below.[2]

Initiations of Love and Anti-Love

How do we connect this enlightening teaching with our initiations in the two-thousand-year cycle of Aquarius?

The ascended masters tell us that the energies of Aquarius are an outpouring of divine love. These initiations have to do with outwitting the forces of anti-love, within and without, and bringing forth the blessings of divine love for the earth and her people.

Our soul is happiest when we are one with love in the highest sense of the word—the love of Christ, of Krishna, of Buddha, of Kuan Yin. And when we are deeply in love with someone, an experience we all cherish, we have a taste of divine love on earth.

Why do we not experience that state of happiness and contentment all the time? Why is it so hard to love unconditionally? I believe it is because we go astray from the path of divine love and the mastery of our human self.

Capricious desires, despite our best intentions, can put us on the road of wrong motives and faulty judgments. We can unwittingly become party to situations that are mentally and emotionally damaging. And we can end up indulging in impulsive or destructive behavior that sets us back for a long time.

The Personal Cost of a Thrill

I remember a client from the early 1970s who was a good person in many ways. Betsy was kind, intelligent and interested in helping other people. She wanted to do the right thing, but she also liked to experiment. She was always trying out the latest fad or psychic adventure. And she slept with several guys who she admitted were "on the dark side" because she found them "intriguing." She liked the thrill of taking chances.

Can you see the setup here? Betsy started running around with people who were doing drugs. She did the psychedelic trip because everyone else was doing it. And she enjoyed the highs she got from her good trips. At Christmas she even gave LSD as presents to her friends.

One night she and some friends had smoked some marijuana and were tripping on LSD, and Betsy had a really bad trip. It started out fine, but all of a sudden she found herself in a crazy world where everything was, literally, upside down. She felt disoriented and crazy. Dark figures that turned into huge black bees were swarming all around her, closing in on her. They started stinging her. She couldn't get away from them. In fact, she could scarcely move. She screamed to her friends to help her, but they couldn't help her come out of it.

Betsy ended up in the emergency room of a hospital under restraints to keep her from clawing herself (she later told me she had been trying to get the black bees off her). She was in agony for hours before it began to wear off. When she finally began to come out of it, she was exhausted, nauseated and still somewhat disoriented.

Unfortunately she had several flashbacks where she would go through the experience all over again. And she began to have panic attacks when she heard any kind of buzzing sound. It took her months to regain a normal sleep pattern.

As you can imagine, while all of this was going on Betsy couldn't hold a job. She had to give up her apartment and move in with her parents, who fortunately were understanding and tried their best to help her. But by the time she had recovered enough to think about going back to work, her employer had already replaced her. She ended up working temporary jobs because she never knew when she might have a flashback or panic attack.

The good news about this whole unfortunate drama is that Betsy's sense of self-preservation won out. She gave up psychedelic drugs and helped several of her friends do the same. As she told me, "I never imagined something like that could happen, even though I've had friends who would occasionally have a bad trip. What I went through was not a bad trip, it was a nightmare trip. I'll never take the chance of it happening again."

Betsy worked hard in therapy to resolve all of this, and she came to realize that the nauseating upside-down world was a graphic depiction of what she was doing to her life through drugs. The black bees were the dark energy she had taken in from her thrill adventures with unsavory characters. Gradually she regained her health, both physically and psychologically. And she became an advocate for others who were trying to shake the drug habit.

The last time I had contact with her, a number of years ago, she was married and had two children. She actually met her husband, Doug, through her work in drug rehabilitation. They knew each other over quite a period of time before they decided to marry.

As she told me in her phone call, "I believe Doug and I are soul mates and that we have a mission together to help people stuck in the drug world. Both of us went through hard times, but it's given us a lot to share with the people we help. They believe us because we understand where they're coming from. It helps them make it through recovery because they can see we made it and are creating a good life."

Most of us have also had some kind of encounter with the dark side, inwardly or outwardly. It's always a wake-up call. Which will we choose: light or darkness, good or evil?

Whatever we may have indulged in that connects us with the dark side, we can do a turnaround. We can turn away from the dark side (just as Darth Vader did in *Star Wars*). We can turn to the light.

Walking the High Road

What do we do when we turn to the light? First and foremost, we ask God to help us. We put our hand in God's hand. And we decide to choose the high road in the face of whatever difficult challenges or negative karmic circumstances we encounter.

Next, we ask the angels, an ascended master or our own Higher Self to be our best friend. And we ask ourselves, "What would Jesus do? What would Gautama do? What would Mary or Kuan Yin do?" By emulating the masters who have already won their ascension, we ready ourselves to return home to God.

Finally, we choose as friends and companions people who are also seeking the high road. When we walk with others who have the same goal, we give and receive support. When we hang around with people who are involved with evil, we put ourselves on a slippery slope. Even if we don't engage in their doings, we can go downhill in a hurry—sometimes not even realizing that it's happening. Why? Because we are subconsciously influenced by their vibes, their attitudes, their destructive take on life.

Yet we are not meant to divorce ourselves from neighbors and business associates and people we meet on the highway of life. Although our spiritual path may be a solitary one, we do not become hermits. An important part of our path is to offer compassion and help to all we meet.

This is a major part of what Jesus came to teach us. This great master taught, "Love thy neighbor as thyself."[3] And he walked his talk. He interacted with people from all walks of life. He dined with the disciples but also with publicans* and sinners. It was a part of his mission.

How was Jesus able to do that and stay on the high road? He had become the living embodiment of God's love freely given to all. He could interact with all kinds of people everywhere because he continually communed with God. He went wherever God sent him as a living example of divine love.

Jesus put his relationship with the Father first in his life. So did the biblical patriarchs Abraham, Isaac and Jacob. So have prophets, saints, sages and devotees of many religions and all walks of life. They walked and talked with God. And they interacted with people of evil without being set back emotionally or dissuaded from their higher calling. The key is this: They kept their hearts and minds stayed on God at all times.

We can learn to quiet our emotions and listen to the

*Tax collectors.

still small voice of God at the same time we interact with others and serve those in need. It's an initiation on the path of divine love. And it brings comfort to our own soul.

The Maha Chohan* says: "The disciplining of the emotions must be found in interaction with others. There is no more certain way to gain mastery of the emotions than to . . . mingle with people from all walks of life and to always prefer to impart the flame of love and of charity toward those who do not have the flame of harmony."[4]

We ask ourselves, "What would my life look like if I were to do that?" We remember that the flame of love and charity originates in the heart of Almighty God, and a spark of that divine love burns on the altar in the secret chamber of our heart. We realize that when we choose to love as God loves, we are one with the heart of God.

So we decide to open our hearts to share that divine love. We walk in Jesus' footsteps. We determine to take Christlike action. We practice the art of forbearance in difficult interactions, yet we do not compromise our principles. We correct ourselves and forgive others. We choose to love God's people everywhere. Now we are walking the high road.

Pursuing Our Higher Calling

How does all this relate to our specific calling in Aquarius?

First, I believe that in Aquarius we are called to identify with our higher consciousness, our Higher Self, and to

*The Maha Chohan (Great Lord) is an ascended master who is the representative of the Holy Spirit.

honor the Presence of God within us. As we meditate on what this means, we more and more realize our divine heritage as sons and daughters of God. We find it easier to follow the precepts of the spiritual path and to obey the guidance of our Higher Self.

Second, I believe we are called to become Aquarian love-conquerors. To me, this means to love ourselves, to love our friends, neighbors and co-workers, to love all that is good, to love the essence of the divine in every part of life. Sometimes that love is gentle, sometimes fiery.

When we love as God loves, we touch our own divine essence. We become like the sun, radiating the warmth and brightness of divine love wherever we go. We discover that we can maintain a stance of loving-kindness in situations that are problematic or hurtful and with people who are unreasonable or unkind. As we develop this emotional resilience, we bless other people as well as ourselves.

Third, I believe we are called to offer God's gift of divine love to the entire planet. This means to invoke God's love and blessings, to counter the dark forces with loving yet fiery rebuke and to care for the portion of earth that is ours.

When we accept our love calling in Aquarius, we are telling God that we will do our best to embrace generous motives, kind thoughts, compassionate feelings, encouraging words and benevolent actions. Yet we also know that we must hone our awareness so that we recognize the forces of anti-love.

Thus, we determine to stand firm against evil. When in doubt about how to counter evil forces, we pray and follow our higher guidance and common sense. Moment by moment, action by action, we move forward to fulfill our destiny in Aquarius.

Creating the Miracle of a Golden Age

Mark Prophet, a twentieth-century adept, had an engaging, positive approach to life. He was a man with tremendous heart and fiery devotion to higher principles. He taught his students to reverse the downward spirals of human consciousness by seeing life as a teacher.

Mark exhorts us to claim our divine heritage and thereby create a golden age, an age of brotherhood and peace:

> Life is a great teacher. And the golden age that is going to come is an age when the anthems in the churches will simply raise you in your consciousness to where you can hardly contain yourself with joy.
>
> And you will not find people out here trying to destroy one another. They will not be bombing one another. They will not be creating hate newspapers against one another, as we are now seeing in the world....
>
> I picked up a paper written by a white man that was completely filled with hatred against the black race. ...I picked up an issue of the Black Panther magazine one day in Santa Barbara; it was filled with invectives against the white race....
>
> All of this is simply a smoke screen to conceal from mankind the real social justice that comes about through having integration with God. If the divine Sonship is realized, we don't recognize race and creed, because race and creed are only compartments that mankind is

assigned, even as Adam assigned labels to the animals.

Adam assigned labels to the animals, and people put labels on one another. But they forget the greatest label of all stamped on them by God's hand: "Made in the divine image."...

Well, people can change a lot of things. And they've changed a lot of things from the divine image to the human image. And I contend that if they can change from the divine to the human, they can change back again, with God's help, from the human to the divine. And this is the whole process that will be the miracle of the golden age.[5]

Born to Manifest the Glory of God

Nelson Mandela, head of the Republic of South Africa, gave the following related teaching. It is a powerful statement of soul liberation:

Our deepest fear is not that we are inadequate.
Our deepest fear is that we are powerful beyond measure.
It is our Light, not our Darkness, that most frightens us.
We ask ourselves, who am I to be brilliant, gorgeous, talented, fabulous?
Actually, who are you NOT to be?
You are a child of God. Your playing small does not serve the World.
There is nothing enlightened about shrinking so that other people won't feel insecure around you.
We were born to make manifest the glory of God that is within us.
It is not just in some of us; it is in everyone.

As we let our own Light shine, we unconsciously give
   other people permission to do the same.
As we are liberated from our own fear, our presence
   automatically liberates others.[6]

Earth Is God's Schoolroom

As we learn our lessons about the fears and folly of
the human consciousness and the fantastic possibilities of
the divine, we realize that earth truly is a schoolroom for
our soul.

We have the opportunity to do all kinds of experi-
ments with God's energy while we are living on the earth.
Some turn out pretty good, some not so good. All of them
are lessons in the cosmic energy flow that moves through
the universe, the earth and the four lower bodies that
house our soul and spirit.

Our very essence is cosmic energy, often spoken of as
divine light. Our individuality is due to the unique crystalline patterning of a portion of that cosmic energy by the
hand of the Creator. And every erg of energy we send out
is stamped with the blueprint of our being.

Thus God has given us, as divine progeny, a certain
portion of divine light and the gift of free will. We get to
choose how we will meter out the energy that is our divine
heritage and we experience the results of our endeavors.

Masters, saints and sages have taught that we are responsible for whatever we create with God's energy and
how it impacts the universe. And the way we spend our
quotient of light either adds to or detracts from our divine
state of consciousness and our level of spiritual attainment.

When we act with benign motives, creative thoughts, generous feelings and kind actions, we add to our cosmic bank account and typically experience positive return. On the other hand, when we are selfish, stodgy, stingy and unkind, we find ourselves on the receiving end of a lot of grief—not to mention the karma we make and the debit on the cosmic ledger.

The Karmic Law of Cause and Effect

Through the great karmic law of the universe, what we send out always returns home to roost. It may not be today or tomorrow, but somewhere along the way the energy we send out comes back to us.

As Paul put it two thousand years ago, "Be not deceived; God is not mocked: for whatsoever a man soweth, that shall he also reap. For he that soweth to his flesh shall of the flesh reap corruption; but he that soweth to the Spirit shall of the Spirit reap life everlasting."[7]

Karmic law is just as true today. When we unwisely invest our energies in actions that are harmful to life, we receive the return of what we have sent forth. Through that law of cause and effect we are given an opportunity to learn and correct our actions.

By the same token, when we wisely invest our energies in actions that bless life, we receive that return as well. And we know that we are on the right track. Even if our outer self doesn't realize it, our soul knows.

Now you might ask, "But what about all the good people on earth who go through terrible experiences?"

That's a hard question, but one that spiritual teachers

and philosophers through the ages have addressed. Sometimes it is the testing of our mettle. Sometimes it is an initiation in endurance and faith. And sometimes it is the balancing of karma from past lives. Yet it always comes back to how we exercise our free will.

Our Creator has given us the gift of free will. How we use it while we are on earth is our choice. Whether or not we use it to bless life and to fulfill our destiny is up to us. We either return to God as an ascended being who has realized oneness with God or as free energy to be recycled for new creation.

Evil does not eternally endure—this is the Creator's love gift to the cosmos. Ultimately, evil and whoever completely embraces evil dissolve into the infinite flow of cosmic energy.

In contrast, those who embrace the path of the ascension may return home to God as individualized God-free beings. Their inner divine blueprint has been fulfilled and made permanent in the cosmos. Truly our destiny is to imprint our unique crystalline pattern in time and space and to realize our individualized oneness with our loving Father-Mother God.

Settle Yourself in Solitude

In the 1500s, the Carmelite nun later canonized as Saint Teresa of Avila instructed, "Settle yourself in solitude, and you will come upon God in yourself." Many of us today follow her instruction and example as we enter into communion with our God through quiet meditation and spiritual contemplation.

In a remarkable book, *Dweller on Two Planets,*
Phylos the Thibetan recounts that from ancient times high
spiritual initiates have walked a solitary path of adeptship.
At some point in their life, these advanced adepts are called
by God to come apart and receive training that quickens
and awakens in them their past accomplishments. They
move on to higher and higher attainment.

The highest of these initiates have been known as Sons
of the Solitude,[8] stalwart ones who have walked and talked
with God and attained spiritual mastery over matter. They
set an example of devotion and self-mastery that is apt for
us today.

Mrs. Prophet teaches that Jesus Christ walked the
earth as a Son of the Solitude. And ancient ones in the
scriptures, such as Melchizedek, King of Salem, and Abraham, biblical patriarch, were also Sons of the Solitude.
The priority of these highest of adepts is service to God
and to God's people on earth.

As Mrs. Prophet says:

> Sons of the Solitude are notable because they
> stand apart from others who may be with them, who
> are seekers, disciples, brothers and sisters on the Path.
> The term that El Morya gave us for these adepts is *the
> lonely ones.*
>
> The fact that they're lonely and in solitude means
> they have an attainment that exceeds that of their
> peers. Therefore they rise to the position of spiritual
> leadership in communities, churches, spiritual move-
> ments. But they are alone and lonely because there is
> still a gulf between them and the next level of initiates

or disciples on the Path.

They are unique individuals who come to lead, who come to deliver dispensations. And they're very much one with the people around them—they enter into a master-disciple type of relationship.

In so doing, they're loving, they're concerned, they minister, they're a part of all these other people. But at the level of their inner attainment, they are alone, and they know they are alone.

Most of them don't have peers that they contact. John the Baptist and Jesus Christ were an exception; both were Sons of the Solitude. That's why it was such an ultimate pain to the heart of Jesus that basically he lost the only other person—at least in the Middle East—who was his equal or greater. . . .

And so, this term *Sons of the Solitude* reminds me that the true initiates of the Great White Brotherhood[9] are called, and call themselves, the lonely ones. To me they are the very same titles.

I think those who are on the Path recognize that one can feel alone midst a crowd when there is no one present who has perception beyond the level of the human soul, who has perception of the Christ. And so, Sons of the Solitude are those who have reached levels of attainment of true adeptship.[10]

In solitude, these climbers of the mountain of Self have moved steadily inward, onward and upward toward the peak of enlightenment—the take-off point for the ascension. Never looking down, always looking up, they ascend, passing each initiation step-by-step.

Set Your Sights on Your Cosmic Future

Climbing upward to the ascension means to aspire to inner and outer God-mastery in all situations. It means developing self-mastery through invoking divine guidance and humbly bending the knee to God. And it means to do good works.

How do we go about it? Here is a seven-step formula to try on a daily basis:

1. Pray for divine guidance.
2. Be humble in heart.
3. Stand for truth and higher principles.
4. Choose higher motives, positive thoughts, right desire and constructive action.
5. Exercise emotional balance and self-restraint.
6. Be an instrument of compassion and loving-kindness.
7. Forgive those who wrong you, and forgive yourself.

Check yourself out at the end of the day. How did you do? Determine to correct whatever mistakes you might have made. Ask your guardian angel to help you. And keep moving upward.

The ascended masters lovingly challenge us to undertake this solitary climb. As lightbearers serving God and God's people on earth, we, too, can be as Sons and Daughters of the Solitude, steadily trekking upward to divine selfhood and the ascension. Ultimately, we too can achieve our victory by passing our initiations on earth and balancing the negative karma we have made throughout our lifetimes.

Climbing the Ladder to Higher Octaves

The ascension can be likened to climbing the rungs of a very high ladder—and not skipping any. Think about it this way: If you removed any one of the rungs of a high ladder, you would likely have to stay where you were or return to ground level. If you attempted to skip over that missing rung, you might very well find yourself hanging in space or crashing downward.

Each initiation on this path to the ascension is like a rung of that ladder. It provides firm footing for the next. If we, as initiates, would ascend to the peak of divine Self-hood, we must pass each initiation in turn and thereby keep moving upward to our victory.

When we fail an initiation we find ourselves on a lower rung of the ladder. Now we must retrace our steps and pass the one we failed in order to keep moving upward. Initiations are like the tests we take in school, the tryouts in athletics, the challenges of moving up the corporate ladder and the finesse we need in difficult interpersonal situations. Our spiritual initiations are cosmic tests; they are all about how we expend our cosmic energy quotient.

We usually have a sense of when we don't pass a test. Our intuition, which is really the inner voice of our Higher Self, tells us. And if we are determined to pass it the next time, we examine carefully the motives, thoughts, feelings and actions that might have caused us to fail. Then we can embark on a path of self-correction.

We usually need to look into whatever impure motives may have started us downhill. That's the most difficult task because often such motives lie hidden in dark crevices of the subconscious or unconscious. So we dig them out and expose them to the light of conscious examination.

Impure motives are usually connected to untoward desires that do not serve our spiritual journey. They take us off on a tangent. Before we realize what's happening, we have set off a chain reaction.

The chain reaction actually goes something like this: We desire something we can't have or think will take too much effort (money, time, sacrifice) to attain. We think discouraging thoughts, such as "I don't think I can make it" or "It's too hard." This kind of thinking triggers feelings of fear, discouragement, frustration and anger. Now we feel even worse, and the next thing you know, we've done something foolish or hurtful. Now we feel guilty and stuck.

At this point we realize we are on a downward spiral, and there's no place to go but up. So we ask God's forgiveness, decide to self-correct and try again.

Our sincere self-correction moves us toward the next rung on the ladder of initiation. Through prayer and total focus on the upward path, we pass that test the next time it is given. And so it continues, step-by-step, until one day we reach the top.

Joy Propels Us to the Ascension

The ascended master Lanello has given specific teaching about climbing the stairway of life to the ascension— and how a sense of joy and daily diligence can propel us swiftly upward.

He tells us:

Joy is the very first principle of the ascension. Take two individuals—one who fulfills his assignments without joy and one who fulfills them with joy. The one without joy, beloved, may lose his ascension for want of joy. And the one with joy may make it even though some elements are lacking.

"That your joy might be full" was the prayer of Jesus—and that you might know and have *his* joy remaining in you. This joy, beloved, can never be satisfied by human companionship alone but by a human companionship wherein those who are together see this as a vehicle for the divine companionship, for a divine joy that sprinkles laughter and merriment and play betwixt the hours of hard concentration. This joy, beloved, that spans all octaves is pleasing to God.

Therefore I say, abandon a sense of martyrdom! Abandon a sense of self-condemnation! Abandon a sense of nonjoy! But take care that your joy puts God first....

Blessed hearts, joy flames go out when you are not in sync with your cycles on the staircase of life. There comes upon you a frantic sense of urgency within. You may connect it to outer responsibilities, burdens and debts, or to not having enough time to do everything you want to do.

Well, time will fall in place and so will space when you dedicate your day to meeting the requirements of the day's initiation on that step of your stairway of life. Then you will go to sleep at night in peace and

Claiming Your Soul's Victory 323

have the peace of angels, knowing you are one step closer to the victory of your ascension or to the point of your adeptship where you may reincarnate again with a full 100 percent of your karma balanced.

Yes, beloved, your daily tasks and obligations and responsibilities have everything to do with your initiations on this staircase of life. Dispatch them well! Guard your time! Seal yourself to accomplish that which must be accomplished....

Only your Christ Self can solve those problems! Only Almighty God can solve them! And when you develop that attitude, you will dispatch those problems and dispense with them in a mighty short time and a mighty short space....

Blessed hearts, take control of your day! For it is a cycle of the sun, it is a cycle of the earth, it is a cycle of your path of the ascension. This is how you make your ascension: I tell you, you score a victory each day! That means you must enter your day with a fierceness and a determination.

Take the end of today to plan for tomorrow, to organize what you will do: when you will arise, who you will see and who you cannot see. Set goals and achieve them no matter what! For to break the patterns of letting things get by you, letting people interrupt you is no small task, but it is accomplished by the surefootedness of the compassionate ones. These compassionate ones, beloved, manage to achieve their victory and also accomplish their daily assignments.

A day's victory can become the victory of a lifetime. Count the days in the year and then the years in the decades of a life span and see how many victories you must achieve to finally step on the dais at the Ascension Temple at Luxor* and feel the caressing love, the white fire of ascension's flame and hear the welcome of the seraphim who surround you and of all the adepts who themselves are candidates for the ascension.[11]

If you don't know exactly where to begin, simply set your sights on the cosmic future as your soul envisions it to be—and catch up to it. Ask your Higher Self to be your guide, your companion, your lifeline and safety belt as you climb upward. Your loving Father-Mother God and the angels will be smiling upon you at ascension's peak. And you will hear the rewarding words, "Welcome home, thou good and faithful servant."

---

*The spiritual retreat known as the Ascension Temple is located in the heaven-world at Luxor, Egypt.

APPENDIX

Spiritual Formulas for the Alchemy of Transformation

As you prepare for alchemical transformation, surround yourself with God's light and protection by invoking the "tube of light." This cylinder of white light descends from the heart of your I AM Presence, the I AM THAT I AM, God individualized for every son and daughter of God. It serves as spiritual protection to you and to your soul.

TUBE OF LIGHT

Beloved I AM Presence bright,
Round me seal your tube of light
From ascended master flame
Called forth now in God's own name.
Let it keep my temple free
From all discord sent to me.

I AM calling forth violet fire
To blaze and transmute all desire,
Keeping on in freedom's name
Till I AM one with the violet flame.

You can also pray to Archangel Michael for protection. Increase the power of your prayers by giving them aloud as a decree, a heartfelt spoken petition directing God's light into our world. You can give this decree when you are traveling or for protection anytime, anywhere. If you are in some public place, simply say it under your breath.

TRAVELING PROTECTION

Lord* Michael before,
Lord Michael behind,
Lord Michael to the right,
Lord Michael to the left,
Lord Michael above,
Lord Michael below,
Lord Michael, Lord Michael wherever I go!

I AM his love protecting here!
I AM his love protecting here!
I AM his love protecting here!

You may also invoke the power of your mighty three-fold flame to help you stand tall and counter evil with God's love, wisdom and power:

O MIGHTY THREEFOLD FLAME OF LIFE

1. O mighty threefold flame of life,
    Thou gift of God so pure,
    Take my thoughts and energy
    And make them all secure.

2. Under bond of brotherhood
    And understanding fair,
    Send thee forth unto my soul
    The gift of holy prayer.

3. Communication's strands of love,
    How they woo by heaven's law
    A tender blessing for the good,
    Releasing holy awe

Lord is used in this prayer as a term of honor, denoting that Archangel Michael carries the power and presence of God.

4. That draws me near the throne of grace
   To now behold thy sacred face
   And without fear dispense aright
   The passions of pure God-delight
   Which set me free from all that's been
   The sinful nature of all men.

5. Christ, raise me to self-mastery,
   The living passion of the free.
   Determination, now arise
   And lift me ever to the skies!

6. I AM, I AM, I AM
   Enfolding life and being all
   With the God-command
   "Amen!" that shatters human pall.

7. I AM, I AM, I AM
   The free—no bondage holds me back;
   I AM the fullness of Love's law
   Supplying every lack,
   And consecration in full measure
   Is my will and God's own pleasure.

8. Saint Germain and Jesus dear,
   Hold my hand with Morya's here
   And let the love of Mary then
   Be the wings to raise all men.

9. Until they all unite in Love
   To serve that purpose from above
   That comes to earth at any hour
   Responding to the call of Power;
   Send thy shining Wisdom then
   That is God's love
   Expanded for all men.

Once you have invoked your tube of light, prayed to Archangel Michael for protection and invoked your three-fold flame, offer a prayer for the dissolving of all anti-love within yourself, your loved ones and everyone you are praying for. And ask the angels of love to fill the vacuum that has been created with God's divine love.

Now you are ready to give a "dweller call" for the binding of all you have ever taken in that is not of love and light.

"I CAST OUT THE DWELLER-ON-THE-THRESHOLD!"

In the name of my beloved Mighty I AM Presence and Holy Christ Self, Archangel Michael and the hosts of the LORD, in the name Jesus Christ, I challenge the personal and planetary dweller-on-the-threshold, and I say:

You have no power over me! *You* may not threaten or mar the face of my God within my soul. *You* may not taunt or tempt me with past or present or future, for I AM hid with Christ in God. I AM his bride. I AM accepted by the LORD.

You have no power to destroy me!

Therefore, be *bound!* by the LORD himself.

Your day is *done!* You may no longer inhabit this temple.

In the name I AM THAT I AM, be *bound!* you tempter of my soul. Be *bound!* you point of pride of the original fall of the fallen ones! You have no power, no reality, no worth. You occupy no time or space of my being.

You have no power in my temple. You may no longer steal the light of my chakras. You may not steal the light of my heart flame or my I AM Presence.

Be *bound!* then, O Serpent and his seed and all implants of the sinister force, for *I AM THAT I AM!*

I AM the Son of God this day, and I occupy this temple fully and wholly until the coming of the LORD, until the New Day, until all be fulfilled, and until this generation of the seed of Serpent pass away.

Burn through, O living Word of God!

By the power of Brahma, Vishnu and Shiva, in the name Brahman: I AM THAT I AM and I stand and I cast out the dweller.

Let him be bound by the power of the LORD's host! Let him be consigned to the flame of the sacred fire of Alpha and Omega, that that one may not go out to tempt the innocent and the babes in Christ.

Blaze the power of Elohim!

Elohim of God—Elohim of God—Elohim of God

Descend now in answer to my call. As the mandate of the LORD—as Above, so below—occupy now.

Bind the fallen self! *Bind* the synthetic self! Be *out* then!

Bind the fallen one! For there is no more remnant or residue in my life of any, or any part of that one.

Lo, I AM, in Jesus' name, the victor over Death and Hell! (give two times)

Lo, *I AM THAT I AM* in me—in the name of Jesus Christ—is *here and now* the victor over Death and Hell! Lo! it is done.

You can also give a fiat for the banishing of the forces of anti-Love. This fiery statement is your soul's repudiation of the forces of evil that oppose divine love. Give the fiat in a posture of absolute peace and equanimity.

In the name of Almighty God, I AM THAT I AM,
be gone, forces of anti-Love!

Now give the "miracle mantra" to intensify the light of divine love and healing within yourself. This decree action is a combination of ruby love fire and emerald healing light. Visualize an intertwined action of brilliant ruby and emerald light flowing through your aura as you give this decree. You can also visualize loved ones enveloped in ruby and emerald light; they will receive it inwardly and manifest it in their own lives in God's timing—and their own.

"I AM THE MIRACLE OF GOD"

In the name of the light of God that never fails:
I AM the miracle of God!
I accept a miracle this day.
I demand a miracle in every level of the chakras of my being and in the five secret rays!
I demand the miracle light of the Eternal Christos, the Sacred Heart of Jesus, and the full power of the Ascended Master John the Beloved:
Blaze forth your miracle light! (give three times) *Burn* through!
I call for Ascended Master Jesus Christ miracle of perfection in my heart, in my third-eye, in my throat, in my crown, in the solar-plexus, seat-of-the-soul, and base-of-the-spine chakras.
Blaze the light of Alpha and Omega! (give three times)
Whirl now the seven chakras! *Spin* them by the power of the seven mighty chohans of the rays!
Blaze the light of the Maha Chohan in the secret

chamber of my heart! (give three times)

> *Lo,* I AM God's miracle this day!
> I AM his miracle made manifest.
> I AM his miracle consciousness in action.
> I AM the blazing light of the Great Central Sun miracle of life—perfecting and resurrecting all in me that is of worth and of sacred fire and of nobility.
> *Blaze* the light through! (give three times)
> I AM God's miracle this day. And I accept his miracle in me as the fullness of that proof of the love of the Father and the Son through the Mother and the Holy Spirit. Amen.

When we call for a miracle, we affirm it and accept it. In God's time and space it will do its miracle work within us and the people we are praying for.

Conclude this spiritual practice by giving these violet flame mantras (or any of the others in the book):

VIOLET FLAME IS...

Breath of God inside each cell
I AM the violet flame
Pulsing out the cosmic time
I AM the violet flame
Energizing mind and heart
I AM the violet flame
Sustaining God's creation now
I AM the violet flame

With all love
With all love
With all love

Shimmering in a crystal cave
　I AM the violet flame
Searching out all hidden pain
　I AM the violet flame
Consuming cause and core of fear
　I AM the violet flame
Revealing now the inner name
　I AM the violet flame

　　With all peace
　　With all peace
　　With all peace

Flashing like a lightning bolt
　I AM the violet flame
Stretching through the galaxies
　I AM the violet flame
Connecting soul and Spirit now
　I AM the violet flame
Raising you to cosmic heights
　I AM the violet flame

　　With all power
　　With all power
　　With all power

Seal and expand your alchemy with this affirmation:

And in full faith I consciously accept this manifest, manifest, manifest (give three times), right here and now, with full power, eternally sustained, all powerfully active, ever expanding and world enfolding until all are wholly ascended in the Light and free![1]

The Chart of Your Divine Self

We can call to God and he will answer because we are connected to him. We are his sons and daughters. We have a direct relationship to God and he has placed a portion of himself in us. In order to better understand this relationship, the ascended masters have designed the Chart of Your Divine Self.

The Chart of Your Divine Self is a portrait of you and of the God within you. It is a diagram of yourself and your potential to become who you really are. It is an outline of your spiritual anatomy.

The upper figure is your "I AM Presence," the Presence of God that is individualized in each one of us. It is your personalized "I AM THAT I AM." Your I AM Presence is surrounded by seven concentric spheres of spiritual energy that make up what is called your "causal body." The spheres of pulsating energy contain the record of the good works you have performed since your very first incarnation on earth. They are like your cosmic bank account.

The middle figure in the chart represents the "Holy Christ Self," who is also called the Higher Self. You can think of your Holy Christ Self as your chief guardian angel and dearest friend, your inner teacher and voice of conscience. Just as the I AM Presence is the Presence of God that is individualized for each of us, so the Holy Christ Self is the presence of the universal Christ that is individualized for each of us.

"The Christ" is actually a title given to those who have attained oneness with their Higher Self, or Christ Self. That's why Jesus was called "Jesus, the Christ." *Christ* comes from the Greek word *christos,* meaning "anointed" —anointed with the light of God.

What the Chart shows is that each of us has a Higher Self, or "inner Christ," and that each of us is destined to become one with that Higher Self—whether we call it the Christ, the Buddha, the Tao or the Atman. This "inner Christ" is what the Christian mystics sometimes refer to as the "inner man of the heart," and what the Upanishads mysteriously describe as a being the "size of a thumb" who "dwells deep within the heart."

We all have moments when we feel that connection with our Higher Self—when we are creative, loving, joyful. But there are other moments when we feel out of sync with our Higher Self—moments when we become angry, depressed, lost. What the spiritual path is all about is learning to sustain the connection to the higher part of ourselves so that we can make our greatest contribution to humanity.

The ribbon of white light descending from the I AM Presence through the Holy Christ Self to the lower figure in the Chart is the crystal cord (sometimes called the silver cord). It is the "umbilical cord," the lifeline, that ties you to Spirit.

Your crystal cord also nourishes that special, radiant flame of God that is ensconced in the secret chamber of your heart. It is called the threefold flame, or divine spark,

because it is literally a spark of sacred fire that God has transmitted from his heart to yours. This flame is called "threefold" because it engenders the primary attributes of Spirit —power, wisdom and love.

The mystics of the world's religions have contacted the divine spark, describing it as the seed of divinity within. Buddhists, for instance, speak of the "germ of Buddhahood" that exists in every living being. In the Hindu tradition, the Katha Upanishad speaks of the "light of the Spirit" that is concealed in the "secret high place of the heart" of all beings.

Likewise, the fourteenth-century Christian theologian and mystic Meister Eckhart teaches of the divine spark when he says, "God's seed is within us." There is a part of us, says Eckhart, that "remains eternally in the Spirit and is divine. . . . Here God glows and flames without ceasing."

When we decree, we meditate on the flame in the secret chamber of our heart. This secret chamber is your own private meditation room, your interior castle, as Teresa of Avila called it. In Hindu tradition, the devotee visualizes a jeweled island in his heart. There he sees himself before a beautiful altar, where he worships his teacher in deep meditation.

Jesus spoke of entering the secret chamber of the heart when he said: "When thou prayest, enter into thy closet, and when thou hast shut thy door, pray to thy Father which is in secret; and thy Father which seeth in secret shall reward thee openly."

The lower figure in the Chart of Your Divine Self represents you as a soul on the spiritual path, surrounded by the violet flame and the protective white light of God, the "tube of light." Your soul is the living potential of God— the part of you that is mortal but can become immortal. The high-frequency energy of the violet flame can help you reach that goal more quickly.

The purpose of your soul's evolution on earth is to grow in self-mastery, balance your karma and fulfill your mission on earth so that you can return to the spiritual dimensions that are your real home.

When your soul at last takes flight and ascends back to God and the heaven-world, you will become an "ascended" master, free from the rounds of karma and rebirth.

Notes

Preface

1. See Eric Roston, "A CEO's Story: All His Office Mates Gone," *Time,* September 24, 2001, p. 82; *People Weekly,* October 1, 2001, p. 67; and "700 Families," at www.atouch-ofgrey.com/Lutnick.html.

2. David Abel, "A Chapel Spared Stirs Talk of Miracle," *Boston Globe,* September 26, 2001.

3. See "Prayer Service at Yankee Stadium," September 23, 2001, at www.cnn.com/TRANSCRIPTS/0109/23/se.03.html.

Introduction

1. Daniel Goleman, *Emotional Intelligence* (New York: Bantam Books, 1995), p. 6.

2. Shakespeare, *Hamlet,* act 1, scene 3, lines 78–80.

Chapter One
Emotional Balance in a Turbulent World

1. Eckhart Tolle, *The Power of Now: A Guide to Spiritual Enlightenment* (Novato, Calif.: New World Library, 1999), pp. 54, 55.

2. "Honoring the Fallen, Comforting Their Friends," *People Weekly,* October 1, 2001, p. 72.

3. Marci McDonald, Josh Fischman, and Mary Brophy Marcus, "Courage under Terrible Fire," *U.S. News and World Report,* September 24, 2001, p. 41.

4. Rick Reilly, "Four of a Kind," CNN SportsIllustrated.com, September 19, 2001; Jaxon Van Derbeken, "Flt. 93: Terror on Board," *Reader's Digest,* December 2001, pp. 72, 73; and Angie Cannon, "Final Words from Flight 93," *U.S. News and World Report,* October 29, 2001, p. 34.

5. Reilly, "Four of a Kind."

6. See Thomas F. Crum, *The Magic of Conflict: Turning a Life of Work into a Work of Art* (New York: Simon and Schuster, Touchstone, 1987).

7. EFT, Emotional Freedom Technique, developed by Gary Craig, is a method of "energy psychology." Based on acupuncture, applied kinesiology and clinical psychology, such meridian-based psychotherapies are rapidly gaining international acceptance.

8. Inner child work has become popular over the past twenty years. It is a therapeutic method of working with the experiences of our younger self through imagery and dialogue. In this work, we guide, comfort and help to heal younger parts of ourselves from those hurtful experiences that lie unresolved in the subconscious or unconscious. I equate the inner child with the soul. I have learned through many years of psychotherapy practice that disturbing thoughts, feelings and habit patterns often arise from our soul's painful experiences. These can surface from childhood, teenage or adult traumas in this or past lives.

9. Martin L. Rossman, M.D., *Guided Imagery for Self-Healing* (Tiburon, Calif.: An H. J. Kramer Book, published in a joint venture with New World Library, 2000), p. 28.

Chapter Two
Mastering the Shadows of Fear

1. I John 3:2.

2. I John 4:18.

3. This exercise is adapted from a technique developed by

Doc Lew Childre and the Institute of HeartMath, Boulder Creek, California.

4. Elizabeth Clare Prophet with Patricia R. Spadaro and Murray L. Steinman, *Kabbalah: Key to Your Inner Power* (Corwin Springs, Mont.: Summit University Press, 1997), pp. 178–79.

5. Dan Millman, *Way of the Peaceful Warrior: A Book That Changes Lives* (Tiburon, Calif.: H. J. Kramer, 1984), p. 113.

6. Ibid.

7. Ibid., pp. 113–14.

8. Gal. 6:7.

9. See Mark L. Prophet and Elizabeth Clare Prophet, *The Science of the Spoken Word* (Corwin Springs, Mont.: Summit University Press, 1991), p. 131.

10. An excellent book on loving-kindness is Sharon Salzberg's *Lovingkindness: The Revolutionary Art of Happiness* (Boston: Shamballa Publications, 1995). This passage is taken from pp. 24–25.

11. I John 3:18.

12. See Patti Becklund, "Little Bit," *Guideposts,* June 2001, pp. 44–49.

Chapter Three
Mustering the Courage to Face Our Dark Side

1. An excellent resource book on the "shadow" concept is *Romancing the Shadow: Illuminating the Dark Side of the Soul,* by Connie Zweig, Ph.D., and Steve Wolf, Ph.D. (New York: Ballantine Books, 1997).

2. Pallas Athena is an ascended lady master whose divine mission is truth. You can pray to her to help you know the truth, speak the truth and to be that truth in action.

3. See Mark 5:1–13.

4. This exercise is an adaptation of HeartMath as taught by

the Institute of HeartMath in Boulder Creek, California.

5. Thomas More, *A Dialogue of Comfort*, in *The Complete Works of St. Thomas More*, ed. Louis L. Martz and Frank Manley (New Haven, Conn.: Yale University Press, 1976), 12:155.

6. Dannion Brinkley with Paul Perry, *At Peace in the Light* (New York: HarperCollins Publishers, HarperPaperbacks, 1995), p. 41.

7. Ibid, p. 212.

8. Ibid, p. 213.

9. Ibid, pp. 219–20.

10. Ibid, p.191.

11. Ibid, p. 201.

12. This dictation from the ascended master of fearlessness, Ray-O-Light, was delivered through the messenger Elizabeth Clare Prophet in Anaheim, California, on December 28, 1975. The quotes in this chapter are taken from this discourse, "Keep Moving!" published in *Pearls of Wisdom*, vol. 25, no. 29, pp. 305–13 (Summit University Press). This master is known as Ray-O-Light because of his transformational experience with a ray of God's light.

13. Spiritually, a Piscean conqueror is one who has mastered human fear, Jesus Christ being the primary exemplar. The last two-thousand-year period (A.D. 0–1999) was known as the age of Pisces. The current two-thousand-year cycle (A.D. 2000–3999) is the age of Aquarius. Fulfilling one's divine plan in Aquarius means to internalize divine love and pass the spiritual initiations of love.

14. President Franklin Delano Roosevelt, first inaugural address, March 4, 1933.

15. *CBS Sunday Night Movie, Scattering Dad*, May 27, 2001.

16. See David Richo, *When Love Meets Fear: How to Become Defense-less and Resource-full* (New York: Paulist Press, 1997), pp. 5–6.

Chapter Four
Banishing Fear-Dragons from the Psyche

1. For further information on the cosmic clock, see Elizabeth Clare Prophet, *The Great White Brotherhood in the Culture, History and Religion of America* (Corwin Springs, Mont.: Summit University Press, 1987), pp. 173–206. See also *Seminar on the Cosmic Clock,* by Elizabeth Clare Prophet, 2-audiotape album, A88087 (published by Summit University Press).

2. The teachings on the four major types of fear in this chapter are taken from Elizabeth Clare Prophet's lecture "On Healing and the Four Types of Fear," given April 3, 1991.

3. *Save the World with Violet Flame! by Saint Germain 1,* 90-min. audiotape with booklet, B88019 (published by Summit University Press).

4. Prophet, "On Healing and the Four Types of Fear."

5. Marianne Szegedy-Maszak, "Cold Sweat and Flashback," *U.S. News and World Report,* September 24, 2001, p. 54.

6. Prophet, "On Healing and the Four Types of Fear."

7. See Viktor E. Frankl, *Man's Search for Meaning,* 4th ed. (Boston: Beacon Press, 1992).

8. Prophet and Prophet, *Science of the Spoken Word,* p. 114.

9. Paramahansa Yogananda, *Autobiography of a Yogi* (Los Angeles: Self-Realization Fellowship, 1974), pp. 131–32.

10. Matt. 10:16.

11. John 2:19.

12. Prophet, "On Healing and the Four Types of Fear."

13. Ps. 23:4.

14. Prophet, "On Healing and the Four Types of Fear."

15. Gen. 5:24; Heb. 11:5.

16. Wayne Muller, *Legacy of the Heart: The Spiritual Advantages of a Painful Childhood* (New York: Simon and Schuster, Fireside, 1993), p. 26.

Chapter Five
Mastering the Furies

1. This version of the ancient tale was taken from Daniel Goleman's *Emotional Intelligence,* p. 46.

2. Elizabeth Clare Prophet, "Teachings on Dealing with the Perversions of the Energies of Winter Solstice," December 20, 1992.

3. Shakespeare, *Hamlet,* act 3, scene 1, line 56.

4. Prov. 16:18.

5. Prov. 16:32.

6. Francis Bacon, "Essay 57" (1625).

7. Rom. 7:19.

8. El Morya, "A Report," December 13, 1992, in *Pearls of Wisdom,* vol. 35, no. 68, pp. 772, 773, 774, 775.

9. El Morya, *Pearls of Wisdom,* vol. 2, no. 27.

Chapter Six
Masks of the Anger-Dragon

1. For a complete look at dream analysis, including nightmares, spiritual dreams, Tibetan sleep and dream yoga, lucid dreaming and techniques to help you more clearly remember and understand your dreams, see my book *Dreams: Exploring the Secrets of Your Soul* (Corwin Springs, Mont.: Summit University Press, 2001).

2. Eph. 4:26–27, 31–32.

3. See Carol Tavris, *Anger: The Misunderstood Emotion,* rev. ed. (New York: Simon and Schuster, Touchstone, 1989), pp. 131–49.

4. See Goleman, *Emotional Intelligence,* pp. 64–65.

5. Elizabeth Clare Prophet, "Darshan with the Messenger: 'Let Not the Sun Go Down upon Your Wrath,'" March 12, 1997.

6. Ibid.

Chapter Seven
Pain as an Inner Teacher

1. Pir Vilayat Inayat Khan, as quoted in Wayne Muller's *Legacy of the Heart,* p. 10.

2. See the following publications by Mark L. Prophet and Elizabeth Clare Prophet: *The Masters and the Spiritual Path* (2001), pp. 81–136; and *Climb the Highest Mountain: The Path of the Higher Self,* 2d ed. (1986), pp. 57–60, 191, 271–72 (published by Summit University Press).

3. See *Fallen Angels and the Origins of Evil: Why Church Fathers Suppressed the Book of Enoch and Its Startling Revelations,* by Elizabeth Clare Prophet (Corwin Springs, Mont.: Summit University Press, 2000). See also *The Book of Enoch the Prophet,* trans. Richard Laurence (San Diego: Wizards Bookshelf, 1976).

4. In Gautama Buddha's first sermon following his enlightenment, he outlined the Four Noble Truths and the Eightfold Path. He explained that by following this path and avoiding the extremes of self-indulgence and self-mortification, one gains knowledge of the Middle Way. The Four Noble Truths state that (1) life is *dukkha,* "suffering," (2) the cause of suffering is inordinate desire, (3) freedom from suffering is in the attainment of nirvana, and (4) the way to this liberation is through the Eightfold Path. The Eightfold Path gives eight precepts for right living: (1) Right Understanding (or Right Views), (2) Right Aspiration (or Right Thought), (3) Right Speech, (4) Right Action, (5) Right Livelihood, (6) Right Effort, (7) Right Mindfulness, and (8) Right Concentration (or Right Absorption of God).

5. Luke 12:32.

6. Prophet, "Darshan with the Messenger: 'Let Not the Sun Go Down upon Your Wrath.'"

7. See Prophet and Prophet, *Science of the Spoken Word,* p. 36.

8. For further information on affirmations and violet-flame mantras, see the following publications from Summit University Press: Elizabeth Clare Prophet, *Violet Flame to Heal*

Body, Mind and Soul (1997); *Spiritual Techniques to Heal Body, Mind and Soul,* 90-min. audiotape, A99038; Mark L. Prophet and Elizabeth Clare Prophet, *Science of the Spoken Word* (1991).

9. Tara Bennett-Goleman, *Emotional Alchemy: How the Mind Can Heal the Heart* (New York: Harmony Books, 2001) p. 296.

10. See Marilyn C. Barrick, Ph.D., *Sacred Psychology of Change: Life as a Voyage of Transformation* (Corwin Springs, Mont.: Summit University Press, 2000), p. 69.

11. Millman, *Way of the Peaceful Warrior,* pp. 201, 202.

Chapter Eight
Ancient Soul Encounters

1. EMDR (Eye Movement Desensitization and Reprocessing) is a method of trauma release discovered by Francine Shapiro, Ph.D., in 1987. As one of the most extensively researched and supported methods for treating trauma, EMDR is now practiced around the world in areas where people have gone through major traumas, such as war, earthquakes, fires, floods, hurricanes, bombings, etc. EMDR practitioners have also successfully treated over a million individuals suffering from the aftermath of assault, domestic violence, rape, "bad trip" drug experiences, combat, loss of loved ones, accidents, serious illness, childhood traumas, natural disasters and recurrent nightmares.

   The method has been extensively researched and is viewed as a highly effective technique for treating immediate trauma and post-traumatic stress disorder. For further information, see *EMDR: The Breakthrough Therapy for Overcoming Anxiety, Stress, and Trauma,* by Francine Shapiro, Ph.D., and Margot Silk Forrest (New York: Basic-Books, 1997).

2. All that seems solid to us is composed of universal energy. Modern physicists regard matter and energy as equivalents, mutually convertible according to Einstein's formula

$E=mc^2$ (i.e., energy equals mass multiplied by the square of the speed of light). Thus, what we think of as solid ground is in reality energy moving at a slow enough speed to be experienced as solid. In essence, matter and energy are one. Therein lies the mystery of the Creator and the creation.

3. Prophet and Prophet, *Climb the Highest Mountain: The Path of the Higher Self,* 2d ed., p. 33.

4. Maitreya, "The Overcoming of Fear through Decrees," in Prophet and Prophet, *Science of the Spoken Word,* p. 14.

5. For further understanding of the Kabbalah, see *Kabbalah: Key to Your Inner Power,* by Elizabeth Clare Prophet with Patricia R. Spadaro and Murray L. Steinman. Chapters 3 and 4 offer a detailed explanation of the sefirot that is the basis of my summary. See also *Anatomy of the Spirit: The Seven Stages of Power and Healing,* by Caroline Myss, Ph.D. (New York: Harmony Books, 1996).

6. Arthur Green, "The Zohar: Jewish Mysticism in Medieval Spain," in *An Introduction to the Medieval Mystics of Europe,* ed. Paul E. Szarmach (Albany, N.Y.: State University of New York Press, 1984), p. 125.

7. Zohar 2:242b, in Isaiah Tishby and Fischel Lachower, comps., *The Wisdom of the Zohar: An Anthology of Texts,* 3 vols., trans. David Goldstein (1989; reprint, New York: Oxford University Press for the Littman Library of Jewish Civilization, 1991), 2:475.

8. Rev. 12: 7–17.

9. Teaching by Elizabeth Clare Prophet.

10. Rev. 19:20; 20:10, 14, 15.

11. For more information on the story of the ancient root races on earth and their departure from innocence, see *Climb the Highest Mountain: Path of the Higher Self,* 2d ed., by Mark L. Prophet and Elizabeth Clare Prophet, pp. 84–93, 493–97.

12. To read Sanat Kumara's personal description of his coming to the rescue of earth, see "The Dispensation Granted," in

The Opening of the Seventh Seal: Sanat Kumara on the Path of the Ruby Ray (Corwin Springs, Mont.: Summit University Press, Summit Lighthouse Library, 2001), pp. 10–15.

Chapter Nine
The Dance of Good and Evil

1. See M. Scott Peck, *People of the Lie: The Hope for Healing Human Evil* (New York: Simon and Schuster, Touchstone, 1983).

2. President George W. Bush, address to a joint session of Congress, September 20, 2001, as published in *MainStreet Journal,* Fall 2001, pp. 15, 17, 22.

3. Peck, *People of the Lie,* pp. 42, 43.

4. In order for fallen angels to be judged, someone on earth must invoke the action of the heavenly hosts. The ascended master Jesus Christ dictated a powerful prayer for God's people to give so that the hosts of the LORD can remove these evil beings from the earth, according to God's timetable, and take them for judgment. Those who give this prayer first prepare themselves by giving the "Tube of Light" decree and invoking the protection of Archangel Michael and his angelic bands. See "Spiritual Solutions," in *Fallen Angels and the Origins of Evil,* by Elizabeth Clare Prophet, pp. 343–56. See also "Spiritual Formulas for the Alchemy of Transformation," pp. 325–32, this volume.

5. Rom. 7:19–23; 8:6–7.

6. For an in-depth description of the initiate's path that leads to the ascension, see the following publications from Summit University Press: *The Path to Your Ascension: Rediscovering Life's Ultimate Purpose,* by Annice Booth (1999); and *Dossier on the Ascension: The Story of the Soul's Acceleration into Higher Consciousness on the Path of Initiation,* by Serapis Bey (1978).

7. Jesus Christ, "'I Have Desired to Be Remembered by You,'" October 8, 1995, in *Pearls of Wisdom,* vol. 38, no. 38, pp. 436, 437, 438.

8. Matt. 11:28, 30.

9. John 8:6, 7.

10. Luke 22:42.

11. See *Spiritual Techniques to Heal Body, Mind and Soul,* by Elizabeth Clare Prophet, 90-min. audiotape, A99038 (published by Summit University Press). Learn how to combine the violet flame with visualization, affirmation and meditation to fulfill greater levels of your own inner potential. To order, call 1-800-245-5445 or check with your favorite bookstore. See also p. 345, n. 8.

Chapter Ten
Keys to Enlightened Self-Mastery

1. Robert Louis Stevenson's "Daily Dozen," as quoted in *Bits and Pieces,* April 19, 2001, pp. 4–5.

2. These criteria were originally formulated by Dr. William C. Menninger and presented in a number of his public addresses. They are printed in a book of his selected papers entitled *A Psychiatrist for a Troubled World* (New York: Viking Press, 1967); see pages 799–807.

3. In the near-death experience, many people describe leaving their bodies and moving up a tunnel of light where they encounter spiritual beings. In a panoramic life review, people experience being on the receiving end of whatever actions they have taken during their lives—both good deeds and otherwise. For further information see Dannion Brinkley's *Saved by the Light* (New York: Villard Books, 1994) and *At Peace in the Light* (New York: HarperPaperbacks, 1995).

Chapter Eleven
Experience Your Inner Joy

1. One successful method I recommend for emotional resolution is trauma-release therapy, or EMDR. It relieves records of trauma through a process of alternating bilateral brain stimulation. For further information, see p. 346, n. 1.

2. I John 3:11; 4:8.

3. Matt. 18:21–22.

4. Matt. 5:43–48.

5. Elizabeth Clare Prophet, "Expanding the Power of the Heart," lecture given in Mexico City, November 29, 1998.

6. This story, which appears in several books on Buddhist teachings, is taken from Mark Epstein, M.D., *Going to Pieces without Falling Apart: A Buddhist Perspective on Wholeness* (New York: Broadway Books, 1998), pp. 176–77. See also Joseph Goldstein and Jack Kornfield, *Seeking the Heart of Wisdom: The Path of Insight Meditation* (Boston: Shambhala Publications, 1987), pp. 211–12.

7. Pema Chödrön, *Awakening Loving-Kindness* (Boston: Shambhala Publications, 1996), pp. 13–14.

8. The nature spirits, or elementals, are beings of earth, air, fire and water. They are the servants of God and man establishing and maintaining the physical plane as the platform for the soul's evolution.

9. Dictation from Saint Germain, recorded by Mark L. Prophet, October 29, 1966.

10. Saint Germain, "We Must Move toward the Crescendo of the Lightning and the Thunder," December 30, 1972, in Keepers of the Flame Lessons, no. 3, pp. 31, 32, 34.

Chapter Twelve
The Fount of Mercy and Forgiveness

1. See Rom. 12:19.

2. Dictation from Kuan Yin, recorded by Elizabeth Clare Prophet, April 13, 1997.

3. Alexander Pope, *An Essay on Criticism,* part 2, line 325.

4. The Dalai Lama, quoted in Mark Epstein's *Going to Pieces without Falling Apart,* p. 93.

5. Jack Kornfield, *A Path with Heart: A Guide through the*

Perils and Promises of Spiritual Life (New York: Bantam Books, 1993), p. 59.

6. Teaching from Elizabeth Clare Prophet's lecture "The Buddhic Essence," given July 3, 1992.

7. See Barrick, *Sacred Psychology of Change,* pp. 162–74.

8. Sidney B. Simon and Suzanne Simon, *Forgiveness: How to Make Peace with Your Past and Get On with Your Life* (New York: Warner Books, 1991), pp. 1–2.

Chapter Thirteen
Claiming Your Soul's Victory

1. The Dalai Lama, quoted in Epstein, *Going to Pieces without Falling Apart,* p. xvii.

2. Prophet and Prophet, *Climb the Highest Mountain: Path of the Higher Self,* 2d ed., pp. 269, 270–71, 272, 273.

3. Matt. 19:19.

4. Maha Chohan, "The High Rope," April 1, 1994, in *Pearls of Wisdom,* vol. 37, no. 15, p. 143.

5. Teaching from a Sunday evening sermon given by Mark L. Prophet, June 21, 1970, in Colorado Springs, Colorado.

6. Nelson Mandela, as quoted in Marianne Williamson, *A Return to Love* (New York: HarperCollins Publishers, 1992).

7. Gal. 6: 7–8.

8. See *A Dweller on Two Planets,* by Phylos the Thibetan (New York: Harper and Row, 1974), pp. 80–81, 135–38, 157–62, 199–200.

9. The Great White Brotherhood is a spiritual order of Western saints and Eastern adepts who have transcended the cycles of karma and rebirth and ascended into the heaven-world. They are known as ascended masters. These magnificent beings work with earnest seekers of every race, religion and walk of life to assist humanity. The word "white" refers not to race but to the aura of white light, the

halo that surrounds these immortals.

10. Teaching from Elizabeth Clare Prophet, June 28, 1990, in conjunction with her analysis of *Dweller on Two Planets,* by Phylos the Thibetan; available on CD on Demand, A91024 (see www.summitlighthouse.org/bookstore).

11. Lanello, "How to Ascend," March 1, 1992, in *Pearls of Wisdom,* vol. 35, no. 10, pp. 121, 122, 123–24. For a thorough understanding of the initiatic path of those who would pursue the goal of the ascension, see Serapis Bey's *Dossier on the Ascension* and Annice Booth's *The Path to Your Ascension.*

Spiritual Formulas for the Alchemy of Transformation

1. The decrees in this section are taken from *Prayers, Meditations and Dynamic Decrees for the Coming Revolution in Higher Consciousness,* published by Summit University Press.

Bibliography

Barrick, Marilyn C., Ph.D. *Dreams: Exploring the Secrets of Your Soul.* Corwin Springs, Mont.: Summit University Press, 2001.

Barrick, Marilyn C., Ph.D. *Sacred Psychology of Change: Life as a Voyage of Transformation.* Corwin Springs, Mont.: Summit University Press, 2000.

Barrick, Marilyn C., Ph.D. *Sacred Psychology of Love: The Quest for Relationships That Unite Heart and Soul.* Corwin Springs, Mont.: Summit University Press, 1999.

Bennett-Goleman, Tara. *Emotional Alchemy: How the Mind Can Heal the Heart.* New York: Harmony Books, 2001.

Booth, Annice. *Memories of Mark: My Life with Mark Prophet.* Corwin Springs, Mont.: Summit University Press, 1999.

Booth, Annice. *The Path to Your Ascension: Rediscovering Life's Ultimate Purpose.* Corwin Springs, Mont.: Summit University Press, 1999.

Brinkley, Dannion, with Paul Perry. *At Peace in the Light.* New York: HarperPaperbacks, 1995.

Brinkley, Dannion, with Paul Perry. *Saved by the Light.* New York: Villard Books, 1994.

Casarjian, Robin. *Forgiveness: A Bold Choice for a Peaceful Heart.* New York: Bantam Books, 1992.

Chödrön, Pema. *Awakening Loving-Kindness*. Boston: Shambhala Publications, 1996.

Crum, Thomas F. *The Magic of Conflict: Turning a Life of Work into a Work of Art*. New York: Simon and Schuster, 1987.

Epstein, Mark, M.D. *Going to Pieces without Falling Apart: A Buddhist Perspective on Wholeness*. New York: Broadway Books, 1998.

Ford, Debbie. *The Dark Side of the Light Chasers: Reclaiming Your Power, Creativity, Brilliance, and Dreams*. New York: Riverhead Books, 1998.

Frankl, Viktor E. *Man's Search for Meaning*. Boston: Beacon Press, 1992.

Gilbert, Rob, Ph.D., ed. *Bits and Pieces*. Fairfield, N.J.: Economics Press, April 19, 2001.

Goldstein, Joseph, and Jack Kornfield. *Seeking the Heart of Wisdom: The Path of Insight Meditation*. Boston: Shambhala Publications, 1987.

Goleman, Daniel. *Emotional Intelligence*. New York: Bantam Books, 1995.

Green, Arthur. "The Zohar: Jewish Mysticism in Medieval Spain." In *An Introduction to the Medieval Mystics of Europe*. Edited by Paul E. Szarmach. Albany, N.Y.: State University of New York Press, 1984.

Inayat Khan, Pir Vilayat. *Introducing Spirituality in Counseling and Therapy*. New York: Omega Press, 1982.

John of the Cross, Saint. *Dark Night of the Soul*. Translated and edited by E. Allison Peers. Garden City, N.Y.: Doubleday and Company, 1959.

Kim, Tae Yun. *Seven Steps to Inner Power: A Martial Arts Master Reveals Her Secrets for Dynamic Living*. San Rafael, Calif.: New World Library, 1991.

Kornfield, Jack. *A Path with Heart: A Guide through the Perils and Promises of Spiritual Life*. New York: Bantam Books, 1993.

Laurence, Richard, trans. *The Book of Enoch the Prophet.* San Diego: Wizards Bookshelf, 1976.

Millman, Daniel. *Way of the Peaceful Warrior: A Book That Changes Lives.* Tiburon, Calif.: H. J. Kramer, 1984.

Muller, Wayne. *Legacy of the Heart: The Spiritual Advantages of a Painful Childhood.* New York: Simon and Schuster, 1992.

Myss, Caroline, Ph.D. *Anatomy of the Spirit: The Seven Stages of Power and Healing.* New York: Harmony Books, 1996.

Paddison, Sara. *The Hidden Power of the Heart: Achieving Balance and Fulfillment in a Stressful World.* Boulder Creek, Calif.: Planetary Publications, 1995.

Peck, M. Scott. *People of the Lie: The Hope for Healing Human Evil.* New York: Simon and Schuster, 1983.

Phylos the Thibetan. *A Dweller on Two Planets.* New York: Harper and Row, 1974.

Prabhupada, Swami A. C. Bhaktivedanta. *Bhagavad-Gita As It Is.* Abr. ed. New York: Bhaktivedanta Book Trust, 1972.

Prophet, Elizabeth Clare. *Fallen Angels and the Origins of Evil: Why Church Fathers Suppressed the Book of Enoch and Its Startling Revelations.* Corwin Springs, Mont.: Summit University Press, 2000.

Prophet, Elizabeth Clare. *The Great White Brotherhood in the Culture, History and Religion of America.* Corwin Springs, Mont.: Summit University Press, 1987.

Prophet, Elizabeth Clare. *The Opening of the Seventh Seal: Sanat Kumara on the Path of the Ruby Ray.* Corwin Springs, Mont.: Summit University Press, Summit Lighthouse Library, 2001.

Prophet, Elizabeth Clare. *Violet Flame to Heal Body, Mind and Soul.* Corwin Springs, Mont.: Summit University Press, 1997.

Prophet, Elizabeth Clare, with Patricia R. Spadaro and Murray L. Steinman. *Kabbalah: Key to Your Inner Power.* Corwin Springs, Mont.: Summit University Press, 1997.

Prophet, Mark L., and Elizabeth Clare Prophet. *Climb the Highest Mountain: The Path of the Higher Self.* 2d ed. Corwin Springs, Mont.: Summit University Press, 1986.

Prophet, Mark L., and Elizabeth Clare Prophet. *The Masters and the Spiritual Path.* Corwin Springs, Mont.: Summit University Press, 2001.

Prophet, Mark L., and Elizabeth Clare Prophet. *Saint Germain On Alchemy: Formulas for Self-Transformation.* Corwin Springs, Mont.: Summit University Press, 1993.

Prophet, Mark L., and Elizabeth Clare Prophet. *The Science of the Spoken Word.* Corwin Springs, Mont.: Summit University Press, 1991.

Richo, David. *When Love Meets Fear: How to Become Defense-less and Resource-full.* New York: Paulist Press, 1997.

Rossman, Martin L., M.D. *Guided Imagery for Self-Healing.* Tiburon, Calif.: An H. J. Kramer Book, published in a joint venture with New World Library, 2000.

Salzberg, Sharon. *Lovingkindness: The Revolutionary Art of Happiness.* Boston: Shambhala Publications, 1995.

Serapis Bey. *Dossier on the Ascension: The Story of the Soul's Acceleration into Higher Consciousness on the Path of Initiation.* Corwin Springs, Mont.: Summit University Press, 1979.

Shapiro, Francine, Ph.D., and Margot Silk Forrest. *EMDR: The Breakthrough Therapy for Overcoming Anxiety, Stress, and Trauma.* New York: BasicBooks, 1997.

Simon, Sidney B., and Suzanne Simon. *Forgiveness: How to Make Peace with Your Past and Get On with Your Life.* New York: Warner Books, 1990.

Tavris, Carol. *Anger: The Misunderstood Emotion.* Rev. ed. New York: Simon and Schuster, 1989.

Tishby, Isaiah, and Fischel Lachower, comps. *The Wisdom of the Zohar: An Anthology of Texts.* 3 vols. Translated by David Goldstein. 1989. Reprint. New York: Oxford University Press for the Littman Library of Jewish Civilization, 1991.

Tolle, Eckhart. *The Power of Now: A Guide to Spiritual Enlightenment.* Novato, Calif.: New World Library, 1999.

Yogananda, Paramahansa. *Autobiography of a Yogi.* Los Angeles: Self-Realization Fellowship, 1974.

Williams, Redford, M.D., and Virginia Williams, Ph.D. *Anger Kills: Seventeen Strategies for Controlling the Hostility That Can Harm Your Health.* New York: HarperPerennial, 1993

Zweig, Connie, Ph.D., and Steve Wolf, Ph.D. *Romancing the Shadow: Illuminating the Dark Side of the Soul.* New York: Ballantine Books, 1997.

Dreams
Exploring the Secrets of Your Soul

Everyone and everything in our dreams is part of us... We spend one-third of our lives asleep—and most of that time we are dreaming. Dr. Marilyn Barrick's fascinating work shows that our dreams are not only meaningful and connected with events in our lives, but they also hold valuable keys to our spiritual and emotional development. In fact, our souls are great dramatists and teachers, and the scripts of our dreams often contain profound and valuable guidance.

ISBN:0-922729-63-8
Trade Paperback $14.00

Dreams: Exploring the Secrets of Your Soul discusses Tibetan sleep and dream yoga, lucid dreaming and techniques to help you more clearly remember and understand your dreams. Learn how to interpret your dreams through the powerful insights in this book and the author's visionary analysis of actual dreams. And discover how to decode the metaphorical messages of your own soul.

> "This unique book on dreams integrates the soul's development
> on the spiritual path with personal dream work....
> It invites us to consider a greater potential of the self beyond
> life's ordinary conflicts and helps us open up to a greater
> understanding of the purpose of life."
>
> —RALPH YANEY, M.D.,
> psychiatrist/psychoanalyst and author of *10,001*

> "Dreams... helps the reader unlock hidden secrets thereby
> opening new vistas to awareness, understanding, healing and
> finally, higher consciousness.... Dr. Barrick carefully, cogently
> and expertly enables the reader to understand the dream
> messages psychologically and spiritually."
>
> —RICHARD FULLER, Senior Editor, *Metaphysical Reviews*

Sacred Psychology of Change

ISBN:0-922729-57-3
Trade Paperback $14.95

Catch the vision of your role in the 21st century. *Sacred Psychology of Change* shows how you can welcome cycles of change and even chaos as transformational opportunities. It is jampacked with helpful information from cutting-edge change theories, psychology and spirituality.

Dr. Marilyn Barrick teaches us how to envision and explore the future while living productively in the present. Discover the importance of a creative mindset, an open heart and the maturing of soul to successfully navigate the waves of change. Learn how to meet the challenges of endings and beginnings and emerge from the darkness of grief and loss into a bright new day.

The storytelling chapters and exercises bring your personal journey to life and suggest practical approaches to the challenging scenarios of our fast-moving world.

"This book asks us to 'focus our attention on the higher intelligence of our heart' and then describes in loving detail ways of doing just that. Those interested in the heart's ability to heal will find encouragement in these pages."

—RUTH BLY, licensed psychologist, Jungian analyst, author

"A profound treasure of spiritual truths and their practical application based on the author's many successful years of personal and professional experience. Written in the language of the heart and with remarkable clarity and sensitivity, this book will lead you, chapter by chapter and step by step, to a profoundly healing dialogue with yourself—and through an exciting spiritual and psychological journey of change."

—KENNETH FRAZIER, L.P.C., D.A.P.A., A.C.P.E.

Sacred Psychology of Love

Searching for your perfect love?
Sacred Psychology of Love unfolds
the hidden spiritual and psychological
dramas inherent in friendships, love
relationships and marriage. It tells the
story of each one's inner beloved and
offers tender ways to spark divine
love in your relationships.

After 35 years as a clinical psychologist and relationship counselor,
Dr. Barrick is uniquely qualified to
reveal the impact of childhood experiences upon adult relationships and to
awaken us to the benefits of the
reflecting mirror of the beloved. She

ISBN:0-922729-49-2
Trade Paperback $12.95

shows the key role your inner "other half" plays in the eternal
dance of love and gives practical self-help exercises to guide you
on your quest for relationships that unite heart and soul.

"A wonderful marriage of the mystical and practical,
this soul-nourishing book is beautiful, healing and thought-provoking."

–SUE PATTON THOELE,
author of *Heart-Centered Marriage*

"In our search for the Beloved, whether inner or outer,
we seek that mysterious blend of beauty and practicality
which Dr. Marilyn Barrick masterfully conveys on every page.
Synthesizing her knowledge of sacred text, her clinical
expertise and her life's wisdom, she has written a book for
anyone seeking to love or to be loved. With compassion and humor,
she gives us an important tool for enriching relationships."

–ANNE DEVORE, Jungian analyst

Marilyn C. Barrick, Ph.D., is the author of a seven-book series on Sacred Psychology, a synthesis of her knowledge of sacred text, her clinical expertise and life's wisdom. The first four books, already published, highlight personal and spiritual growth through understanding the ins and outs of love, change, dreams and emotions. Dr. Barrick will complete the series with three books offering her professional and spiritual insights on the soul, children and family, and past lives.

FOR MORE INFORMATION

Summit University Press books are available at fine bookstores worldwide and at your favorite on-line bookseller.

For a free catalog of our books and products or to learn more about the spiritual techniques featured in this book, please contact:

Summit University Press
PO Box 5000
Corwin Springs, MT 59030-5000 USA
Telephone: 1-800-245-5445 or 406-848-9500
Fax: 1-800-221-8307 or 406-848-9555
E-mail: info@summituniversitypress.com
www.summituniversitypress.com

MARILYN C. BARRICK, PH.D., is a clinical psychologist, minister and transformational therapist. She has authored three spiritual/psychological self-help books: *Dreams: Exploring the Secrets of Your Soul, Sacred Psychology of Change: Life as a Voyage of Transformation* and *Sacred Psychology of Love: The Quest for Relationships That Unite Heart and Soul.*

In her fourth book, *Emotions: Transforming Anger, Fear and Pain,* Dr. Barrick offers psychological expertise and in-depth spiritual understanding to guide us through the emotional ups and downs of today's turbulent world. Her therapeutic repertoire includes past-life analysis, soul work, trauma release techniques, imagery and self-help exercises.

In addition to her writing and private practice, Dr. Barrick conducts seminars in the U.S.A., Canada and Europe. Over her 37-year professional career, she has consulted as a psychological expert to schools, churches, government agencies, professional advisory boards and mental health facilities. Early in her career, she taught graduate psychology courses and served with the Peace Corps as a training development officer and field counselor.

Dr. Barrick is also a minister in a church that integrates the spiritual teachings of the world's major religions. Thus, her perspective on emotional transformation and the case studies featured in *Emotions: Transforming Anger, Fear and Pain* are drawn from her ministry as well as her clinical practice.

Visit Dr. Barrick's web site at www.spiritualpsychology.com.